THE STATE POLITICS OF JUDICIAL AND CONGRESSIONAL REFORM

Recent Titles in
Contributions in Political Science
Series Editor: Bernard K. Johnpoll

Disarmament Without Order: The Politics of Disarmament at the United Nations
Avi Beker

The Liberty Lobby and the American Right: Race, Conspiracy, and Culture
Frank P. Mintz

The Liberal Future in America: Essays in Renewal
Philip Abbott and Michael B. Levy, editors

A Change of Course: The West German Social Democrats and NATO, 1957–1961
Stephen J. Artner

Power and Policy in Transition: Essays Presented on the Tenth Anniversary of the National Committee on American Foreign Policy in Honor of Its Founder, Hans J. Morgenthau
Vojtech Mastny, editor

Ideology and Soviet Industrialization
Timothy W. Luke

Administrative Rulemaking: Politics and Processes
William F. West

Recovering from Catastrophes: Federal Disaster Relief Policy and Politics
Peter J. May

Judges, Bureaucrats, and the Question of Independence: A Study of the Social Security Administration Hearing Process
Donna Price Cofer

Party Identification, Political Behavior, and the American Electorate
Sheldon Kamieniecki

Without Justice for All: The Constitutional Rights of Aliens
Elizabeth Hull

THE STATE POLITICS OF JUDICIAL AND CONGRESSIONAL REFORM

Legitimizing Criminal Justice Policies

THOMAS CARLYLE DALTON

Contributions in Political Science, Number 135

Greenwood Press
WESTPORT, CONNECTICUT • LONDON, ENGLAND

Library of Congress Cataloging in Publication Data

Dalton, Thomas Carlyle.
The state politics of judicial and congressional reform.

(Contributions in political science, ISSN 0147–1066 ; no. 135)
Bibliography: p.
Includes index.
1. Criminal justice, Administration of—United States. 2. Criminal procedure—United States. 3. Criminal registers—United States. I. Title. II. Series.
KF9223.D35 1985 364′.973 84–29763
ISBN 0–313–24549–5 (lib. bdg.)

Library of Congress Catalog Card Number: 84–29763
ISBN: 0–313–24549–5
ISSN: 0147–1066

First published in 1985

Greenwood Press
A division of Congressional Information Service, Inc.
88 Post Road West, Westport, Connecticut 06881

Printed in the United States of America

10 9 8 7 6 5 4 3 2 1

To Arthur and Beverly Dalton

About the Author

THOMAS CARLYLE DALTON holds a Ph.D. in Political Science from the University of Massachusetts. He has worked as Director of Research and Lecturer at the Institute of Public Service, Seattle University and for the State of Washington Governor's Office. His writings have appeared in *Policy Studies Review* and other publications.

Contents

Tables and Figure ix

Preface xi

Introduction xiii

1. Understanding the Implementation and Outcomes of Federal Policy 3

THE STUDY OF POLICY IMPLEMENTATION 3

DETERMINING RESPONSE AND POLICY OUTCOMES 5

COMMON CONDITIONS OF EFFECTIVE IMPLEMENTATION 9

THEORETICAL PERSPECTIVES UNDERLYING STUDIES OF POLICY IMPLEMENTATION 17

REFORMULATING LEGITIMATION THEORY 35

2. The Growth of Judicial and Congressional Intervention: Civil Liberties and Criminal Records Privacy Policy 39

THE CIVIL LIBERTIES DECISIONS: WARREN COURT REFORMS AND BURGER COURT RETRENCHMENT 41

FEDERAL AND STATE COURT STRUCTURE AND ROLES 51

CRIMINAL RECORDS PRIVACY: TECHNOLOGICAL INNOVATIONS AND THE PROBLEM OF CONGRESSIONAL CONTROL 57

POLITICAL CONSTRAINTS TO FEDERAL REGULATION OF STATE AND LOCAL CRIMINAL JUSTICE PROCESSES 65

3. National Patterns of State Policy 75

IMPLEMENTING *MAPP* AND *MIRANDA* 75

STATE CRIMINAL RECORDS POLICY AND PERFORMANCE 85

PRELUDE TO ADDITIONAL INQUIRY 97

4. California and Colorado: Contrasting Styles of Populism 101

CIVIL LIBERTIES POLICY: THE ELECTORAL IMPLICATIONS OF STATE COURT ACTIVISM 105

CRIMINAL RECORDS POLICY: THE ATTORNEY GENERAL AND STATE COURT IN LEADERSHIP ROLES 116

5. Washington and Massachusetts: The Politics of Ambivalence and Activism 125

CIVIL LIBERTIES POLICY: THE INCIPIENT CONSEQUENCES OF STATE COURT INACTION 129

CRIMINAL RECORDS POLICY: THE PROBLEM OF AUTHORITY IN INDEPENDENT AGENCIES 140

6. Understanding the State Implementation of Judicial and Legislative Policy 155

EXPLAINING VARIATIONS IN STATE RESPONSE AND PERFORMANCE 156

AN EXPLANATORY FRAMEWORK: RELATIONSHIPS AMONG VARIABLES INFLUENCING OUTCOMES 172

7. Criminal Justice Policy and American Politics: Reform and the Dilemma of Legitimacy 177

THE CYCLE OF REFORM AND RETRENCHMENT 178

THE APPEARANCE AND REALITY OF REFORM 197

References 207

Case Index 219

General Index 223

Tables and Figure

TABLES

1. Applied Studies Related to Minimal Threat of Change 10
2. Applied Studies Related to Unambiguous Mandate 12
3. Applied Studies Related to Supportive State and Local Elites 14
4. Applied Studies Related to Possibility of Enforcement 16
5. Extent of Utilization of Information Technology in Criminal Justice 59
6. State Court Rulings on Civil Liberties Policies, 1966–1982 86
7. Variations in State Dissemination Policy and Management, by Year of Adoption 91
8. Court Disposition Reporting 93
9. Audits and Accuracy Checks of CCH Records 95

FIGURE

1. Explanatory Framework for Policy Implementation 173

Preface

The ideas for this project originated several years ago when I was an administrator in a state planning agency. The agency was responsible for the allocation of federal grants sponsored by the Law Enforcement Assistance Administration (LEAA). My responsibilities included the development of state regulations and the implementation of the federal criminal records privacy mandate.

My academic training had been in political theory so my theoretical knowledge of politics and policy making far outstripped actual experience. What I found particularly intriguing (if not troubling) about this experience was that the promise of representative government accountable to the people is possible only to the extent that our elected and governmental officials are committed to such ideas in the implementation of public policies. Unfortunately, all too often, more effort goes into saving the appearances of democratic ideals than into making them a working reality. Therefore, this book is an effort to understand factors which tend to accentuate or reduce the gap between the promise and reality of democratic politics.

I am indebted to several people for helping me give order and coherence to my ideas and experiences. William E. Connolly provided some early inspiration about how to theorize about politics, and Chris Webster showed me how to use theory to understand political realities. Without Kenneth Dolbeare's insights and continuous support, this project would never have come to fruition. Kenneth Laudon graciously provided some data regarding state performance under criminal records privacy, which was indispensable to this work. Finally, the faculty and staff at the Institute of Public Service, Seattle University, provided the luxury of time and the academic context necessary to reflect about the politics of policy implementation.

I would also like to thank several persons who, as respondents for the study, provided important insights about the state politics of national reforms and other important contacts. They include Edward Pringle, Daniel Jaffe, James Vogt,

Andrew Klein, Doug Cunningham, Walter Trefry, James Joy and James Sullivan.

Finally, I would like to express special thanks to Pandora for her help on the index and to my wife, Linda, whose skills in editing and help in every aspect of this work understate the true magnitude of her assistance, which goes far beyond the pages of this book.

Introduction

Studies of the implementation of public policies have provided new insights about a variety of factors shaping outcomes. Interesting conceptual schemes of varying theoretical rigor have been advanced to help identify the consequences of national policies. Yet little effort has been made thus far to undertake studies which might help us adjudicate between rival theories or identify implications for the American political system.

All too often the methodologies employed and policy focus impose artificial limits on the development of adequate explanatory theory. Narrow gauge studies limit our ability to generalize about policies involving different policy systems and originating institutions. Self-imposed limits in inquiry also tend to obscure underlying institutional realities, often reinforcing preconceived notions about the distribution of power, accountability and legitimacy of our political institutions.

Arguments about the efficacy and desirability of different forms of federal intervention in state and local criminal justice processes epitomize our inability to generalize about the implementation of federal policy. Over the last two decades the Supreme Court and Congress have attempted to enlarge civil liberties and privacy protections and increase federal oversight as well as to reduce crime, increase the effectiveness of criminal justice organizations and promote state policy discretion and enforcement. These policies have been controversial and the subject of governmental and academic studies with conflicting findings.

The principal social policy objective of the Warren Court (1953–1969) was the achievement of greater equality of treatment under the law. The *Mapp v. Ohio* (1961) and *Miranda v. Arizona* (1966) decisions express how the Court attempted to achieve this objective through the nationalization of suspects' and defendants' due process rights. *Mapp* applied the so-called exclusionary rule to the states, holding that the Fourth Amendment prohibited the admission of illegally seized evidence in state and trial court criminal proceedings. The ruling in *Miranda* applies Fifth and Sixth Amendment guarantees against self-incrimination and for adequate legal representation by specifying the conditions under which a suspect's statements may be considered voluntary. Unless police have given several designated warnings (e.g., the right to remain silent and to have an attorney present during interrogation), a suspect's statements cannot be considered voluntary and cannot be introduced as evidence by the prosecutor at trial. The policies differ in two important ways with respect to clarity and specificity. Compared to *Miranda*, *Mapp* does not define the procedures which police must follow to comply. Nor does *Mapp* define the conditions which constitute when a search or seizure is legal—only subsequent case law defines these conditions. *Mapp* also imposes supervisory responsibilities on courts (e.g., approval of warrants) absent in *Miranda*. A subsequent analysis in Chapter 3 examines how these differences in form and content have contributed to fundamental differences in implementation and outcome.

The other element of the Warren Court strategy consisted of the extension of federal district court jurisdiction to oversee state court determinations of criminal cases involving due process challenges. Defendants could subsequently obtain federal court review of issues concerning not only the appropriateness of state court interpretations of Constitutional rights but also the adequacy of fact finding processes.

The Burger Court (1969–) and Congressional policy have been directed at different substantive goals involving law enforcement and reduction of crime. Their primary strategies have been the enlargement of state and local policy making capacity, discretion and accountability, and the contraction of federal court and bureaucratic intervention. Thus, the Burger Court civil liberties policies since 1969 and the Congressional Omnibus Crime Control and Safe Streets Act of 1968 share a common approach of establishing minimum standards for the administration of criminal justice. Congressional regulation of criminal justice information systems was begun with an amendment to the Crime Control Act in 1973, followed by LEAA regulations (Title 28) to improve the management, increase the quality and control the exchange and dissemination of criminal records. A primary purpose of that policy is the protection of privacy and due process rights of the subjects of criminal records.

Comparative analysis of the civil liberties and criminal records privacy policy provides us with an important opportunity to bring into sharper focus several issues now engaging the attention of observers who wish to understand the outcomes of national policies regulating criminal justice processes.

Legislatures and courts do differ fundamentally with respect to organization and processes by which policies are adopted and implemented. The implementing environment also may have a different impact on court and legislative policy. However, an exhaustive review of institutional similarities and differences is not the point of this analysis. Instead, this comparison of civil liberties and privacy policies, which happen to be initiated by different institutions, is designed to discover what they suggest together about common factors and interests involved in the implementation of the national policies, and what that implies about American politics.

This comparative analysis focuses upon state court justices and state executives (e.g., governors, attorney generals, state agency administrators) because they are important intermediaries in the intergovernmental system by which national guidelines are converted into state policy and local practice. State officials' responses to federal policy strongly influence how the policy is perceived, understood and interpreted, implemented and enforced.

Therefore, this study undertakes an historical and comparative examination of the state implementation of Supreme Court civil liberties and Congressional criminal records policy in order to address several related issues: What are the political constraints (and supports) to the state implementation of national policies in criminal justice? What are the interests and institutional dynamics involved? How do the outcomes of the *Mapp*, *Miranda* and criminal records privacy policies compare, and which factors contributing to effective policy implementation are most salient? How do we explain implementation processes and outcomes in political-theoretical terms? How do these theories contribute toward our understanding of the efficacy and consequences of judicial and Congressional policy? Finally, what are the implications for the American political system?

In order to answer these questions, I have employed a two-tiered methodological structure for the inquiry. The first tier consists of establishing the national patterns of state response, performance and impact, based on existing studies of the implementation of civil liberties and criminal records regulations. The second tier consists of detailed analysis of several state responses and implementation processes to explain variations in state response and outcomes of these national policies.

Several criteria were employed to select four states—California, Colorado, Washington and Massachusetts—reflecting the actual diversity among all states. They exhibit a range of policy responses and performance, regions, size, urbanization and political culture.

In addition, I tried to include examples of states which had *anticipated* federal mandates through prior adoption of state policies. I did so in order to see if that contributed to any significant differences in implementation processes or outcomes. For example, the California and Washington state courts adopted the exclusionary rule guidelines established for federal courts by the U.S. Supreme Court decision in *Weeks v. U.S.* (1914) well before *Mapp* (1961) imposed it on state courts. The Massachusetts state court adopted a rule similar to the *Miranda* warnings before the states were required to do so. The states of California and Massachusetts adopted criminal records privacy policies in anticipation that they would have to do so eventually. Interestingly, these policy innovations did not exempt the states from having to make subsequent revisions in their policies in response to federal mandates. This fact, among others, provides useful insights about the political implications of policy implementation processes examined in Chapters 6 and 7.

The states were also chosen according to differences in policy development and implementing authority, type of enabling policy and organizational structure. Policy development and implementing authority refers to those state officials and/or agencies exercising authority to implement and enforce state policy. For example, Massachusetts and Colorado represent extremes with respect to criminal records privacy because Massachusetts uses an independent commission while Colorado policy does not involve any executive or administrative role, relying instead on mechanisms of judicial review. The states also vary with respect to methods the state courts employ to influence policy affecting adminstrative and judicial functions. For example, the chief justice of the Colorado Supreme Court has personally handled executive-legislative liaison while the Washington state court has tended to delegate this responsbility to the court administrator.

The type of enabling policy is characterized by its comprehensiveness, consistency with past policy, and compatability with related state policies. For example, the criminal records privacy policy adopted by the Colorado legislature failed to address many elements presented by federal policy, advancing only incremental changes from the past, yet was compatible with prevailing public disclosure policy. Other states such as Massachusetts and Washington adopted comprehensive statutes involving significant departures from past policy, thus challenging the presumption favoring public disclosure. In civil liberties policy, states which represent extremes along this dimension would include California whose state court has systematically advanced prescriptive search and seizure and interrogation policies while Massachusetts has chosen to express these policies in a fragmentary manner.

Finally, the states were selected according to differences in the organizational capacity of courts or executive bureaucracies to implement public policies. The state courts selected for analysis exhibit important differences in appellate structure and degree of administrative unification. Colorado has a unified court structure with centralization of administrative rule-making and budget control. Massachusetts is at the other extreme in which unification is lacking, access to intermediate appellate courts is limited and the state court has very little administrative control over trial court functions.

The implementation experiences of the states selected were compared and contrasted along several lines in order to generate sufficient evidence to support an explanation of variations in outcomes. Points of comparison included state institutional relations, policy interpretation and enforcement, and ideological positions and style of policy-making of state intermediaries. Policy making style refers, in part, to the characterization of decision making by such terms as procedural, substantive (result-oriented), pragmatic or managerial. Finally, the state cases are compared with respect to whether conflict or consensus is the characteristic mode of response to federal policy, and regarding the influence of public opinion and interest groups in criminal justice policy development and implementation.

I have used a number of sources to supplement the analysis of national patterns and to document the state cases. Several reports sponsored by LEAA (now the Bureau of Criminal Justice Statistics), the Congressional Office of Technology Assessment (OTA), and SEARCH Group Incorporated have been particularly useful for the analysis of criminal records privacy policy. Also, the modest but impressive literature regarding the use and impact of information technology in criminal justice contributed to the study. The analysis of Supreme Court and state court decision making on civil liberties benefited from the voluminous academic literature on the subject, including a number of law review articles written by state court justices and other state officials involved in state policy development and/or implementation processes.

I have exercised restraint in elaborating on the details of the numerous federal and state court cases covered in this study. There are important reasons for this. The focus of this book is on the analysis of the state implementation of federal mandates. If I were concerned with the dynamics of policy formulation or constitutional law per se, then more detail on the facts of the cases would be appropriate. In addition, what I attempt to examine is how policies evolve over time, the effects of factors such as elite support, clarity, and enforceability, and implications for institutional change. Thus, what is important is understanding how the reciprocal relationships between federal, state and local officials contribute to outcomes. In this effort I had to exercise judgement about what cases appeared most significant in shaping state policies. As the reader can see, judicial and Congressional policies do not have uniform consequences for each state, partly for reasons of political culture as discussed in Chapter 7.

I conducted a number of on site and telephone interviews with state and local criminal justice officials (including state court justices, local judges, prosecutors, police and public defenders) as well as gubernatorial assistants, legislative aides, assistant attorney generals, and state agency administrators. Also, I had discussions with representatives of civil liberties (e.g., the ACLU) and other interest groups active in the formulation, implementation and litigation of policies involving criminal justice issues. The selections of interview respondents was governed by the focus on state intermediaries, representation of criminal justice functions and governmental institutions, and familiarity with how the policies were implemented.

The interviews were used not only to reconstruct decision making and implementation processes over time, but to probe whether and why discrepancies emerged between initial perspectives about authority and legitimacy, images of law enforcement practices, attitudes about the policies, expectations about impacts, and actual experience. Unfortunately, only a small selection of comments and explanations could be included in the text. When reporting information from these interviews throughout this book, publicly known officials are identified by name and title. Otherwise, I refer to individuals only by their general region, position, role or relationship to the policies in order to observe confidentiality.

Two important considerations in a study of this kind are how to account for the extent and direction of change over time; and how to explain differences between states with respect to the implementation of similar policies.

First, policies initiated in an environment of controversy, widespread defiance, and little elite support can undergo transformation with the passage of time, increasing public support and elite commitment, and thereby increasing the possibility of change. The reverse is also equally possible. Factors such as the clarity and specificity of a policy are also likely to undergo change through federal and state rule-making changes. While there is no optimum time frame, the inquiry should cover at least a ten to fifteen year period. By these standards, it is not surprising that early studies of the *Brown v. the Board of Education* (1954) decision, eager to document outcomes and impacts, found little compliance and much evasion when conducted only two to five years after the Supreme Court decision. While studies which immediately follow policy adoption provide significant information about factors shaping initial response, it would be premature to draw conclusions about ultimate performance or change. The structure of this study accommodates this need by tracing the development and implementation of the civil liberties decisions over two decades and federal and state activities involved with the implementation of criminal records privacy since 1973.

Second, the multiple case study approach is a useful strategy when complex phenomena must be examined in real world contexts. A study limited solely to available data on national patterns of compliance would not provide a sufficient basis by which to explain why things happened the way they did. The processes by which policy is implemented are perhaps best understood through a case study approach because it allows us to determine whether there are underlying institutional forces at work in a political culture. The presence of such forces might help explain differences between states with respect to the implementation of Congressional and judicial policies. Although it may be difficult to precisely assign causal relations among factors, case analysis facilitates construction and testing of alternative explanations (Yin, 1981).

The nature of a state political culture constitutes an important underlying dimension influencing state policy making processes. Although acknowledging it to be a complex factor, many observers concur in its potential to deepen our understanding of policy and political change (see especially Elazar, 1972; Litt, 1965; Patterson, 1968; Rosenthal and Moakley, 1984; Verba, 1965), In an effort to synthesize the literature on political culture, Rosenthal and Moakley contend that applied studies must distinguish between the *manifestations* of a political culture (e.g., partisan orientations, expections and support); its *sources* (e.g., ethnic distribution, economics, demographics); and its *effects* (e.g., general political behavior, policy styles of political elites) (1984: 13).

My study examines the relationship between the manifestations and effects of political culture. More specifically, it analyzes the relationship between the distribution and exercise of policy making authority and policy making styles of political elites. Therefore, what will be of particular interest is the identification of the resources political elites draw upon to implement and legitimize their policies, and the determination of how institutional factors and expectations of other intermediaries as well as participants in policy processes (e.g., implementers, consumer advocates and secondary populations such as the press) affect the level and availability of those resources.

The politics involved in the implementation of federal policy presents many appearances to its observers as well as participants. This makes the explanation of the processes of policy innovation and reform an elusive and vexing task. The search for an explanation based on an understanding of appearances rather than underlying realities may understate or exaggerate the participants' comprehension of and ability to influence factors shaping outcomes. Political appearances may not only reinforce the observer's preconceptions about prospects for reform and the function of the political system but serve to reconstitute the behavior of policy participants in self-fulfilling ways.

Appearances play an important strategic role in political conflict involving policies and their consequences. An essential purpose of politics is to strike an acceptable relationship between the distribution of power and affected interests. Importantly, the results of political conflict may both redistribute power among the participants and result in a differential distribution of burdens and benefits, responsibilities and opportunities. Parties to a political dispute therefore have important incentives to trade upon purported discrepancies between appearance and reality in ways calculated to advance their favored policy positions. Contending interests involved in a policy issue are unlikely to reveal their real interests or power positions in order to gain leverage over consequences of policies they favor.

The outcomes of the state implementation of federal policy may require agents to reconcile or alter their beliefs about authority and revise their interpretations of institutional realities to conform with newly discovered political necessities. These images of institutional structure, capacities of role-bearers within them and perceived possibilities of change are sustained by underlying beliefs about political legitimacy. Thus, conceptions about legitimacy play an important role in establishing the possibilities and limits of reform.

The possibility of analyzing policy implementation processes and generalizing about political implications is enhanced to the extent that descriptive terms are available to capture the complex relationship between the responses of the participants and the ultimate outcomes. I contend that the compliance perspective is too narrow and ill-suited to handle this complexity. Consequently, in Chapter 1 I propose and distinguish several terms (i.e., response, impact, performance and change) which guide my analysis in subsequent chapters. Next, I identify the emergence of a conventional wisdom from applied studies regarding several factors likely to influence the effectiveness of policy implementation processes. These factors include the extent of change, clarity of mandate, supportiveness of state and local elites, and the possibility of enforcement. Applied studies weigh the explanatory significance of these factors differently because of underlying theoretical differences. Finally, therefore, the assignment of Chapter 1 is concluded with a review and critique of the theoretical underpinnings of applied studies to illustrate how they view the significance and political implications of these common factors.

Each theory contributes in important but incomplete ways toward helping us to see the significance of legitimacy in understanding the state implementation and institutional consequences of federal policy. Nonetheless, I show why the problem of regime legitimacy cannot be effectively assimilated into existing theoretical frameworks but must be developed as a separate and distinctive theory. I go on to indicate what the contours of such a theory entail and briefly illustrate its explanatory power.

Chapter 2 traces the evolution of national policies regulating criminal justice processes and presents an analysis of the institutional, intergovernmental and organizational dimensions of those policy reforms. This effort concludes by identifying several political constraints to the implementation of these policies. These factors, which include Constitutional rights, law enforcement practice, cross-cutting policy, separation of powers, federalism and governance, serve as important referants in our subsequent analysis of the state cases in Chapter 6.

In Chapter 3 an attempt is made to use available studies and data to establish nationwide patterns of state policy impact and performance. This analysis challenges the importance of clarity and change, suggested by organizational and communication theory to account for outcomes, while raising other issues about the role of state intermediaries and possibility of enforcement for additional exploration.

Case studies of four state processes by which national civil liberties and criminal records policies are converted to state policy are presented in detail in Chapters 4 and 5. In particular, they attempt to identify the importance of state political culture, ongoing institutional relationships and differential elite support in determining state responses.

Chapter 6 uses the state cases to explain variations in performance. The explanation identifies the ways in which conflicts over Constitutional rights, interest group pressure resulting from cross-cutting policies and problems of balancing the needs of law enforcement against the social costs of discrimination maintain the appearance of pluralist politics while concealing underlying institutional constraints and power structural conflict. Such constraints are reflected in elite conflicts over the separation of powers, federalism and governance processes.

I contend that the outcomes of these policies are the products of reciprocal relationships between originating institutions, state intermediaries and implementers. Key variables include whether the policy involves substantive, procedural or structural change; the beliefs of state elites and implementers regarding the structure of routine organizational practices; the interests and priorities of state executives, legislators and court justices with respect to political consequences or risks of action (or inaction); and on-going formal and informal institutional relationships.

Finally, Chapter 7 draws together the elements of explanation into a general theory of policy-making processes with which to understand the relationship between public policy and American politics. That theory includes several related propositions. First, the form that federal policy takes strongly influences the ability of state elites to legitimate their policy choices and actions. More specifically, structural policies, which involve the alteration of institutional relationships in a policy system, influence the *actual* distribution of burdens and benefits. Moreover, conflicts among institutional elites over structural policy contribute to recurring legitimation problems manifested in a cycle of reform and retrenchment.

Second, there are important power structural and institutional constraints at work within a state political culture which establish the threshold and direction of change. Progressive change is more likely to be sustained in states in which there is a strong elite support, compatible policy making styles and consistent and continuous enforcement. Nonetheless, national policies with structural implications tend to get displaced into conflicts over policy making authority and administrative capacity. Consequently, this only further exacerbates legitimation problems by dispersing and fragmenting the authority and accountability of national and state elected officials while reinforcing the concentration of power and discretion of administrative elites and implementers in policy subsystems.

Finally, the problems of reform and legitimation which confront the intergovernmental policy system have certain paradoxical consequences. These paradoxes are both symptomatic of the deeper ambivalance toward freedom and rights rooted in the philosophical foundations of liberalism and dependence upon judicial intervention to compensate for the weaknesses in mechanisms of democratic accountability.

THE STATE POLITICS OF JUDICIAL AND CONGRESSIONAL REFORM

1

Understanding the Implementation and Outcomes of Federal Policy

THE STUDY OF POLICY IMPLEMENTATION

Studies of the policy implementation process have progressed through several stages involving closely related points of inquiry. The traditional disciplines of administration theory and organizational behavior supplied the initial impetus to investigate why policies fail to be translated into neutral rules of program execution (Hargrove, 1975; Rabinovitz, Pressman and Rein, 1976).

Studies of the impact of Supreme Court decisions, demonstrating a gap between intent and actual performance, invited closer inspection of how a legislative policy gets translated into behavior (Dolbeare, 1974). As the field of policy implementation has developed, the focus of judicial and legislative studies has converged around some common factors affecting outcomes.

The second stage of policy implementation analysis has been characterized by a plethora of case studies identifying factors hindering program implementation. Studies by Bailey and Mosher (1968), Derthick (1975), Lowi (1969) and Pressman and Wildavsky (1973) document how statutory ambiguity, guideline development processes and organizational complexity (including variations of state and local official support) may contribute to failure to achieve intended goals. These studies have exercised caution about the implications of their findings for the nature of the political system.

This restraint has been justified because we lack the explanatory theories necessary to identify factors shaping outcomes, and how they contribute to institutional change. In addition, there has been no common agreement on how to measure the implementation and outcomes of public policy. Some studies have been content to measure procedural compliance while others seek to trace the relationship between output, impact and ultimate change processes (Dolbeare, 1974). Without such agreement we are unable to evaluate the extent to which policy outcomes contribute to or detract from the accountability of the electoral process, assess what that implies about the distribution of political power or determine the consequences for prevailing beliefs about the legitimacy of American governmental institutions. Therefore, this chapter attempts to identify and distinguish such terms as *response, impact, performance,* and *change* to facilitate the evaluation of alternative explanations of policy outcomes.

Studies to date have resulted in general agreement on several factors likely to influence policy effectiveness. Although differing with respect to the relative significance of individual factors, the conventional wisdom of policy implementation now holds that policies involving minimal threat of change, a clear mandate, supportive state and local elites and the possibility of enforcement are more likely to be successful. These factors or conditions are generally held to be invariable regardless of policy characteristics, nature of the policy system, institutional origin and implementing environment. Each of these factors will be discussed in more detail in the context of the applied and theoretical literature.

Recently, efforts to develop conceptual frameworks of implementation processes have been launched to determine the relationship between these and other factors in explaining outcomes. These frameworks cover a wide range of policy systems and draw upon several theoretical bodies of knowledge such as psychological theories of cognitive dissonance and expressivism, utility theory, organizational behavior, communications theory, systems theory, and legitimation theory. There are major variations among applied studies with respect to theoretical self-consciousness, explanatory power and applicability, rigor and testability. Some schemes constitute interesting conceptual frameworks but lack systematic application (e.g., Bardach, 1977; Baum, 1981; Berman, 1980; Edwards, 1980; Elmore, 1978). Others specify operational measures of key variables (Tarr, 1977; Wasby, 1970; 1974–1975); or causal relationships between factors (C. Johnson, 1979; Ripley and Franklin, 1982; Van Meter and Van Horn, 1975). In some instances they develop predictive theories of policy success or failure (Baum, 1976b; Brown and Stover, 1977; Mazmanian and Sabatier, 1983).

While progress in applied studies has been extensive, several limitations remain. Little effort has been directed at testing the strength of underlying theories to explain variations in the outcomes and effects of public policy. Consequently, there is a failure to document whether and why a characteristic pattern of performance emerges in the implementation of similar policies in a particular policy area and how that pattern is likely to vary or change given the presence or absence of key factors.

Next, as C. Johnson and Canon (1984) observed recently, most theories of judicial policies purport to explain the responses and behavior of and policy consequences for all relevant populations typically involved in implementation (such as federal and state officials; implementers, direct recipients and secondary publics). However, their empirical application has been limited to one or two of these potential actors, within specific studies.

Finally, there have been only limited efforts thus far to develop explanatory frameworks using psychological and/or social science theories capable of integrating our knowledge of policy implementation processes across policy *settings* and *institutions*. While the attempt to develop a theoretically integrated explanatory framework presupposes further progress in applied studies of Congressional and judicial policies, the development of a unified theory is not precluded by these limitations. Policies involving similar mandates and a common policy system have been implemented by Congress and the Supreme Court in several areas, offering the opportunity to conduct comparative policy research. Moreover, conceptual frameworks construed in the broadest institutional terms are a necessary corrective to conclusions dictated largely by policy areas in which particular frameworks are applied. Examples of limited attempts in this regard include works by Baum (1977; 1981); Elmore and McLaughlin (1982); Horowitz (1977); Mazmanian and Sabatier (1983); Nakamura and Smallwood (1980); Rabinovitz, Pressman and Rein (1976); Shapiro (1968), and Shapiro and Hobbs (1974).

It is my contention that legitimacy theory is uniquely suited to explain the outcomes of judicial and Congressional reforms in the administration of criminal justice, and potentially those in other policy areas as well. I shall try to support this contention later in the chapter.

DETERMINING RESPONSE AND POLICY OUTCOMES

There is little agreement in the literature on policy implementation regarding ways to best characterize outcomes of public policy. The terms compliance, response and impact, for example, are used in inconsistent and often overlapping ways. Each implies different implications regarding scope and measurement. Thus, there is a need to employ a common terminology in order to compare the implementation of policies originated by different institutions, actors and implementing environments.

Wasby (1970) has argued that the term compliance involves a narrower focus than impact. Assessments of compliance turn upon judgments about the policy originators' intentions as well as the implementers' awareness, understanding and attitude toward what is expected. Implementers' perceptions or expectations about a policy's effects may influence their willingness to comply with the policy directive. In addition, the impacts or effects of the policy may not be intended and often involve second or third order consequences which complicate judgments about causal relationships among policy, behavior and attitude (Dolbeare, 1974).

Further, the use of the term compliance involves normative assumptions regarding hierarchy, obedience and acceptable vs. unacceptable behavior. Yet policy is usually implemented in state and local contexts in which there are wide variations in political culture, in the distribution of power among elites and in perceived authority and public support. Therefore, while the implementation of judicial policy may involve formal, hierarchial relations between the Supreme Court and state courts, states or localities do not always bear a subordinate relation to Congress with respect to policy implementation. In addition, state executives and justices may exercise substantial discretion in the way they choose to respond to policy requirements. Consequently, they may satisfy policy objectives in varying ways and through behavior neither required nor intended by the policy originator.

Several terms therefore may be employed to characterize policy results, which help bypass some of the more vexing problems associated with the measurement of compliance. These terms are *response*, *impact*, *performance* and *change*. The terms *results* and *outcomes* are used generically when more than one of these specific terms applies.

First, the term *response* appears to capture two dimensions of behavior: the consistency of implementers' behavior with the direction intended by goals and the intensity of the implementers' attitudes toward the policy. Both the *direction* and *intensity* of response may be influenced in turn by how the policy is interpreted and by perceptions of expected effects of that policy. Direction of response pertains to the avenue the implementer chooses to "satisfy" policy demands. Thus, response to policy demands is not necessarily the same thing as compliance. Some state courts, for example, have chosen to interpret a Supreme Court policy by ruling in a way that is inconsistent with the principles and objectives yet more limited or expansive in scope. In some circumstances, state courts and legislatures may have anticipated the Supreme Court or Congressional policy with policies comparable to but not the same as subsequent federal policy. Therefore, under these circumstances it would be incorrect to conclude that state policy has failed to *comply* with the directives of its federal superiors.

The relation between behavior and attitude is often asymmetrical, which may reflect the intensity of response. State courts have exhibited wide variations in response toward the Supreme Court criminal procedure decisions. In some instances, criticism of the decisions also entailed refusal to implement the decision. In other circumstances, subsequent state court decisions were consistent with the Supreme Court ruling despite negative attitudes that had been expressed publicly. Similary, in policy responses to Congressional regulations, where state executives are indifferent with respect to enforcement, that attitude can encourage procedural adoption, perfunctory behavior and yet result in little or no change in performance.

Finally, the direction and intensity of responses are influenced by how state elites and local implementers interpret the policy as well as their expectations of impact. While clear and precise policies are expected to facilitate communication and increase the accuracy of interpretation and, thus, fidelity to required behavior, the expectation is not necessarily warranted. Policy interpretations are formulated and mediated through the screen of prevailing beliefs, predispositions and existing organizational practices. For example, state court responses to Supreme Court policy are conditioned in significant ways by beliefs about the legitimacy of judicial roles and the scope of supervision as well as by perceptions of the change or disruption that these policies can create in existing state practice.

Similarly, state executives are unable to respond unilaterally to federal policy but must contend with legislative responses while anticipating and weighing the electoral consequences of their responses. Therefore, state officials' responses to federal policy and willingness to enforce them are conditioned to a significant degree by state and local environmental and political circumstances.

Policy *impacts* refer to the effects of a policy with respect to individual conduct, organizational structure, intergovernmental and interorganizational relations and even characteristics of a particular policy system. When intended effects are achieved, this usually implies that at least some of the policy goals or objectives have been met. Unintended consequences, although frequently contributing to policy failure, may sometimes contribute to the realization of policy goals as well.

There is, however, a problematic relationship between objectives sought by policy originators, impact and the expectations and behavior of implementers. There are inherent difficulties involved in determining whether policy outcomes are the *cause* or *effect* of implementers' perceptions and attitudes. This is so because implementers anticipate and sometimes even precipitate the outcomes which occur whether or not they are intended. This problematic characteristic of policy implementation is exemplified well by the analysis of law enforcement responses to federal and state civil liberties and criminal records privacy guidelines discussed in Chapter 3 and further illustrated in Chapters 4 and 5.

When faced with policies they do not support, implementers have several options. They can develop interpretations of policy consistent with the impact they expect—thereby both misinterpreting policy intent and behaving inconsistently with it. On the other hand, they can make adaptations in behavior and organizational structure in ways which do not involve overt evasion or resistance to the policy and which inadvertently implement some aspects of the policy. They may also choose to comply in the short run with the expectation of future changes in the political environment more supportive of resistance. Moreover, some circumstances may prompt defiance as a way to test the probability of actual enforcement. Given these alternatives, it should be clear that there is an important reciprocal relationship between policy impact and response. The direction of response may be influenced by perceptions of expected effects and vice versa. What policy recipients expect to happen as a result of implementation may influence their subsequent behavior and attitudes and, thus, their ultimate performance.

These examples suggest that discrepancies or inconsistencies are likely to emerge between analyses of response and impact. The importance of reconciling such inconsistencies in this regard cannot be overstated, especially when the inquiry draws heavily upon one of these sources of data about policy outcomes such as performance limited to procedural or behavioral actions. There may be important intervening factors which are missed by this approach.

The policy implementation literature is replete with instances of narrow focus which result in treating unexplained phenomena as anomalous and marginal. For example, many studies of *Miranda* conclude, based on widespread departmental adoption of procedures and use of warnings by police, that the decision has been effective. Yet this study finds that conclusion premature when evidence of impact and change is included in the investigation. Or, consider the inconsistency between state court responses to the Warren Court civil liberties decisions and subsequent state court decisions. While criticism was overwhelming (Canon, 194b), most state court decisions were nonetheless consistent with Supreme Court policy. This leaves an important question unresolved: what effect did these critical responses have on the willingness of criminal justice implementers to implement the decision?

Differences in the attentiveness to the problem of coherence and completeness is likely to be accentuated when studies arrive at different conclusions concerning the same policy. This is particularly conspicuous in the case of studies by Dolbeare and Hammond (1971) and R. Johnson (1967) of the Supreme Court school prayer decision. In a study focused on the implementing population, R. Johnson concludes that non-compliance by local school officials and teachers is explained by cognitive dissonance theory. His explanation holds that non-compliance among other strategies is likely to reduce tensions resulting from opposition to policics (for which hc has no undcrlying bclicf or commitmcnt) originated by institutions the individual respects. But when the focus is enlarged to include the actions of state officials as well as the implementing populations, the explanation changes. Thus, Dolbeare and Hammond found that non-compliance to school prayer occurred not because of cognitive dissonance but because of state executive indifference to a "style" issue which did nothing to alter their power or preferences. This conclusion is corroborated by additional evidence that school prayer was not really a visible or controversial issue because of a general lack of any information or guidance from state officials.

Another term to distinguish is *performance*. We are interested not only in knowing what happened as a result of the implementation of public policy, but whether there has been some improvement in the nature and conduct of decision processes and outcomes. Issues of effectiveness as well as efficiency, including fairness and due process, must figure into an appraisal of performance. Information concerning impact is often the only source of information available by which to infer performance and determine the extent of change. Moreover, when objective data is available it may only provide evidence of procedural adoption but little evidence of actual utilization. Therefore, data about impact can provide an important source of inferences about actual performance, as long as it is used cautiously and judiciously.

In addition to these elements of outcome, policy implementation studies must also document the extent of *change*. Policy related changes are difficult to measure, for change can occur on many different levels and may vary over time. Change or the absence of it may be manifested in beliefs, behavior, attitudes, procedure and organizational structure, power relationships and so forth. It is unlikely that policies will produce simultaneous changes in all these dimensions;

rather, such changes that do occur as a result of implementation of policy will be limited to one or two dimensions. Those dimensions *least* likely to change (for reasons discussed in Chapter 7) include beliefs, attitudes and organizational structure. In contrast, behavior and procedure are potentially more amenable to alteration. The reason why behavior and procedure are more likely to change is that they constitute the formal and visible aspects of the implementers' contact with the policy process. Moreover, as state policies implementing federal criminal records regulations and the *Miranda* decision show, there are few costs to formal ratification of policies necessitating procedural change and perhaps substantial benefits if these are the *only* types of actions upon which assessments of compliance are made.

But as judicial impact studies stress, judgments about change based solely on procedural compliance are of limited utility in assessments of the efficacy of public policy. The Supreme Court civil liberties decisions were not only expected to produce behavioral and procedural change but also were expected to improve the quality of fact finding processes and fairness of subsequent case outcomes. Federal criminal records privacy policy has involved similar objectives.

Inferences about improvements in record quality resulting from changes in record management procedures are easier to document than the consequences of the *Miranda* warnings on the conduct of evidence gathering. Therefore, inferences about change resulting from the two court decisions are more hazardous and potentially misleading if based solely on official outcomes of criminal justice processes such as rates of arrest and conviction, number of warrants issued, or motions to suppress evidence. Changes in case outcomes may result from factors unrelated to adoption and use of due process guidelines.

Thus, the more relevant measure of results of policies such as *Mapp* or *Miranda* might be changes in elite attitudes and support, interorganizational processes, organizational structure, judicial outcomes or frequency of appellate review. Other measures such as change in the proportion of decisions not to arrest or charge, or plea bargaining, or other non-judicial decision making would also be an important source of information on the extent of change. Such measures would tell us more about how reform-oriented policies affect the configuration of informal processes where, as Horowitz (1977) contends, the change or lack of it is most likely to be manifested.

COMMON CONDITIONS OF EFFECTIVE IMPLEMENTATION

Some consensus has been reached in the policy implementation literature regarding the importance of the extent of change, clarity, elite support and enforcement in determining the outcomes of public policy. These factors are briefly described here in the context of the literature on Congressional and judicial policy. The importance of these conditions in theories which generalize about

TABLE 1.

Applied Studies Related to
Minimal Threat of Change

Variables	Studies
Extent of goal consensus	Van Meter and Van Horn (1975); Mazmanian and Sabatier (1981)
Amount of public support*	Van Meter and Van Horn (1975); Mazmanian and Sabatier (1981)
Organizational complexity increases magnitude of change	Pressman and Wildavsky (1973); Rabinovitz, Pressman and Rein (1976)
Conflicting values affect utility and/or intensity of opposition	Brown and Stover (1977); Rodgers and Bullock (1976)
Extent of conflict between attitudes and behavior (creates dissonance)	R. Johnson (1967); Muir(1967)
Extent to which policy is anticipated	Wasby (1970); Krislov (1971)

*Baum (1981) says an environmental perspective is not as useful in understanding court implementation.

their implications for understanding the political system will be developed in the next section.

Minimal Threat of Change

The implementation literature holds that judicial and legislative policies which involve extensive change are less likely to be effectively implemented than those in which change is minimal. Significantly, while courts may be less constrained than legislatures by political environmental factors in making rulings involving profound social change, they are no less affected by problems in implementation. Table 1 lists applied studies related to the role of change which are discussed below.

Policies which involve extensive change but low goal consensus are more likely to encounter difficulties of implementation than policies with little change and high goal consensus (Van Meter and Van Horn, 1975). This is so because policy is largely a product of incremental decisions; short-term policies build on past ones deviating only slightly from prior goals and practices. Legislative policies involving extensive institutional change require an enormous amount of initial public support and continuous special interest support over time to insure they are faithfully and effectively executed. This support is especially vulnerable to dissipation over time, so subsequent erosion of initial success is likely a byproduct (Mazmanian and Sabatier, 1981). Unlike legislative policy, court decisions can involve extensive change with little public support. Therefore, implementation processes depend less on interest group support over time than on other factors internal to the judicial process and organizational context into which the decisions are injected (Baum, 1981).

Regardless of these important institutional differences, the amount of expected change does have a bearing on responses. There are at least three factors which reinforce the importance of change in influencing policy outcomes. These factors include complexity of organizational process involved, stability of the policy system, and the values, attitudes and expectations of implementers.

First, policies which entail organizational change and interorganizational coordination are likely to be perceived by implementers as involving more extensive change than those minimizing such effects (Pressman and Wildavsky, 1973). Even policies with high goal consensus are likely to be ineffective if they also require organizational change.

Next, policies involving policy systems characterized by instability and fluctuation will generally be less capable of effectively implementing policy involving extensive change than systems which are stable and tightly coupled (Rabinovitz, Pressman and Rein, 1976). This is so because consensus and decision-making processes are more likely to be weak in "loosely-coupled" systems than in those which are not. Extensive bargaining and compromise is necessary before policies can be executed with the predictable result that as the policy nears implementation, ambiguity replaces clarity and specificity.

Finally, the values, attitudes and expectations of implementers influence the extent of policy change. If implementers do not share values underlying a decision or statute, then cognitive dissonance is more likely to result than if policy values are compatible with implementers' beliefs (R. Johnson, 1967; Muir, 1967). Moreover, policies involving extensive change in values may affect the perceived utility of and the intensity with which the policy is supported or opposed by target groups (Brown and Stover, 1977; Rodgers and Bullock, 1976). Policies involving extensive change which produce intense opposition are less likely to be effectively implemented than those involving neutrality or weak opposition. (Van Meter and Van Horn, 1975). Expectations also affect the way the magnitude of change is characterized. For example, court decisions which are not anticipated by target groups may produce greater expectations of change than decisions and trends which build slowly over time (Wasby, 1970; Krislov, 1971). Importantly, regardless of the actual amount of change, policies can produce expectations about outcomes which differ markedly from actual effects.

TABLE 2.

Applied Studies Related to Unambiguous Mandate

Variables	Studies
Identifies what is expected (e.g., behavior, performance)	Van Meter and Van Horn (1975)
Limits distortion, delegation	Lowi (1979)
Provides resource to supporters	Mazmanian and Sabatier (1981)
Affects efficacy of judicial communication process	Wasby (1970; 1973)
Limits bureaucratic discretion through guidelines; facilitates oversight	Rabinovitz, Pressman and Rein (1976)
Complexity of legislation and limitation of judicial decisions necessitates detailed and specific guidelines	Van Horn (1979); Baum (1981); Shapiro (1968)

Unambiguous Mandate

Another tenet of successful implementation is that the policy objectives should be stated clearly, intended behavior identified and performance specified (Van Meter and Van Horn, 1975; Mazmanian and Sabatier, 1981). Table 2 summarizes the findings of the following applied studies with respect to clarity.

Clarity of policy is important for three reasons. It tells implementers what is expected of them and, therefore, limits delegation (Lowi, 1979). It provides a way to deter deliberate distortion or misrepresentation by those seeking to evade implementation. And, an unambiguous policy provides a resource to supporters of the policy (i.e., clients and special interests) to influence implementation process (Mazmanian and Sabatier, 1981). Judicial opinions are somewhat more limited than statutes in the potential for clarity. While statutes provide general rules for action, judicial decisions prohibit certain acts and are deliberately narrow in scope. Little is said about alternative behavior (Baum, 1981).

However, the complexity of legislative processes and necessity for compromise make intentional vagueness and delegated discretion inevitable byproducts of statutes (Van Horn, 1979). To the extent that both courts and legislatures face similar problems of complexity, intermediate and lower level implementers are given responsibility for the development of more detailed guidelines to provide the clarity lacking in original policy (Baum, 1981; Shapiro, 1968). State appellate courts sometimes generate principles and precedents of broad scope and clarity from cases based on extremely narrow factual situations. However, most decisions are not stated unequivocably nor do they consistently specify how implementers' conduct should be changed to conform to rulings protecting defendants' rights.

Further, policy clarity affects the efficacy of processes by which policy is transmitted from superiors to subordinates. In this respect, it is held that courts are less able than legislatures to control the way decisions are transmitted. Thus, courts are more dependent on communication processes which are directly influenced by numerous participants in a judicial process (Wasby, 1970; 1973). Consequently, clarity is essential to limit distortion by lower level implementers. Thus, the exercise of oversight powers is essential to obtain feedback regarding bureaucratic fidelity to legislative intent (Rabinovitz, Pressman and Rein, 1976).

Supportive State and Local Elites

Next, the literature holds that initial and continous support by state and local elites is crucial to effective implementation of federal policy. There are two sources of elite support: (1) governors, legislators, judges and local elected officials; and (2) state and local agency administrators. Table 3 provides a summary list of the applied studies regarding the role of elites discussed below.

State and local elected officials are especially important to the success of federal intergovernmental policy because such officials exercise direct control over agency resources and activities. These resources provide an important source of patronage by which political executives can reward supporters and influence outcomes. While support for federal programs is determined by the national political environment, support by state and local elected officials is especially crucial to initial implementation (Baumer and Van Horn, 1984). In addition, over the long run a "fixer" (a legislator or executive who controls resources important to the program) should be ready to intervene on a continuous basis in order to protect the program from destruction (Bardach, 1977). In this regard, in recent years the devolution of decision making to state and local elected officials has been urged as a strategy to increase elite support by strengthening accountability and representation processes at state and local levels (Van Horn, 1979; Porter and Tarr, 1982).

Another way in which state executives and legislators can influence policy implementation processes is through their power to interpret policy intent and objectives for lower level implementers. Such interpretations can decisively influence attitudes of subordinates in the policy system. As Dolbeare and Ham-

TABLE 3.

Applied Studies Related to
Supportive State and Local Elites

Variables	Studies
State and Local Elected Officials	
Control of resources for patronage	Baumer and Van Horn (1984)
Strong support by state and local officials crucial to initial implementation	Baumer and Van Horn (1984); Ripley and Franklin (1982)
Extent of aggressive and continuous oversight ("fixer")	Bardach (1977)
Nature of interpretation (e.g., narrow, broad, accuracy)	Dolbeare and Hammond (1971)
Extent of devolution of policy-making and discretion	Porter and Tarr (1982)
State and Local Administrators	
Whether new agencies created	Mazmanian and Sabatier (1981)
Mobilization of supportive interest groups	Mazmanian and Sabatier(1981); Rourke (1976)
Consistency of statutory goals with agency staff preferences (or lower court judges)	Brown and Stover (1977); Rodgers and Bullock (1976)

mond (1971) found, elite predispositions toward a policy can reinforce misinterpretation of policy in which the lack of positive action is rationalized away.

In addition to state executives and other state officials, state and local agency administrators with direct responsibility for implementation can influence outcomes. Federal policies which create new agencies and organizational processes by which policy is implemented are more likely to achieve initial policy objectives because implementers may be chosen who are supportive of its aims and statutory purposes. In addition, agency administrators must be skillful in the use of resources and mobilization of interest group support to persuade executives to continue to support efforts toward implementation (Mazmanian and Sabatier,

1981). If these skills are lacking, little success can be expected in securing support and cooperation in implementation (Rourke, 1976).

One final factor in determining the degree of support by agency administrators is the extent to which statutory goals are consistent or compatible with their preferences (Brown and Stover, 1977). For example, policies which impose costs with little payoff for administrators with respect to continued interest group support and long term agency survival will find little support, so resistance becomes an acceptable alternative (Rodgers and Bullock, 1976).

Possibility of Enforcement

As Richard Neustadt declared, decisions are not ''self-executing'' (1960), and policies adopted by legislatures and courts are no exception. Any policy will encounter some indifference or resistance which must be overcome to achieve goals and objectives. Therefore, effective policy implementation requires that some means be available to ensure that intended policy objctives are implemented. Thus, enforceability is an important factor in the applied studies listed in Table 4.

In this respect, the implementation of legislative and court-originated policy is thought to differ in a fundamental respect. Legislative policy objectives are primarily achieved through an inducement system in which conditions are attached to grants-in-aid. In contrast, courts must rely primarily on sanctions to enforce their decisions (see Baum, 1981, for a succinct comparison).

Inducement through the allocation of resources is intended to make observance of policy more attractive; the benefits are meant to outweigh the costs (Rodgers and Bullock, 1976; Brown and Stover, 1977). Factors likely to affect the efficacy of inducements include policy salience to implementing agency unit members (Elmore, 1979; Berman, 1980); the proportionate effect on its budget (Van Horn, 1979); and the likelihood of actually suffering the loss of funds (Baumer and Van Horn, 1984).

The most direct means of enforcement available to legislatures—withdrawal of funds and intervention by superiors in the activities of subordinates—are rarely employed. In fact, they need not be because there are a variety of other indirect but effective approaches to achieving implementation (Van Meter and Van Horn, 1975).

The statute itself constitutes an important source of leverage to legislators and bureaucrats to enable enforcement. New agencies may be created or existing ones designated for policy execution that are sympathetic to the policy objectives, likely to build professional and client alliances and willing to pursue aggressive agendas. Decision rules of implementing policies (e.g., grant allocation formulas and regulatory procedures) can also be structured to minimize veto points and insure organizational consistency with intended objectives (Mazmanian and Sabatier, 1981).

Grant-in-aid programs secure advance compliance by requiring detailed plans

TABLE 4.

Applied Studies Related to
Possibility of Enforcement

Variables	Studies
Inducement Systems (Legislatures and Bureaucracies)	
Policy benefits exceed costs of non-compliance	Brown and Stover (1977); Rodgers and Bullock (1976)
Salience to implementers	Elmore (1979); Berman (1980)
Budget effect	Van Horn (1979)
Probability of loss of funds	Van Meter and Van Horn (1975); Baumer and Van Horn (1984)
Extent statute structures implementation (e.g., limits veto points)	Mazmanian and Sabatier (1981)
Extent of plan requirements and guidelines	Nieman and Lovell (1981)
Congruence of values of national officials and local implementers	Gray and Williams (1980)
Sanction Systems (Courts)	
Make costs of non-compliance less attractive	Baum (1976b); Brown and Stover (1977)
Credibility and zone of acceptance	C. Johnson and Canon (1984)
Intensity of demands	Krislov (1971)
Number and type of target groups affected (e.g., potential for litigation)	Brown and Stover (1977); Scheingold (1982)
Likelihood of reversal of decisions	Baum (1976b)

for the administration and allocation of funds. In addition, guidelines may be promulgated to carefully specify acceptable expenditures, intergovernmental and interpolicy responsibilities and relationships, reporting requirements and other areas. Regulatory intrusiveness may therefore be an important surrogate for the direct hierarchical control lacking in a federal system involving decentralization of power and state and local autonomy (Nieman and Lovell, 1981).

Finally, exchange strategies which try to maximize shared values (utility) between superiors and subordinates can be an important substitute for approaches based on power and dependence (Gray and Williams, 1980). Funding can be used to foster policy innovation and demonstration projects designed to cultivate mutual support for change. Moreover, to the extent that state and local officials can be encouraged to address common problems through federal initiatives, the need for active enforcement is diminished. Thus, recent federal policies have emphasized the strengthening of state and local relations under revenue sharing in order to devolve accountability and thus, enforcement, to lower levels of power.

Sanctions, on the other hand, are meant to make a negative response less attractive. Sanctions increase the cost of resistance without altering the benefits of acceptance (Baum, 1976b; Brown and Stover, 1977). Therefore, to be effective, sanctions must entail the threat of substantial loss and credibility of use; that is, the recipient must value the object forfeited and must perceive that the sanction is likely to be inflicted for failure to implement (Baum, 1976b; Brown and Stover, 1977). Factors likely to affect the credibility of the sanction and likelihood of implementation include zone of acceptance (C. Johnson and Canon, 1984), intensity of enforcer's demand (Krislov, 1971), number of target groups affected (Brown and Stover, 1977), number and intensity of groups willing to challenge officials for resistance or evasion (Brown and Stover, 1977; Scheingold, 1982), and likelihood of reversal (Baum, 1976b).

In sum, each of the factors discussed here provides some purchase for understanding policy implementation. Yet applied studies weigh the significance of these factors differently because of differences in the social and pyschological theories which underpin their analysis. Therefore, next I will describe, contrast and identify strengths and weaknesses in these theories with respect to how these factors of implementation are employed to explain the political system as a whole.

THEORETICAL PERSPECTIVES UNDERLYING STUDIES OF POLICY IMPLEMENTATION

Three observations should be made before examining differences among theoretical perspectives. First, the close conceptual connection of some theories to the compliance perspective discussed earlier seriously compromises their explanatory range. This is particularly the case with utility theory, some versions of organization theory, and to some extent, cognitive dissonance theory.

Second, applied policy studies rarely exhibit a self-consciousness about theoretical commitments, often employing or mixing more than one perspective. Consequently, the theory or theories being illustrated and tested by the empirical data are not always clear. Therefore, one purpose of this exercise is to identify the most central theoretical underpinnings of selected works in order to illustrate how they view the significance and political implications of particular factors.

Third, most of the theories reviewed here explicitly or tacitly advance some conception of political legitimacy as a functional necessity for the maintenance of the political system. This means that citizens' acceptance and support of the political regime and its policies must rest on prior conceptions about the legality of its authority as well as the appropriate use of its institutional power and policy-making prerogatives. I contend that issues regarding the legitimacy of regime structure and policies cannot be assimilated effectively into existing theoretical frameworks (as C. Johnson and Canon claim, see especially, 1984: 189–202), but must be developed as an independent and distinctive theory. Legitimation theory suffers not from its lack of promise but from its relative underdevelopment as a plausible alternative theoretical perspective for applied studies of policy implementation.

Utility Theory

Social and political scientists rarely employ utility theory with the same rigor as economists. Instead, some policy analysts advocate a looser, less stringent version. Such practitioners include Wilson (1977) who attempts to demonstrate its ability to explain the motives for crime and Posner (1982) who shows how crime policy, including civil liberties decisions, is governed by utility maximization. Brown and Stover (1977) use it to explain the responses of criminal justice officials including judges, while Rodgers and Bullock (1976) use it to explain responses of school officials to federal desegregation policy.

The basic presupposition of utility theory is that people are primarily motivated to maximize pleasure (or gain) and to minimize pain (loss). This is based on the assumption of economic rationality that people are endowed with a complete and consistent set of preferences which are continuous over time and primarily selfishly motivated. For example, implementers and consumers of public policies will calculate and weigh the value of expected outcomes or benefits of compliance against the loss from the risks of non-compliance (potential punishment). Social and political scientists generally relax the requirement of quantification of value by including attitudes toward outcomes as well as other non-quantifiable variables such as behavior and beliefs. Expectations generally refer to the perceived probability of a course of behavior resulting in a benefit or cost.

Utility theory is beset with difficulties in theory and application. First, there is a large and impressive literature challenging the viability of both cognitive and moral dimensions of utility theory and utilitarianism. Criticisms of the cognitive aspect of utility theory include its over-rationalized view of individual choice (Elster, 1983; Sen and Williams, 1982); the tenuousness of its assumptions of transitivity (consistency) and stability of preference (Dyke, 1981; Hollis, 1983); its inability to account for policy outcomes contrary to real interests

(Connolly, 1983; Goodin, 1982); and the limitation of its assumption of selfishness for an adequate theory of collective action (Parfait, 1984).

The moral dimension of utilitarianism suffers from related defects which include a perverse obliviousness to individual rights (Dworkin, 1977; Hampshire, 1983) and an insensitivity to the possibility of choosing a coherent life plan or project over short term want satisfaction (Rawls, 1971).

In applied policy studies utility theory is vulnerable on a number of counts including important limitations in its view of political legitimacy. First, utility theory is unable to shed problems associated with its compliance perspective. There continues to be, therefore, a tendency to oversimplify the characteristics of the policy system (e.g., hierarchical relationships) and to equate policy failure with the absence of tangible incentives or credible means of enforcement or sanction. Moreover, its applicability appears limited to implementing or consuming populations where enforcement has some purchase in explaining behavior. However, cognitive dissonance theory suggests that analyses limited to behavioral responses generally fail to explain just how inducements and sanctions influence the motivations and attitudes of policy participants and recipients. Thus, behavioral indicators construed in terms of wants or preferences may tell us more about the acceptability of inducements or sanctions than about attitudes toward the policy or its consequences. Thus, we may learn more about the symptoms rather than the determinants of policy outcomes.

Rodgers and Bullock (1972) illustrate this deficiency well in their discussion of the relationship between general law-abidingness and policy-induced acts of compliance. The authors maintain that there is no inconsistency between general law-abidingness or the belief in the legitimacy of the political system and specific acts of non-compliance such as tax resistance or evasion of school integration by school officials or parents. Importantly, these responses occur when consumers or implementers believe they benefit from non-compliance *and* that they do not expect to be caught or punished. Thus, the primary consideration is the estimate of whether the regime cares enough about the policy to actually enforce it rather than that of its appropriateness or authoritativeness. This proposes a very strange and cynical view of legitimacy which collapses it into coercion. For, if governmental officials are unable to depend upon or generate sufficient voluntary support for their policies because they are suspected of hypocrisy, then they are already suffering from a legitimation problem. This reasoning generates a kind of perverse logic which holds that the more coercion and/or repression a government uses, the more sincere its policy commitment and the more legitimate its authority.

The notion of enforcement and legitimacy advanced here finds little support in studies of the implementation of federal policy. For example, Baumer and Van Horn (1984) argue in their analysis of the politics of employment and training policy that the state and local implementation of the Comprehensive Employment and Training Act (CETA, 1973) suffered from the overuse of Congressional oversight, precipitated, in part, by incorrect and exaggerated perceptions of fraud and abuse. The tightening of eligibility rules and addition of new layers of regulations in 1978 underscored the counterproductive effects of the substitution of sanctions for incentives in precipitating the withdrawal of elected officials active in leadership and supervision of the local prime sponsor activities. Decisions such as this helped damage CETA's image and undermined public support of it as a legitimate governmental activity.

Communication Theory

In contrast to utility theory, theories of communication place more emphasis on the form and substance of the mandate than on enforcement mechanisms. Although communication theory awaits further use in applied policy studies, Neustadt (1960); Deutsch (1966; 1970); Wasby (1974–1975; 1976); and Lowi (1979) have developed systematic theories to date.

Neustadt's theory of the importance of the persuasiveness and finality of communication in policy effectiveness grew out of his analysis of presidential leadership. Given limited time and resources and the need to conserve political capital, effective communication becomes an essential element of presidential power. Therefore, intentions must be made clear, goals clearly enunciated, objectives carefully specified, and the decision must be perceived as final. However, one of the weaknesses of Neustadt's theory is the difficulty executives face given only indirect control over bureaucratic implementation processes. While the power to exploit the rule-making process is an important tool available to executives to achieve their intent, as is control over cabinet or high level agency appointees, there is no guarantee that regulatory revision will contribute to greater clarity or finality in advancing policy objectives (Hargrove and Nelson, 1984; Rabinovitz, Pressman and Rein, 1976).

Deutsch has charted the most elaborate and comprehensive theory of information flow in the political system. His ambitious theory unites systems theory (discussed later) with cognitive dissonance and Freudian theory. Deutsch argues that the governmental and policy process function analogously to the model of cybernetic theory proposed by Weiner (1950). Contrary to Neustadt, Deutsch contends that the political system has the capacity to steer itself and maintain equilibrium (e.g., political stability).

According to Deutsch, the political system is constituted, in essence, by a combination of decision points, each with different functions for screening information to achieve policy outputs. The screening function performed by the political system will produce policies which are simultaneously feasible as well as acceptable to both the regime and its citizens.

The problem with Deutsch's theory is that it presents a theory of the political and policy process which is disembodied. He does not explain the roles of officials, institutions or implementers anywhere. Consequently, we are never sure whose interests are served by the policy process and just how institutions and policies are legitimized by a self-governing system.

Wasby has advanced a more realistic and tentative analysis of the relationship between the *channels* used to communicate policy and the *context* in which the messages are received. There are, in fact, a variety of means by which policy objectives can be communicated which include existing hierarchies, attentive publics, advisory opinions, training and other means. Factors pertinent to the context include visibility of the decision, who responds, organizational size and form, community beliefs, and others. Wasby documents the interplay of channels and contexts in his 1976 study of how communication processes affect responses of small town police departments to civil liberties decisions. He found numerous defects in the match between channels and contexts contributing to a failure to change police conduct.

Other studies of judicial policies, however, question the possibility of achieving finality in policy interpretations as Neustadt contends and challenges the possibility of controlling appropriate channels of communication. Tarr found in a test of the Neustadt doctrine that decisions characterized by persuasivness, clarity of argument and perceived finality *do not* curtail the range of state court responses to successively more specific U.S. Supreme Court school prayer decisions nor produce greater compliance (1977: 103). In another study, Milner (1971a) discovered that police responses to *Miranda* were more heavily influenced by internal departmental information sources even though police were exposed to more accurate and less distorted information sources outside the department (e.g., prosecutors and judges).

Nowhere does the doctrine of clear and effectively communicated policy achieve greater significance than in Lowi's (1979) analysis of the liberal, welfare state. Lowi argues that the combination of ambitious but ambiguous and uncoordinated policy, involving excessively delegated discretion to unaccountable bureaucracies, is responsible for massive policy failure (e.g., of the War on Poverty) and has exacerbated problems of legitimacy of the American political system. The rule of law has been replaced by "interest group liberalism" putting the state in an unacceptable role of "receivership" for entrenched interests and questionable policy.

Lowi's prescription for the restoration of law is the establishment of a "juridical democracy." The Supreme Court would assume an enlarged role of overseeing Congressional laws to insure that they are unambiguous, minimize bureaucratic discretion, maximize Congressional oversight, and address issues affecting the common good. Lowi's conception is problematic because he assumes that the judiciary can easily overcome legislators' proclivity toward compromise and ambiguity and is capable of crafting a role for courts which does not overstep the constitutional separation of powers. Moreover, increased judicial activism has exacerbated rather than reduced problems of legitimation facing the American political system.

Organization Theory

The classic literature on organization theory holds that there are significant organizational constraints to policies regardless of how clear the mandate, favorable the inducements or severe the sanction for implementation. Organizational structures tend to be inertial (e.g., dominated by routine and rigid rules), reinforcing predispositions toward maintenance of existing policy or incremental changes which stabilize their budget, mission, jurisdiction and measures of performance (Downs, 1967). This theory has been used to demonstrate the incremental character of policy-making (Lindblom, 1968) and budget processes (Wildavsky, 1979), and constitutes an important element in studies of constraints to organizational innovation (Yin, Heald and Vogel, 1977). Therefore, the most significant factor affecting implementation processes emerging from these studies is the extent of change.

But the somewhat stereotypical image of organizations projected by classic theory has undergone some important revisions. Wilson's (1968) study of police department styles and routine discovered that variations in local government structure and community political environment within which police operate contribute to differences in the perception and conduct of law enforcement activities. And, in a path-breaking work Allison (1971) determined that differences in organizational structure contribute to differential responses to policy implementation processes. An important implication is that differences in organizational structure can contribute to variations in performance measures, as demonstrated by Jacoby's (1980) study of offices of prosecution.

As organization theory has further evolved, analysts have focused more attention on factors shaping unit member attitudes and behavior. Some of the most significant contributions in this regard have included the work of Kaufman (1960), Davis (1969), and Lipsky (1980). Kaufman's study of the forest service ranger contended that centralizing policies fail to understand the importance of discretion in motivating individual performance. Lipsky criticizes this view by suggesting that too much policy-making authority is delegated to "street level bureaucrats" (especially in law enforcement and client-centered social services), enabling them to exercise enormous power affecting the rights, privacy, welfare and life chances of those at the receiving end.

Davis takes a more legalistic and cautious approach than the others, arguing that we shuld be careful to avoid confusing the difference between abolishing discretion and "structuring" it. Proposals to structure discretion should acknowledge the importance of procedure and rules in establishing a common set of expectations about conduct among implementers as well as consumers. Structured discretion identifies standards of conduct by which performance can be measured rather than prescribing or circumscribing detailed behavior. Davis concludes that the problems of accountability of an administrative state can be handled best by making it possible to identify, evaluate and challenge the use and abuse of discretion. Proposals to eliminate discretion run the risk of producing a bureaucratic state insensitive to individuality and intolerant of freedom.

In a similar vein, other recent approaches to organizational behavior contend that properly channeled discretion may be conducive to innovation, experimentation and adaptation of policy to unforseen circumstances. For example, Elmore (1979) contends that a compliance perspective ignores the importance of institutional learning and fine turning that a policy must undergo to be effective. Therefore, he recommends a more tolerant attitude toward state and local variations in response and performance under national policies.

One crucial deficiency in organization theory (especially classic theory) is its almost exclusive development and application in the context of executive bureaucracies. Consequently, little knowledge has been developed thus far as to whether and how it applies to judicial policy implementation. While Shapiro (1968) and Baum (1981) have provided some interesting preliminary lines of comparison, few studies have examined similarities or differences in applied settings. I believe that an additional significant barrier to comparative studies is the preoccupation with stereotypical bureaucratic routine organizations to the exclusion of other forms such as professional expertise or collegial whose structures, incentive systems and conduct differ in significant respects (Dalton and Fitzpatrick, 1985).

Next, the emergent preoccupation with discretion (e.g., Elmore, 1979), exaggerates the importance of unit member conduct at the expense of examining ways in which elites operate as a positive or negative force in creating an environment conducive or inhibiting to innovation. Where innovation is tied too closely to discretion it also exaggerates the control of unit members over policy execution compared to other environmental factors. Moreover, it unjustifiably collapses the distinction between policy formulation, implementation and reformulation processes upon which ideas about democratic accountability are based. My subsequent examination of the state implementation of civil liberties policies illustrates the dilemma that control of discretion poses for achieving institutional change without sacrificing accountability. It examines how the preoccupation of civil liberties interests and law enforcement with discretion locks them into the comfort of appearances with self-fulfilling and paradoxical consequences for the possibility of progressive reform.

Systems Theory

In *A Framework for Political Analysis* Easton proposed that we define politics broadly as the "authoritative allocation of societal values with binding effects" (1965a: 49–50). In addition, he proposes (similar to Deutsch, but absent the psychological analogy) that we conceive of the allocation process in terms of a "system" whereby environmental policy demands and supports are processed by the political system to produce policy outputs. Feedback mechanisms in the form of elections and general purpose evaluations of policy effects continuously lead to new demands and supports *and* provide information to decision-makers as to potentially necessary alterations in either policies or institutional rules or structures. Construed in its broadest terms, systems theory constitutes an important corrective to narrow gauge focuses on organizational behavior by conceptualizing a more general way to understand the relationship between elite support, regime continuity and institutional change.

In a companion book, *A Systems Analysis of Political Life* (1965b), Easton attempts to unite systems and legitimation theory. The obvious care and thoughtfulness with which he develops the concept of legitimacy stands not only in stark contrast to the crude psychological reductionism of the Deutsch model, but has provided the basis for the development of more recent theories of state legitimation by Habermas (1973) and others.

Easton's notion of legitimacy is elaborated in his description and appraisal of the role of "supports" in stabilizing the political system (see especially Part IV, chapters 18–21). Easton identifies two types of ideologies which provide system support—*partisan ideologies* (e.g., liberal, conservative) and *legitimating ideologies* (e.g., expressive, instrumental). Partisan ideologies, which pertain to beliefs about societal norms such as freedom, equality, and participation are oriented toward public policies and their effects, providing a source of "specific support" to the political system. Legitimizing ideologies provide "diffuse support" and are defined as ethical principles and constitutional foundations which limit institutional roles, power and responsibilities of elected officials and administrators. Instrumental ideologies pertain to justifications officials provide to demonstrate how their use of institutional power satisfies constitutional norms. In contrast, expressive ideologies capture, in Easton's words:

> . . . The emotional roots of appeal found in a vision of life, society and politics lie in the capacity of the belief system to establish a firm link to the motivational structure of members of the system; to their conception of feelings about their own needs, interests and place in the political and social system or to their convictions that the ideology correctly or truthfully explains the real world (1965b: 295).

The importance of expressive ideologies in their partisan form (e.g., through party affiliation) lies therefore in their twofold purpose of establishing personal identity and facilitating identification with the political system. This implies at a minimum that an important requisite to system stability is the voluntary allegiance of its citizens.

One challenge which confronts governmental elites is how to effectively mobilize sufficient levels of both "specific" and "diffuse" support in order to execute governmental functions with respect to the adoption and implementation of public policies. Easton's explanation of how elites reconcile differences between partisan ideologies while maintaining support from the regime (e.g., constitutional order and norms) is unsatisfactory in that he tends to collapse the distinction between specific and diffuse support into concepts such as the "common good" and "political division of labor" (1965b: 316, 327).

A difficulty which stems from the use of such bridging concepts is the mistaken assumption that partisan ideologies can never conflict over issues pertaining to regime structure (e.g., separation of powers) (1965b: 339). Another is his apparent assumption that regime legitimation is maintained by elites at the input rather than output end of the system. This limits citizen challenges to official policies as a source of feedback for the evaluation of public policy. However, institutional elites are just as apt to come under fire for the way they use their offices and mobilize political resources to *implement* as well as to adopt public policies.

Since Easton's work, scholarly interest has shifted substantially away from systemic conditions toward the factors influencing implementation and shaping outputs in policy specific areas such as criminal justice, education, health care and employment and training. Theoretical and applied studies by Rabinovitz, Pressman and Rein (1976); Rein and Rabinovitz (1977); and Berman (1980), for example, seek to determine the political dynamics of policy subsystems in the context of the policy cycle.

The findings which emerge from these and other studies are that policy implementation processes (especially guideline development) are somewhat self-contained worlds insulated from wider political accountability. As Ripley and Franklin (1982) aptly put it, "subgovernments" composed of a constellation of clientele interests, bureaucrats, politicians and professionals determine the interest served and excluded. From this perspective the notion of a national political system may be a misnomer for what in reality are loosely connected power structures dominated by single-issue interests.

These findings also tend to undermine assumptions about the independence of a system legitimating resources and processes from elite dominance, for they suggest that the policies which are legitimated are those which serve dominant interests rather than those which are most effective in addressing problems. Paul Starr's (1982) recent analysis of the medical profession provides an excellent example of the power perpetuating consequences of domination by a singular professional perspective in effectively de-legitimizing competing alternatives. This suggests that the traditional wall of separation between the authority and governance responsibilities of elected officials and the power of bureaucratic and special interests has been increasingly eroded.

Cognitive Dissonance

Since its emergence in experimental studies conducted by Leon Festinger (1957), cognitive psychology has provided a very powerful theory for explaining the significance of change as a factor in policy implementation (e.g., Huntington, 1981). However, it has been employed sparingly in applied studies (R. Johnson, 1967; Muir, 1967). According to Festinger, persons are compelled by an internal drive to establish harmony or consistency among their opinions, knowledge, attitudes and behavior. Conflicts among these usually result *following* a decision involving a choice between two or more alternatives which involve inducements or sanctions for specified behavior. Dissonance occurs when the positive characteristics of the rejected alternative and the negative effects of the chosen alternative are revealed after the action is taken. In other words, any choice is bound to involve an element of uncertainty and ambiguity as to whether it was correct or appropriate. Further, choice is likely to expose conflicting beliefs and commitments.

Therefore, people exhibit a strong impulse to reduce dissonance by justifying (or rationalizing) their choice by either increasing the desirability of the chosen alternative or decreasing the value or advantages of the rejected choice. For example, police may reconcile the inconsistency between their duty to faithfully execute laws and their commission of civil liberties violations by the greater benefits to public safety derived from denying the factually guilty their Constitutional rights. They might also reduce the dissonance associated with punishment for illegal behavior they consider legitimate by downgrading the probability of actual enforcement by the courts or departmental superiors.

There are several difficulties with cognitive dissonance theory and its use in applied studies which should be stressed. First, positing the origin of dissonance reduction in unconscious psychological states strips the agent of the capacity for autonomous choice and rationality—characteristics essential for distinguishing between inconsistencies between beliefs and between beliefs and behavior—assumptions upon which cognitive psychology is partly predicated. Elster's (1983: 24–25) attempt to save this theory from these insurmountable difficulties by treating autonomy and judgment as residual capacities after sources of distortion of preference formation have been eliminated is not persuasive. For it unjustifiably reduces the capacity for intentional action and critical reflection to a secondary status.

Second, it is not altogether clear what reasoning process the subject employs to distinguish between conflicting beliefs and to sort out dissonant elements from those which are consonant with one's behavior. Festinger correctly acknowledges that consistency cannot serve as the criterion because of its logical connotations (1957: 2). Therefore, he contends that "reality" performs this orienting function by exerting pressure in the direction of bringing the appropriate cognitive elements into correspondence with that reality (1957: 11). But this only creates additional difficulties because we want to be able to distinguish between responses to conflicts between beliefs and behavior unconstrained by power or conditioning and those stemming from, say, projection, paranoia, repression, wishful thinking or transference.

Finally, cognitive dissonance theory arbitrarily limits the potential strategies available to the subject to reduce dissonance. The contention is that subjects show a stronger inclination to alter beliefs in line with behavior than the reverse, and that they are unlikely to attempt to change the environment or political ideologies which condition their choices. Yet one strategic behavioral response available to implementers who oppose a policy but fear sanctions for resistance is perfunctory execution. Accordingly, the appearance of conformity is presented to superiors while maintaining consistency with underlying beliefs. Another route available to policy opponents is to change the formal or informal rules affecting participation (such as a change in voter registration laws or electoral processes). Also, alternative institutions may be created such as private schools to escape integration or communes which nurture alternative life styles at odds with the dominant culture.

Unhappiness with some of the defects of cognitive dissonance theory prompted Elster (1983) to identify two other potential manifestations of dissonance reduction, acknowledged but undeveloped by Festinger. In doing so, Elster provides a more complete elaboration of what he believes are the implications of cognitive dissonance theory for social theory, politics and public policy.

Elster distinguishes between two types of impulses persons externalize to reduce cognitive dissonance in a political system incapable of completely satisfying each individual's preferences. One strategy which Elster considers a recurring feature of human conduct is "adaptive preference formation" (1983: 111–117). This cognitive drive is based on the theory that individual preferences typically reflect anticipatory reactions to the available possibilities. In other words, persons are apt to downgrade the inaccessible options. In essence, persons will limit their aspirations at or below the level of possible choices.

In contrast, "character planning" constitutes the attempt to improve personal welfare without the loss of autonomy. Instead of downgrading the inaccessible, the possible is upgraded. Elster contends that excessive expectations are functionally necessary to sustain the motivation necessary to achieve economic growth and political stability. They provide temporary contentment with and justification for the energy put into striving after unrealized goals. The paradox of character planning, however, as Elster suggests, is that as the real possibilities of attainment are increased, so is the level of frustration because people will tend to overshoot the actual possibilities, generating irrational expectations which cannot be satisfied (1983: 139).

Elster contends that for these reasons persons seek a release from the dissonance they experience because of conflict between their expectations and the possibilities. Freedom consists essentially in being able to choose *not* to do things which one may want to do. Therefore, the act of legitimation comes about through adaptive preference formation so that justifications are created which legitimate the social distance between and unequal power of political leadership and subjects (1983: 118, Chapter IV).

Elster cautions, however, that there is a problematic interdependence between frustrations due to irrational expectations and those due to new levels of expectations. In other words, there may be a double tendency to base one's preferences on misperceptions of the real possibilities (and therefore unreasonably suppress aspirations) or to irrationally exaggerate the probability of attainment of wants.

While Elster does not address this problem directly, he fails to provide an adequate defense of his conclusion that political stability can only be achieved when adaptive preferences prevail. Nor, for that matter, is it clearly demonstrable that either public policy or recipients' responses reflect primarily an adjustment to the currently available options. The New Deal and War on Poverty are excellent examples of aspiration-striving rather than resignation-acceptance policy strategies. Moreover, as Chapter 6 will demonstrate, the conflict between policy proponents constantly tending to upgrade the regulatory reach of ambiguous mandates while opponents (e.g., implementers) attempt to scale them down may have more to do with the politics of power than with cognitive dissonance.

Cognitive Expressivism

An alternative theoretical approach to understanding the cognitive capacities and actions of persons originates from the philosophical work of Wittgenstein (1953), Winch (1958), and Goffman's sociological investigations (1968; 1969). Their work contends that the language and ideas we use to express individual intentions, beliefs and aspirations and to characterize and understand our social existence partially constitutes the self-understandings (personal identity) and institutions which comprise a way of life. They do so because language (and knowledge claims upon which it is based) is governed by rules or coventional understandings about meaning in the social context of its use. I have chosen to designate this theoretical approach as cognitive expressivism.

Connolly (1983) and Harre (1980) have extended and strengthened the expressivist thesis in two significant directions. Connolly contends that key terms found in our political vocabulary (e.g., interests, power and freedom) express and reflect pre-understanding about shared moral judgments and standards which embody a way of life. In other words, the use of political vocabularies is rooted in more fundamental ideas about our capacities as autonomous and responsible agents. Connolly is not contending that there is universal agreement about the moral content of these background conventions. Rather, he advances a looser claim which stipulates only that some concepts would not be formed unless they expressed underlying views about the capacity for autonomy as well as responsible action (1983: 24–25, 213–214).

Political disputes over the terms of power, for example, simply reflect underlying differences over the best way to understand the relationship between the context in which the term is employed and the point of characterizing a set of institutional practices one way rather than another. The appraisive feature of political language provides the space for conflicts over the application of the terms of power (e.g., between persuasion, manipulation and coercion) in a particular context. Therefore, the contention that power has been exercised, resulting in the limitation of the recipients' choice or capacity to act, shifts the burden of responsibility to the power holder to justify that limitation (1983: 214).

Harre has used expressivist theory in order to develop a theory of institutional change. He contends that the public-collective dimension of human life is a product of the interplay between the *practical* and *expressive* orders. The practical order is constituted by the technological and material modes which sustain life while the expressive order pertains to the ways in which persons organize the system of values of honor, respect and contempt (1980: 4–5).

The expressive and practical orders rarely coincide, contributing to the tendency of individual aspirations to outstrip the possibility of their fulfillment. This may give rise to incongruities or discrepancies between, for example, the official doctrine or ideology upon which the institution is based (such as equal opportunity or freedom) and their actual attainment. These conflicts or inconsistencies occur partly because the limited positions available in the practical order must be modified and enlarged to fit expressive aspirations of its role-bearers. Consequently, new "moral careers" emerge for those who make innovations in the conduct of institutional roles.

In fact, as Harre contends, the continuity of an institution does not really require equivalence between the expressive and practical order. If it did, as Goffman's (1968) description of total institutions such as the asylum suggests, a transparency between self and official roles would result in an empty formalism of perfunctory performances (Harre, 1980: 360). Instead, institutions provide the space between the official and unofficial beliefs, attitudes and expectations of its members. Institutional change occurs when the load of latent beliefs and aspirations of its members are converted into new moral careers which help reconstitute official roles and remove limits to personal achievement. Institutional change will therefore reflect both modifications in the perceptions, beliefs and aspirations of its role-bearers and the actual distribution of respect and contempt, or other values, among available roles and positions (1980: 346–402).

An illustration of Harre's thesis would include the history of the labor movement. Locked into demeaning and insecure roles dictated by the technical imperatives of the economic order, workers organized around a set of aspirations designed to bring about not only increased economic security but greater respect from management. This new respect was then embodied in key changes in labor-management relations such as the contract and right to collective bargaining. Or, as Connolly might argue, these changes expressed underlying aspirations for freedom and politicized latent grievances about power and responsibility, reshaping the distribution of economic opportunities, burdens and benefits. In Chapter 7, I will suggest how we might understand criminal justice reform in these terms.

The theory of cognitive expressivism has spawned recent attempts by some of its proponents to explain political integration and conflict in terms of a theory of legitimacy. The most notable effort thus far has been made by Habermas (1973). Synthesizing the insights of both Marxist and systems theory, Habermas contends that the political stability of contemporary liberal, capitalist societies is threatened by multiple crisis tendencies which may issue from any of its institutional subsystems. These subsystems include the *economic*, *political-ad-*

ministrative and *socio-cultural* (see especially Held, 1982: 181–189, upon which my interpretation of Habermas is based).

According to Habermas, an "economic crisis" stems from insufficient consumable values; and a "rationality crisis" from inappropriate and ineffective intervention by the political-administrative system. A "legitimation crisis" stems from the contradictory tendency for increased intervention by the state in the economic sphere without the requisite resources of legitimacy (justifying ideologies) to do so; and a "motivation crisis" results from the erosion of traditional beliefs in privatism, competition and aspirations of success by a process of technocratic rationalization. For, as the state must increasingly intervene to address questions of fair distribution, the more citizens lose faith in the capacity of the market to distribute scarce resources, making a legitimation crisis inevitable.

Habermas has developed an insightful theory beset with many ambiguities and difficulties discussed more thoroughly elsewhere (see Thompson and Held, 1982). For our purposes, however, Habermas advances three important, although undeveloped ideas which could strengthen legitimation theory. First, Habermas acknowledges that there can be multiple sources of conflict within the political system, and no one source by itself is capable of causing a systemic crisis. Therefore, for example, under-performance of the economy or governmental over-regulation would not necessarily undermine support of constitutional foundations or belief in the capacity of the voters to elect new officials capable of adequately addressing these problems.

Second, Habermas recognizes that deficits are likely to occur in system support if the outcomes of its decisions or policies, for example, fail to coincide with the principles of its regime ideology or rationale for economic development and growth. From this perspective, in contrast to cognitive dissonance, the dominant institutions themselves can be a source of aspiration inflation, creating pressures for dissolution and the withdrawal of allegiance. Yet institutional officials may compensate for these deficits by supporting strategies designed to reduce the distance between regime values and practice. One avenue, of course, is a narrowing of goals and promises which the ideology advances (see Huntington, 1981) while another might consist of dismissing the credibility of the source of disaffection.

Third, Habermas acknowledges that the political system has the capacity to "absorb" or "displace" legitimation conflicts which might undermine regime stability. He has been criticized for failure to develop the notion of displacement more completely, instead of exaggerating the importance of "motivation crises" in explaining legitimation problems (Held, 1982: 188). Habermas has subsequently acknowledged this difficulty with his theory, concurring that "motivation" and "legitimation" crises are best kept analytically distinct. He concedes that cultural factors may intervene to sustain system legitimacy in part by enlarging instrumental attitudes and tolerance of cynicism and indifference (Habermas, 1982: 280–281).

Unfortunately, this concession increases the plausibility of the claim of cognitive dissonance theory that adaptation to institutional possibilities indeed represents a rational response to real institutional constraints. The more that institutional structures and cultural-ideological values present an interlocking character, the greater the need to adjust beliefs to coincide with the inescapable order of things. (See Huntington, 1981, for the application of cognitive dissonance theory to explain the inevitability of cynicism following periods of progressive reform.)

Connolly (1981) persuasively confronts this problem of the reality of appearances in the theory of legitimation issuing from the assumptions of expressivist theory. The rejoinder that his theory proposes consists of two contentions. One is that prior beliefs about individual autonomy, freedom and reflexivity provide the logical space within which dissonance can arise. This is illustrated by the fact that dissonance theory holds that cognitive pressures stem from the need to retain the appearance of consistency between outer conduct and inner convictions. Connolly contends that this impulse toward coherence embodies the image one wants to *project* to oneself and others as one who is acting freely instead of being driven by inner compulsion or outer necessity. Second, this psychological impulse is problematic because the identity of the self is bound up with the appearances one constructs serving to strengthen the reality of constraints to personal achievement and institutional reform.

For example, the more one perceives the barriers to achievement of aspirations as constituted by a set of interlocking institutional constraints whose alteration imposes unacceptable alterations in exisiting roles and/or the redistribution of resources toward more productive uses, the more unrealistic and irrational one's aspirations appear. Thus, the comfort of appearances locks individuals into self fulfilling behavior intransigent to change. As we shall see, this provides an important way to comprehend the barriers to institutional change.

Connolly develops these themes in the context of the problems of performance and allegiance which constrain the policies of the welfare state because the national government occupies a secondary status to that of the private economy which is geared toward the goal of increased productivity. Caught in a bind to both assist as well as discipline marginal, unproductive populations in the political economy, the welfare state becomes a screen upon which the disaffection from the civilization of productivity is projected. As that disaffection intensifies, regime values and norms come under pressure by reactionary policies and laws to support new economic imperatives which substitute the politics of utility for the promoting of a common good.

We can see the distinctions between expressive, dissonant and pathological modes of response more clearly by examing the psychological processes involved. The capacity for *introspection* and *projection* are essential ways in which individuals express, interpret and validate the personal and social reality of their attitudes and predispositions as well as their beliefs and convictions. Each of these psychological processes establishes avenues by which personal identity emerges and by which bonds are forged with the larger society and political community.

Nevertheless, the materials from which self-images and social possibilities are constructed are potentially vulnerable to distortion by internal (e.g., desires) and external constraints (e.g., ideology, institutional structure) operating on the beliefs and aspirations which form one's character or personality.

The process of introspection enables the individual to gain insights into the relationship which obtains between a given mental state (beliefs) and a disposition (desire). For example, if an individual experiences fear and resistance when encountering people in authority, the act of introspection helps call up past experiences of the kind which formed a belief upon which the disposition is based. Subsequent reflection upon the characteristics of past and comparison with present contexts involving authority enable the suspension of the belief to judge whether fear or resistance may be an appropriate response. While resistance may be an appropriate reaction in some contexts (e.g., when the legitimacy of the authority is being challenged), generally it would be considered a compulsive or obsessive predisposition to react that way toward authority always. *Introjection* describes a state of mind in which particular reactions to external objects are internalized in the form of dispositions which perpetuate behavior long after the original feelings about the object have subsided. Such behavior is often manifested in the form of persecutory anxiety and self-admonishments when these internalized dispositions surface (Wollheim, 1984: 120–128).

Projection is also a characteristic psychological capacity which manifests itself in both normal and pathological forms. Freud's discovery of pathological forms of projection has largely overshadowed (until recently) the non-destructive, creative forms of projection which strengthen social bonds and contribute toward change in our ideas and beliefs. Freud's concept of projection grew out of his experience with clients who attributed their own feelings or mental state to some other person. Projection allows individuals harboring unwanted dispositions to deposit them in other people. This helps alleviate frustration and anxieties created by incompatible desires by castigating others who manifest these traits.

However, the more severe forms of projection, originating from fantasies, require more than just rearrangement of mental states but adjustment of the external world to satisfy these fantasies. This acting out of desire helps to normalize and rationalize the fantasy. As Wollheim (1984: 270–271) characterizes it, this form of projection involves two interdependent components: derealization and depersonalization. Derealization involves the actual denial of the reality of part of the environment; depersonalization involves the denial of part of oneself (desire or beliefs). Operating in tandem, these elements of projection breed intolerance, confusion and insensitivity. In this state, locked into a paranoid world, the individual is literally unable to identify or sympathize with others or to find a meaningful place in society. Therefore, what makes *identification* possible is the weakening of feelings of persecution, increased acceptability of internal attitudes and judgements, and removal of the perceived gap between internal dispositions and their external manifestations.

Forms of projection which facilitate identification with others in contexts which differ from one's own involve the attribution of one's own beliefs, judgements or imagination to others. The world is viewed in metaphorical rather than literal terms. Other persons' needs and interest are acknolwedged in empathetic terms rather than on the basis of suspicion and self doubt. Cavell (1979) advances perhaps the strongest argument in behalf of the projective imagination in contending that it enables us to challenge and alter the basic presuppositions of knowledge and language—thought and action. In addition, Wollheim (1984) argues that our capacity for projection advances a form of "self concern" consistent with the need for community, precisely because it enables the concern for the future (e.g., care about the significance of our lives) to overcome the influence of the past.

This brings us to the role of interpretation in overcoming the conflicts between inner life and the imperatives of outer conduct which undermine a sense of personal security achieved through development of coherent beliefs and compatible desires. As the foregoing account suggests, external constraints to personality development may distort or otherwise inhibit self-interpretation and understanding by fostering an unreflective allegiance and adaptation to social conduct established within the limits of institutional roles.

The potential for conflict under the conditions of adaptation (as Elster, 1983, defines the mode of response) is endemic to institutional structures predicated on conflicting dispositions or motivations which cannot coexist. Under these conditions, the criterion of consistency is not sufficient to justify or sustain adaptation. (See Wollheim, 1984: 172–182, for a more detailed development of this idea.) The more that these conflicts are exacerbated by competing institutional demands and ideological differences, the stronger the pressures on the individual to either abandon those beliefs which hold conflicting desires in check (creating potential openings for coercive forms of social control); alter prescribed roles in line with one's aspirations (but risk appearing idiosyncratic); or act out unresolved conflicts in pathological ways described above.

Each response involves uncertainty and ambiguity which can be avoided by maintaining the *appearance* of consistency in the face of conflicts which remain unresolved. This response captures a natural inclination toward ambivalence and indecision inherent in situations in which the conflict resulting from the gap between individual aspirations and institutional opportunities finds no acceptable alternatives to existing channels of expression and conduct. The appearance of change afforded by projecting insecurity presents a kind of consoling reality both to those whose self-image and privilege depends upon the status quo as well as to those who lack the resources to locate the source of self doubt and anxiety in underlying institutional dynamics.

As the projection of insecurity suggests, those who conform to a political system undergoing social and economic change, but remain ambivalent and frustrated by their inability to achieve their aspirations, retain the appearance of freedom and dignity by supporting the exclusion of marginal populations from the exercise of their sovereignty. For, if part of the achievement of a secure identity necessitates the suppression of doubt and ambiguity of feelings about the legitimacy of the political order, then that doubt is partly dispelled by defining those who fail to exhibit the self-discipline and sacrifice required to sustain social and economic change as irrational and irresponsible. This reaction can have the double effect of saving the appearance of freedom to affirm one's own ends by denying the chance to others. Also, it has the effect of redistributing the resources of respect and contempt by redefining the legal, economic and civil rights of some of its citizens. This may reinforce the belief in the necessity of emerging institutional structures while rendering the underlying power and prevailing interests more transparent to all.

The Problem of Legitimation within Other Theories

Our review of alternative theoretical perspectives which underpin applied studies of implementation underscores the importance of legitimacy as an underlying theme in explanations of American public policy processes. However, there are several difficulties in current formulations of legitimation theory. First, it is not altogether clear why legitimation problems must originate principally from political conflicts stemming from underlying economic sources as Habermas holds. Nor is it explained why this is the primary source (cause) of the softening of motivation for support of or disaffection from governmental institutions and policies as contended by Habermas and Connolly. Yet, legitimation conflicts do not appear to be limited to just economic issues. Regime support can also be undermined by morally symbolic issues such as abortion, school prayer or saliency of civil liberties issues. These latter issues, endemic to conflicts over social policy, contribute to differences over Constitutional issues such as the Bill of Rights, separation of powers or federalism.

Second, current formulations about legitimation do not explain why disaffection should find expression in a common political vocabulary with unified and/or unidirectional responses (e.g., directed toward national governmental institutions). It may be equally plausible, as cognitive dissonance theory (or utility theory) would argue, that there are no such common interests or tendencies and that response is dependent upon salience of policy or perceived dissonance by the individuals involved. Moreover, a high degree of national regime support can coincide with a low level of policy support. There can also be a low degree of support for state governmental institutions such as state courts with a high level of support for national policies and institutions. This suggests that the expression of attitudes toward policy has *differential* rather than unified effects on institutional structures and their legitimating ideologies. For example, the pressure on Constitutional norms and appropriateness of court policy making functions involved in school prayer, integration or abortion may be offset by court decisions affecting the civil liberties of criminal defendants, or by Congressional policies increasing the resources available for crime control.

A third difficulty confronting systems and expressivist notions of legitimacy is their inability to account for periodic reversals in the dominance of partisan ideologies of political elites and variations in the strength and assertiveness of governmental institutions in formulating public policy. Critical elections involving major realignments of political coalitions frequently occur at intervals which coincide with periods beset with substantial social-economic problems and political conflict (Burnham, 1970; Key, 1959). During such periods, disaffection often finds expression in third party movements which contribute to reversals of partisan positions such as that between traditional positions of Republican and Democratic parties following the critical election of 1896, or of the party affiliations of Democrats in the South after the 1964 and 1968 Presidential elections. Or, consider the differences between the judicial conservatism of the Supreme Court during the New Deal compared with the activism of the Warren Court in the 1960's. These reversals not only underscore the absorbancy of governmental institutions but suggest a flexibility and responsiveness to problems and constituencies likely to be most disaffected from the political system.

Finally, another problem exhibited by most theories is the exaggeration of the importance of the national government and its policy making institutions, and the underestimation of the significance of subnational differences in political culture in explaining the source of legitimation problems. The use of the concept of state or regime often carries with it connotations of omnipotence and centrality which may outstrip its actual importance or salience in explanations of governance problems, institutional conflict and change.

This is no more clearly illustrated than with the persistence of substantial variations and discrepancies between state policy and practices and national policy or regime values. They range from the most obvious instances in which the South maintained a policy for several decades of massive disenfranchisement of black voters or school segregation vastly at odds with the practices of other states and the Constitution, to the more subtle but persistent variation between state courts with regard to the standing of criminal defendants to bring motions to suppress evidence (discussed in Chapters 4 and 5). These examples suggest that legitimation conflicts may have more to do with the dispersal of authority in the federal system than with its concentration. It also suggests that the factors which shape state responses to national policy may be rooted in part in the power concentrating features of policy subsystems as well as in characteristics of state political culture.

REFORMULATING LEGITIMATION THEORY

I shall save a more detailed examination of how the analysis of state cases supports a reformulation of legitimation theory along the lines suggested by these criticisms for Chapter 7. What emerges from our analysis of these theoretical perspectives is that there appear to be several elements or conditions with which we could forge a separate theory of legitimation. No current theory adequately addresses all of the following elements nor do current formulations agree on the significance of individual factors for the maintenance of political stability.

1. *Justification of authority and generation of support*. National and state officials must be able to establish and justify their authority (and achieve political integration) not merely on the basis of personal charisma or by virtue of an electoral mandate, but by conforming to perceived regime values (e.g., Constitutional norms and founding values). Support for national or state policies must be based in part on beliefs in their appropriateness as a prerogative of originating institutions as dictated by regime norms or by expression through subscription to a partisan ideology.
2. *Personal identification with the political system*. Citizens must have the capacity to pursue individual aspirations, realize their interests or satisfy wants or preferences. They also must command respect for their choices, achieve a secure identity and be able to freely express their beliefs through participation in political processes (e.g., through parties, interest groups or direct involvement). To the extent that national or state authorities satisfy or observe these conditions of personal identity, citizens will identify with the collective goals and purposes of the regime.
3. *Interests served—distribution of burdens and benefits*. Public policies must also reflect and serve some combination of interests other than *solely* the regime leadership or implementing officials or organizations, or class or single interest group (i.e., target group). The burdens and benefits of the outputs and outcomes of public policy must reflect, as much as possible, a random distribution among its implementers and recipients.
4. *Process for adoption and evaluation of policy change*. Changes in regime values and public policies must be adopted through some explicit and accessible process (e.g., elections, Constitutional amendments, legislation, or initiatives). The policy must be be capable of implementation and oversight, and its outcomes evaluated.
5. *Capacity to implement/enforce public policy*. Both governmental institutions and/or the private sector must have the *capacity* (e.g., resources to achieve support, and enforcement powers) to execute public policies and to achieve mandates which satisfy some actual or possible set of wants, interests or aspirations of its citizens.

I shall illustrate briefly how each current theory constructs a framework using different ones of these five elements as necessary or merely contingent features conducive to political stability. In addition, they exhibit differences in how they view the scope of political conflict, the possibility of democratic accountability, and the prospects for institutional change, discussed in Chapter 7.

Cognitive dissonance theory contends that regime stability can be maintained only if institutions advance policies which satisfy some possible and realizable set of wants that are within their capacity to achieve (element 5). One potential difficulty with this perspective is the inability to distinguish whether the policies adopted stem from the aspirations, needs and interests of some sector of the public or simply reflect the interests of elites in promoting existing positions and privileges. This violates element 3 and assumes away the necessity of satisfying element 1.

Utility theory takes a slightly different but inconsistent approach. It holds that the success of public policies predicated on want satisfication (element 2) depends upon the construction of incentives and rewards back ultimately by coercive sanctions (element 5). What this does is underestimate the importance of the necessity of institutional leadership to justify the exercise of authority in terms of regime values or partisan ideologies (element 1). A likely outcome of this bias (as noted earlier) is to violate element 3 by privileging the interests of implementers (or a target group), thereby undermining regime support.

The emphasis of communication theory as proposed by Deutsch is roughly equivalent to that of cognitive dissonance with its stress on the capacity of the regime to promote stability. However, Deutsch provides little detail as to how his information processing system satisfies element 4, nor how public policy-making processes satisfy element 3. On the other hand, Lowi makes element 3, and to some extent 5, the pivot upon which a political system must turn. But he fails to be explicit about how his themes about the common good and new institutional role for the court satisfy elements 2 and 1.

Classic theories of organization (e.g., Downs, Wildavsky, Lindblom) see the inability to satisfy element 3 as a reality of the political system. This deficiency is compensated, in part, by the effectiveness with which institutional elites depart from element 1 by appealing to utilitarian considerations. In addition, further compensation is derived from the increased partisan political support gained from satisfying a strategic combination of the interests of client groups and public benefiting directly from agency controlled policies (e.g., distributive policy) which sustains a dominant policy-making majority.

Revisionist organization theories (e.g., Allison, Wilson), while acknowledging the deficiencies in satisfying element 3, attribute a strong compensating influence to the external environment vis à vis element 5 with regard to protecting (unreconstructed) regime values and norms (element 1). They also attribute a stronger role to the evaluation of the output (element 4) of policies implemented by organizational elites.

Finally, competing theories of unit member discretion appear to agree on the deficiencies this creates with respect to element 3, but so far have not developed its broader implications for the American political system.

Unlike the other theories reviewed here, the systems theory advanced by Easton attempts a comprehensive treatment of the elements of legitimacy theory. However, as already noted, Easton fails to develop an adequate and convincing account of element 2 (in his analysis of expressive ideologies) as well as to demonstrate how evaluations of the outputs of public policy (originating from partisan ideologies) (element 3) provide an independent and continuous source of legitimation of the regime. Easton's theory subsequently puts too much emphasis on the continuous nature of regime support and the legitimizing role of an underlying consensus about the common good.

Cognitive expressivists also stress the importance of elements 1 and 2, as do proponents of cognitive dissonance, albeit for very different reasons as discussed earlier. Habermas considers the principal threat to the legitimacy of the political system to issue from an undermining of regime values by technocratic values (ascendancy of policy making by implementing officials, element 3, without requisite justification, element 1). Legitimacy is also threatened by the failure or incapacity of the private sector and/or governmental institutions to satisfy aspirations as defined by traditional regime and capitalist ideology (element 2). In contrast, Connolly argues that the legitimacy of the political system is challenged by a displacement of the load of disaffection, created by the discrepancies between individual freedom and institutional imperatives, onto governmental institutions (element 2). Consequently, perceptions increase regarding the nonrandom distribution of burdens and benefits of policies (element 3), effectuating the erosion of regime values (e.g., rights) upon which institutional authority is based (element 1).

Connolly (1981: 16–17) downplays the significance of elections or processes by which policy is implemented and evaluated and other forms of political participation as compensating mechanisms (element 4) for legitimation deficits. He does so because he assumes that political alternatives are monopolized by the two parties suppressing the expression of aspirations for institutional change while increasing cynicism and disaffection. Therefore, public policies will typically fall short of those possible sets of wants and aspirations involving significant institutional change. In contrast, Habermas contends that the aspiration-substituting tendencies of the political-administrative state (e.g., the attempt to allocate market values through public policy) necessitates adoption of policies that it is unable to implement and requires response to pressures for increased participation it is unable to accommodate (1973: 68–75).

2

The Growth of Judicial and Congressional Intervention: Civil Liberties and Criminal Records Privacy Policy

Over the last two decades, the Supreme Court and Congress have undertaken ambitious initiatives to both enlarge civil liberties protections as well as reduce crime through innovation and experimentation. These reforms have involved the state incorporation of constitutional guarantees and strengthening of state leadership to plan and coordinate criminal justice policy. The *Mapp* (1961) and *Miranda* (1966) decisions and the Omnibus Crime Control and Safe Streets Act (1968) noted the onset of a period in which the Supreme Court and Congress, through the Law Enforcement Assistance Administration (LEAA), greatly enlarged their role and policy development and oversight of the administration of criminal justice.

Significantly, the Crime Control Act was used not only to advance a reform agenda (e.g., through appropriation of block grant money for allocation to the states), but also to bring about limited federal and state regulatory control (through conditions of aid) of criminal justice processes. Congressional regulation of criminal justice information systems was initiated by an amendment in the early 1970's to improve the management, increase the quality, and control the exchange of criminal records. A central purpose of that policy is the enlargement of privacy protections and due process rights for subjects of criminal records.

The civil liberties policies embodied in the *Mapp* and *Miranda* decisions and the criminal records privacy mandate involves similar efforts by the Supreme Court and Congress to articulate national policies for due process protections in the criminal justice system. Both Court and Congressional policies were part of a broader movement to strengthen policy making and accountability mechanisms at the state and local level. Yet, the policies were implemented in contrasting political environments, involving different underlying institutional relationships and intergovernmental philosophies. The Supreme Court decisions involving suspects' and defendants' rights in the 1960's were made in spite of widespread opposition to the increased "federalization" of state court procedures. The civil liberties decisions were intended to increase federal court oversight and intervention as means to insure that the state courts provided adequate forums for the adjudication of violations of the constitutional rights of the accused.

In contrast, the regulation of criminal records management was one of many conditions of aid involved in a widely supported program used to strengthen state and local capacities to deal with crime. These grants and conditions were intended not only to underwrite innovation in crime control but to increase state discretion, control and accountability for policy making processes. Policies for the management and control of criminal records were a part of a larger LEAA agenda to upgrade state information technological capacities sufficient to enable effective participation in a national computerized criminal history system.

A significant feature shared by these policies is that they marked the federal government's first attempt to regulate the administration of criminal justice. This has presented some novelty for intergovernmental relations and criminal justice over the last two decades. On the one hand, the Department of Justice has assumed a de facto regulatory role through LEAA; and, on the other, the Supreme Court and lower courts have greatly enlarged their policy-making and supervisory role over the administration of criminal justice. Thus, to the extent that both LEAA (following Congressional mandate) and the state courts have exercised regulatory control over the administration of justice, they have become involved in the *implementation* of intergovernmental policy.

These Court and Congressional initiatives have followed two distinctly different reform traditions. The Warren Court civil liberties policies were part of a broader effort toward nationalizing reform policies aimed at redistributing power and realizing greater equality under the law. Thus, these policies are rooted in the liberal New Deal reforms of the 1930's and their 1960's counterpart which ushered in basic changes in economic and civil rights designed to eliminate the sources of insecurity, powerlessness and inequality in society.

Shapiro captures these linkages very effectively:

> First, the Warren Court was pursuing the equality value fairly consistently, and it was doing so along lines that had been clearly laid down by the New Deal. Indeed, the Warren Court showed promise of carrying the New Deal program to its ultimate conclusion in the welfare state and an egalitarian political process at a time when legislative and executive branches were faltering. Both in terms of values and interests, the program toward which the Warren Court seemed to be moving was identical to that last great outbreak of the New Deal, Lyndon Johnson's "War on Poverty" and "Great Society" (1983: 236–237).

In contrast, the sources of Burger Court and Congressional policy in the 1970's, aimed principally at crime control, originate with the progressive reform era. The primary strategy of this tradition has been to strengthen the policy-making, management and enforcement capacity of state and local government agencies to deal more efficiently with local needs and to increase their accountability to the public. In this respect, Burger Court post-civil liberties policy and Congressional initiatives designed to reduce crime share a common theme of new federalism. That theme is that the role of the federal government is limited to establishing *minimum standards* below which states and localities should not fall (Porter, 1982: 3–4). Therefore, the responsibilities for reform initiatives and policy development now lies with state and local executives, legislators and courts rather than the Congress and Supreme Court.

This chapter traces the history of these policies through the 1960's and 1970's. First, the interpretation of search and seizure policy (the exclusionary rule) and of interrogation and confession policy (the *Miranda* rights) reveals the philosophical basis of contrasting approaches of the Warren and Burger Courts. Next, the role and importance of federal district courts are examined to illustrate some of the power structural implications of differing concepts of federalism on state court policy-making. Third, some of the organizational and jurisdictional reforms undertaken by state supreme courts are examined to establish their significance for understanding responses to Supreme Court civil liberties policies analyzed in Chapters 3 through 5. Fourth, efforts by the Congress and LEAA to control the technological development of criminal information systems and to protect the privacy and due process rights of criminal records subjects are examined in terms of organizational, intergovernmental and Constitutional implications. Finally, some common underlying themes which emerge in the analysis of these policies are united in a discussion of six political constraints thought to inhibit the regulation of the criminal justice system. Later, Chapter 7 will examine the significance of these contrasting policy approaches in broader historical terms by situating them in a recurring dynamic of legitimation conflicts lodged in a cycle of reform and retrenchment.

THE CIVIL LIBERTIES DECISIONS: WARREN COURT REFORMS AND BURGER COURT RETRENCHMENT

Pre-*Mapp* Doctrine and the Warren Court: The Exclusionary Rule

The origins of conflict over the exclusionary rule can be traced to differences over the framing of the Fourth Amendment to the Constitution. James Madison had proposed language for the amendment reflecting the prevailing sentiment of the colonists against the issuance of general writs of assistance (warrants) which lacked "probable cause" and judicial approval. The version ultimately adopted, however, distinguished between prohibitions against unreasonable searches and seizures (the "privacy standard") and requirements for the issuance of warrants (the "warrant requirement") (Bloom, 1982).

Subsequent Supreme Court decisions including *Mapp* have generally held that the Fourth Amendment is designed to protect against government invasions of individual privacy. Consequently, a warrant is considered instrumental to securing that protection. Therefore, in *Weeks v. U.S.* (1914) the Supreme Court prohibited all federal courts from admitting evidence at trial if secured in the absence of a legal search warrant. In doing so, the Court stated the responsibility of the judiciary in unmistakable terms by declaring:

> The effect of the Fourth Amendment is to put the courts of the United States and federal officials, in the exercise of their power and authority, under limitations and restraints as to the exercise of such power and authority and to forever secure the people, their houses, papers and effects against all unreasonable searches and seizures under the guise of law (*Weeks*, 1914: 389).

However, the Supreme Court was soon confronted with a dilemma in adhering to an absolute rule in the face of rapidly changing social and technological circumstances. The mobility of automobiles created the need to define exceptions to the "warrant requirement." Thus, in *Carroll v. U.S.* (1925) the Court permitted police to search a car without a warrant only when there was *both* (1) "probable cause" to believe the car contained evidence of a crime *and* (2) "exigent circumstances" which made it impractical to obtain a warrant (Kamisar, 1983). What the Burger Court has done (among other things), is alter the *Carroll* doctrine by expanding the "exigent circumstance" exception.

In several cases between 1946 and 1950, culminating with *U.S. v. Rabinowitz* (1950) the Court continued to debate the relative significance and relationship between the "reasonableness" and "warrant" clauses of the Fourth Amendment. At one point in the debate, with *Johnson v. U.S.* (1948) the Court appeared to subscribe to the point of view that only a neutral magistrate detached from the competitive business of ferreting out crime would make a "warrant requirement" workable *and* satisfy the need for "reasonableness." But with its decision in *Rabinowitz* the justices concluded that the two clauses were distinct by holding that the "relevant test (for reasonableness) is not whether it is reasonable to procure a search warrant but whether the search was reasonable" (*Rabinowitz*, 1950: 65–66). Unhappy with the drift of the court, Justice Frankfurter dissented by arguing that only a warrant makes a search "reasonable" and that the Court's erosion of the "warrant requirement" would eventually make the exceptions swallow the rule.

The Supreme Court decision in *Wolf v. Colorado* (1949) seemed to extend the line of reasoning taken in *Rabinowitz* as well as many subsequent cases decided by both the Warren and Burger Courts. The decision in *Wolf* indicated a reluctance on the part of the Court to link the constitutional right to privacy to a universal rule by which potential erosions of privacy could be held in check. While *Wolf* declared that the right to privacy applied to the states through the Fourteenth Amendment, it conceded that important policy considerations made the imposition of an exclusionary rule an unnecessary remedy. The Court specifically noted (in an appendix to its opinion) the progress many states had shown in adopting rules of their own which afforded the protection of privacy. Moreover, the pressure of local public opinion was thought to be a more effective tool against police abuse of citizens' rights than a uniform national rule (*Wolf*, 1949: 32).

It took another decade before the Supreme Court undertook a reexamination of state practices in light of *Weeks* and *Wolf*, concluding that a uniform national policy was necessary, making all evidence obtained from unconstitutional searches and seizures inadmissible in a state court. In justifying its decision, the Court not only found state progress in adopting *Weeks* unimpressive but found compelling evidence that many states had already reached the conclusion that other remedies had completely failed to secure compliance. Interestingly, the California state court decision in *People v. Cahan* (1955) was specifically cited as an example of a state court decision which had found citizens' privacy rights inadequately protected by state law against police abuse.

Although acknowledging that recurring issues of "reasonableness" remained unresolved by their decision, the Warren Court tried to anticipate criticism of *Mapp* by making its underlying rationale clear. Yet significantly, nowhere in the decision does the Court explicitly recognize deterrence of police conduct as the primary or even secondary objective of *Mapp*:

> There are those who say as Justice Cardozo that under our constitutional exclusionary doctrine the criminal is to go free because the constable blundered. . . . In some cases this will undoubtedly be the result. But as was said in *Elkins*, "there is another consideration—the imperative of judicial integrity." The criminal goes free if he must, but it is the law that sets him free. . . .
>
> Our decision founded on reason and truth, gives to the individual no more than that which the Constitution guarantees him, to the police officer no less then that to which honest law enforcement is entitled, and to the Courts, that judicial integrity so necessary in the true administration of criminal justice (*Mapp*, 1961: 659–660).

While *Mapp* established a national guideline regulating investigative, prosecutorial and judicial processes, two additional but tangential decisions provided added tools to ensure its implementation and enforcement. In *Jones v. U.S.* (1958) the Court ruled that a defendant could claim automatic *standing* to challenge the search or seizure of contraband or stolen goods even though there is no technical ownership of such property. Since *Jones*, however, the Burger Court has generally restricted the right to automatic standing in *Rakas v. Illinois* (1978) and *U.S. v. Salvucci* (1980) to include only those instances where the defendant can claim ownership and, therefore, justify expectations of privacy.

In addition to *Jones* the Warren Court proposed a two-pronged test in *Aguilar v. Texas* (1964) by which a magistrate could determine whether a warrant should be issued on the basis of police use of an informant's tip. The test required that the magistrate be informed of (1) the underlying circumstances from which the informant concluded the contraband was where it was claimed to be ("basis of knowledge" test) and (2) some of the underlying circumstances which established the credibility or reliability of the informant's information (''veracity'' test). Nonetheless, the scope of the *Aguilar* test has been undermined by a recent Burger Court decision in *Illinois v. Gates* (1983) which repudiates overly technical determinations for the issuance of warrants in favor of the ''totality of circumstances'' justifying ''probable cause.''

Some confusion was created late in the Warren Court's decade of reforms with three decisions which reflected lingering uncertainty about issues of the reasonableness of privacy expectation expressed in *Mapp*. The decisions also formed the basis of the renewal of criticism of the exclusionary rule which lay dormant in the decade following *Mapp*. First, with *Katz v. U.S.* (1967) the Warren Court abandoned the *Olmstead v. U.S.* (1928) test of physical trespass as a basis of illegal search and seizure in favor of individual expectation of privacy. The Court argued that what the Fourth Amendment protected was *people* not *places*. Therefore, what a person seeks to protect as private, even where accessible to the public, could be constitutionally protected from search and seizure. Consequently, the ''expectation of privacy standard'' was used solely to decide whether a search had taken place, *not* whether a warrant was required. Nonetheless, the Warren Court held that warrants were generally required if the ''expectation of privacy'' was implicated, ''subject to only a few specifically established and well delineated exceptions'' (*Katz*, 1967: 357).

Second, the attempt to establish what constitutes the *exceptions* to the exclusionary rule has been most problematic and thankless task. In its decision in *Terry v. Ohio* (1968) the Warren Court established an important opportunity to apply the principles enunciated in *Katz* in a case involving a ''stop and frisk'' search of a suspect. In the attempt to avoid inconsistency the Court equivocated. *Terry* held that random questioning and searches were not as intrusive as arrests and therefore did not involve the issue of ''reasonableness.'' The Court stated somewhat inconclusively that there was no available test for ''reasonableness'' other than ''balancing'' the need to search or seize against the invasion which the search and seizure involved. The Court did stress, however, that the ''balancing'' test only applied to situations in which there was less than ''probable cause'' for arrest and that warrants would normally have to be obtained.

In its last related decision in *Chimel v. California* (1969) involving the delineation of exceptions to the warrant rule, the Warren Court finally dispensed with the ambiguity of *Rabinowitz* and equivocation in *Terry*. The decision specifically overturned a California state court decision which had justified ''good faith'' exceptions involving seaches incident to arrest. But the case is ironic because California's adoption of the exclusionary rule prior to *Mapp* was singled out as the justification of why other states should do likewise. With *Chimel*, the Warren Court suppressed evidence incident to arrest but obtained without a search warrant on the grounds that it failed to satisfy those exceptions which it delineated. These might include the seizure of weapons, prevention of destruction of evidence or circumstances which might jeopardize the safety of the officer.

The Burger Court's Post-*Mapp* Decisions

In an attempt to distance itself ideologically from its predecessor, the Burger Court initiated the 1970's with a rhetorical salvo challenging the efficacy of *Mapp* and culminating in several significant decisions eroding and limiting the expansion of defendants' due process rights. In cases better known for their extensive and argumentative *dicta* than their practical consequences for state administration of criminal justice, the Burger Court decisions in *Bivens v. Six Unknown Agents* (1971), *U.S. v. Calandra* (1974), *U.S. v. Janis* (1976), and *Stone v. Powell* (1976) have become obligatory reference points for detractors of the exclusionary rule. These decisions all challenge the *efficacy* of the rule. This seems a successful way to challenge the policy, if only evidence could be found to confirm such charges. But since convincing direct evidence is hard to come by (as shown in Chapter 1), the Court has followed a different tactic.

Instead, the Court has redefined the goal or purpose of the rule so as to shift the burden of responsibility for compliance away from courts (and towards police) while making confirmation of the criminal justice system's performance even more problematic than before. The claims of inefficacy are particularly disingenuous because they are self-fulfilling. The Burger Court has been busy for over a decade making decisions which undermine the probability of acceptance and implementation of *Mapp*. Yet, as the post-*Mapp* rulings indicate, the Burger Court has exhibited a peculiar inability (unlike its post-*Miranda* decisions) to fashion restrictions to *Mapp* which would actually loosen the limits it had allegedly imposed on effective law enforcement.

The Burger Court's dissatisfaction with the scope of exceptions imposed by the Warren Court in *Chimel* with regard to the use of warrants was clearly expressed in *Chambers v. Maroney* (1970). In *Chimel*, the Warren Court held that warrantless searches of automobiles could be justified only in instances of "probable cause" stops. In contrast, the Burger Court decided that warrantless searches could be conducted long after a vehicle had been stopped and impounded. The Burger Court relied on *Carroll* (1925) to justify a constitutionally-based difference in the Fourth Amendment privacy protections between houses and cars. Yet, the following year in *Coolidge v. New Hampshire* (1971), the Burger Court appeared to renege on its overly broad view of "exigent circumstances." There, it found that when a vehicle is parked in a private driveway a warrant must be secured to justify a search.

Additional problems were immediately raised however with respect to the conundrum posed by auto searches and searches of persons incident to arrest. In several cases beginning with *U.S. v. Robinson* (1973) the Burger Court greatly expanded the perimeter of warrantless searches of persons incident to arrest. The Burger Court had been eager to find a simple formula or "bright line" rule which police could apply to avoid having to analyze whether a search was justified, and *Robinson* presented that opportunity. In that case, the Burger Court upheld a warrantless body search of a person incident to arrest for a traffic violation (revocation of a license) on the grounds that there is a need to find evidence of the crime charged before that evidence is destroyed. The dissent by Justice Marshall points out, however, that *Robinson* failed to satisfy the circumstance because the search could not be justified to either prevent the destruction of evidence, since none existed, nor by the possibility that the suspect was armed and dangerous. The majority evaded these inconsistencies by distinguishing *Robinson* from *Chimel* as involving a search of a person not the vehicle itself. Sidestepping the inconsistency of selective application of rules to suit the circumstances, the Burger Court held that some warrantless searches were "reasonable" *per se*, regardless of the facts as long as they were preceded by a lawful arrest (one involving "probable cause").

Notwithstanding the attempt to end the confusion wrought by the post-*Chimel* world with a "bright line" distinction, *U.S. v. Chadwick* (1977) presented the need to address the warrant requirement once again, but from a new perspective. *Chadwick* appeared to involve circumstances not easily assimilated by the so-called "bright line" exception fashioned in *Robinson*. A locked footlocker was seized from an open trunk of a parked car during the arrest of its owner. Only subsequently at the police station was the footlocker searched and contraband found. Ironically, the government's argument that the defendant had a lesser "expectation of privacy" in the trunk than in his home or office, therefore justifying a warrantless search, unwittingly contributed to the creation of a new Burger Court doctrine. The Court incorporated the theory but used it to reverse the conviction of the defendants.

The Burger Court applied this new principle of expectation of privacy retroactively to distinguish *Chadwick* from the earlier *Chambers* decision. That principle consisted of the idea that searches incident to arrest involved varying degress of "privacy expectation." Therefore, warrantless searches of persons incident to arrest may be justified, given the irreversible intrusiveness of the preceding arrest, compared to those of possessions (not within the arrestee's direct control), because of the difference in the degree of the "reasonable expectation of privacy" involved.

The adoption of this new rationale however has not remedied the difficulties of distinguishing when warrants are necessary but has only further complicated the matter. The *Robbins v. California* (1981) and *N.Y. v. Belton* (1981) and *U.S. v. Ross* (1982) decisions exemplify the inconsistency in applying the "bright line" and "reasonableness" standards to cases involving nearly identical circumstances. The cases differed only with respect to *where* the contraband was discovered. In *Robbins* contraband was discovered in a wrapped container in the trunk; in *Belton* contraband was discovered in a plastic wrapper in the pocket of the defendant's jacket. The *Robbins* case however required a warrant where *Belton* did not because of differences in the "expectation of privacy." Although the distinction seems workable in these cases, in *Ross* the Burger Court demonstrated its inability to apply the distinction consistently. The Court held that ''moveable containers'' once locked in a car trunk met the diminished ''expectation of privacy'' doctrine, justfying a warrantless search. Seemingly contradicting *Robbins*, the Burger Court signaled its desire to return to *Robinson* and *Chambers* standards of effective law enforcement by contending that the ''exigent circumstance'' of potential vulnerability of a vehicle's contents to theft or vandalism justified a warrantless search and seizure of its contents. In proposing multiple, confusing if not contradictory standards, the Burger Court has helped create a perplexing situation for police and courts alike by making it even more difficult than before to determine under what conditions a legal search and seizure has been properly executed.

This inclination toward avoidance of specifying rules regarding the issuance and use of search warrants is well illustrated in *U.S. v. Leon* (1984). The case is extremely significant, for not only does it recognize police invocation of ''good faith'' exceptions to the exclusionary rule but it clearly exempts judicial responsibility for violations of the rule. The Court ruled in *Leon* that evidence should not be barred from use at trial if it was obtained with a search warrant subsequently found to be invalid.

In justifying their decision, the majority not only took the opportunity to denounce the inefficacy of the exclusionary rule as a deterrent of police misconduct but concluded for similar reasons that judges and magistrates should not be held responsible for committing errors in the issuance of warrants (p. 16–17). The recent studies which the majority cites to prove that the social costs outweigh the deterrent value of the rule do more to undermine than support their arguments. For example, the majority cites a 1979 U.S. Government Accounting Office study of the effects of the exclusionary rule on motions to suppress, which showed that 80 to 90 percent were denied. A compendium of studies of the costs and benefits of the rule with respect to convictions, sponsored by the American Bar Foundation Research Journal in 1983, also found little evidence of adverse effects. Similarly, the National Institute of Justice study of California (1982) found that the number of cases declined for prosecution was negligible, affecting only 4.8 percent of all cases and 0.8 percent of all arrests (*Leon*, 1984: 8).

The argument that the majority makes to immunize the judiciary from sanctions for failure to uphold the rule in the review and issuance of search warrants is simply that they are not a part of the law enforcement team. The dissent filed by Justices Brennan and Marshall criticized the majority opinion for its extremely narrow reading of the exclusionary rule ''relegating the judiciary to the periphery'' of the Fourth Amendment based upon ''an impoverished understanding of judicial responsibility'' (pp. 4, 8).

The dissent goes on to argue that the Fourth Amendment does not single out any particular agency for compliance, nor exempt others such as the executive or judiciary. Further:

> If the Amendment is to have any meaning, police and courts cannot be regarded as constitutional strangers to each other; because the evidence gathering role of the police

is directly linked to the evidence admitting function of the courts, an individual's Fourth Amendment rights may be undermined as completely by one as by the other (1984: 1).

Interrogation and Confession Policy: The *Miranda* Decision

Unlike *Mapp*, the Warren Court had provided several signals prior to *Miranda* that it intended to protect the rights of suspects and defendants against abuse inherent in the interrogation process. Prior to the Warren Court era, determination of whether a confession was voluntary was dictated by the "totality of circumstances" doctrine first elaborated in *Johnson v. Zerbst* (1938). In that decision, the Court held that the voluntariness of a confession should be determined by the particular facts and circumstances surrounding the case including the background, experience and conduct of the accused. Unhappy with the open-endedness of the principle, the Warren Court elected to move beyond this doctrine by proposing a "selective incorporation" of constitutional rights through the Fourteenth Amendment due process clause. First, in *Gideon v. Wainwright* (1963) the Court contended that the availability of counsel was essential to the accused to effectively apply his Sixth Amendment right to be represented in a court of law. Second, in *Malloy v. Hogan* (1964) the Court held that a defendant could not be required to confess to a crime, testify or otherwise incriminate himself in violation of his Fifth Amendment right against self incrimination.

These two decisions in turn, contributed to a third in *Escobedo v. Illinois* (1964) in which the Warren Court attempted to clarify the circumstances under which these rights would apply in the context of police investigative practices. The upshot of *Escobedo* is that when a police inquiry into an unsolved crime shifts from the investigatory to accusatory stage, the defendant must be warned of his absolute "right to remain silent" and must acknowledge his "request for counsel." If these rights are not observed then any subsequent incriminating statements or confession could not be considered "voluntary" or used against him.

When *Miranda* was eventually decided in 1966, it consolidated these earlier decisions. Suspects questioned while in custody were to be advised of their "right to remain silent;" that any statements made could be used against them at trial; that they had a "right to consult counsel;" that an attorney would be provided and that these rights could be waived for the purposes of making a confession. By custodial interrogation, the Court meant "questioning initiated by law enforcement officers after a person has been taken in to custody or otherwise deprived of his freedom of action in any significant way" (*Miranda*, 1966: 444). In their opinion, the Warren Court indicated its unhappiness with progress under *Escobedo* and the apparent intransigence of prevailing police practice, which invited abuse of the suspect through the inherently coercive custodial interrogation process. The majority also insisted that the decision was not intended to obstruct legitimate law enforcement practice. Rather the decision constituted an invitation to adopt non-coercive approaches to the investigatory process. Nonetheless, dissenting opinions strongly challenged the ruling, asserting that it created a new public policy going far beyond constitutionally warranted application. Moreover, *Miranda* became a visible political target for the 1968 presidential campaign and provided Congress an opportunity to express its criticism with the passage of the Crime Control Act of 1968.

Notwithstanding the unpopularity of the decision, the clarity and specificity of the decision appears to have constituted an important asset as well as liability with respect to its ability to withstand the Burger Court attempts to undermine its principles and limit its application. The tight focus of the decision at a particular stage in the criminal justice process has been an asset because it has deflected post-*Miranda* challenges to issues of marginal or peripheral consequence to the main objectives of the policy. Cases decided by the Burger Court which have involved tangential issues such as use of statements made to subsequent to *Miranda* warnings for impeachment purposes include *Harris v. New York* (1971), *Oregon v. Hass* (1975) and *U.S. v. Calandra* (1974).

But in other cases, when the Burger Court has focused directly upon the nature and the scope of the rights of the accused, the specificity of *Miranda* has become a primary liability. We see this most clearly in its decisions with respect to "voluntariness," "availability of counsel" and custody. In an important case in 1974, the Burger Court ruled in *Michigan v. Tucker* that under certain specified circumstances, police may resume their questioning of a suspect who has asserted his "right to remain silent" and use the fruits of that questioning to either obtain a confession or use the statements to impeach his testimony at trial. The upshot of this ruling was to separate the issue of "voluntariness" of the waiver of one's rights from the assertion of the right. Therefore, police can resume questioning of a suspect (after being informed of his rights) without first charging or arraigning him for a crime and need not obtain a waiver before questioning the suspect about additional crimes. In *Tucker*, a case involving the issue of "consent to search," the Burger Court exhibited the strong desire to return to the pre-*Miranda* "voluntariness" test ("totality of circumstances") first enunciated in *Johnson v. Zerbst* (1938). Such a move has encouraged many states to continue to cling to the pre-*Miranda* doctrine long after it has served its usefulness.

The point at which the "right to counsel" should be acknowledged by police has also led the Burger Court to adopt somewhat inconsistent positions. Also in *Tucker*, the Burger Court held that the failure by police to advise a defendant of "right to counsel" does not render an interrogation illegal, involuntary nor inadmissible in court. In writing the opinion for the majority, Justice Rehnquist contended that the *Miranda* warnings were not rights protected by the constitution but only "prophylactic standards" to provide reinforcement against self-incrimination. The decision has come closer than any other in an explicit rejection of the principles upon which *Miranda* is based.

Yet by 1981 in *Edwards v. Arizona* the Burger Court suddenly decided to take a different tack toward the issue of "counsel," signaling a willingness to reexamine the premises of *Tucker*. Unlike *Michigan v. Mosely* (1975) in which silence is evidently not sufficient to terminate questioning, *Edwards* held that once a suspect requests counsel questioning cannot be renewed until counsel has been made available, unless the suspect chooses to initiate further communication with police. Although the decision doesn't abrogate *Mosely*, it may serve as an important counterbalance to the steady erosion of a suspect's in-custody rights.

With the exception of *Edwards*, the Burger Court's post-*Miranda* decisions have been conspicuous for their clever exploitation of essentially contested meanings likely to emerge no matter how precise the policy strives to be. But the exploitability of ambiguous language can work both ways, especially if the Court decides to search for meanings which support instead of undermine policy objectives. This was the case with the Burger Court's interpretation of the interrogation process in *Rhode Island v. Innis* (1980). In this case, the Court held that *Miranda* warnings are activated whenever a person in custody is subjected to either express questioning or its functional "equivalent." Such functional "equivalents" include communication which takes place in transit to police headquarters involving comments not addressed to the suspect but nonetheless having the effect of a psychological inducement to make incriminating statements. While this decision seemed pregnant with implications for reinvigoration and strengthening of post-*Miranda* policy, that expectation has not been fulfilled.

In a far reaching case decided in 1984, *New York v. Quarles*, the Supreme Court held that in situations where public safety is at risk a suspect's statements may be admitted into evidence in the absence of the observance of the *Miranda* warnings. Although acknowledging that their decision "lessened the desireable clarity of the rule," the majority contended that the decision was justified because it reduced the necessity of on-the-scene balancing of public safety and individual rights (1984: 8–9). However, instead of designating what constitutes a "public safety exception," the Court defers to the instinctive good judgment of the officer. With a reassuring gesture, the majority claims:

> The exception will not be difficult for police officers to apply because in each case it will be circumscribed by the exigency which justifies it. We think police officers can and will distinguish almost instinctively between questions necessary to secure their own safety or the safety of the public and questions designed to elicit testimonial evidence from the suspect (1984: 9).

What the dissenting justices found particularly disconcerting about the majority opinion is that it shifts the burden to the defendant to establish that public safety considerations were not sufficiently compelling to override his privilege against coercive interrogations. Moreover, as the dissent stresses, the decision condemns the judiciary to conducting post facto inquiries into the propriety of custodial interrogations—a decided step in the direction of imposing pre-*Miranda* standards of judicial decision-making.

FEDERAL AND STATE COURT STRUCTURE AND ROLES

Contrasting Views of Federalism: The Expansion and Contraction of Federal Court Jurisdiction

The role of the federal district courts has been neither acknowledged nor well understood but is no less important to understanding the state implementation of national reforms in criminal justice. The role of federal courts has been reflected in and shaped by politics ever since the constitutional convention in 1787 (Ball, 1980). Article Three of the Constitution broadly specifies the scope of powers of federal courts. Congress, however, has the power to decide the scope of federal court jurisdiction over criminal and civil cases. These powers have been broadly defined by Congress, producing overlapping jurisdiction with state courts. Thus, federal courts provide a potential forum (especially when state cases involve federal issues) for federal review of defendants' due process violations (Glick, 1983: 32–33). The extent of federal court review of state court determinations has been particularly strategic and controversial in advancing or impeding court-originated criminal justice reform.

The Warren Court drew upon the potential power of the federal courts to advance the agenda of egalitarian reform. One strategy effectively used to oversee the implementation of the desegregation decision in *Brown* (1954) and reapportionment in *Reynolds v. Sims* (1964) was the use of a federal *injunction* to overcome resistance or evasion by responsible officials. The effect of federal injunctive relief is that it establishes compulsory bargaining between litigants and defendants to negotiate the terms of future conduct. This process can result in the creation of state plans identifying time tables and actions to accomplish the remedies required by the courts. The use of federal court injunctive relief, as some recent studies suggest, has spurred additional Congressional action and subsequent Supreme Court decisions which have had some modest success. (For a discussion of the implementation of voting rights, see Ball, Krane and Lauth, 1982; and Mazmanian and Sabatier, 1983, for analysis of implementation of desegregation.)

Although such remedial strategies would have been available to the Warren Court to enforce the civil liberties decisions, that opportunity was expressly rejected in *Dombrowski v. Pfister* (1965) which defered to federal statutes which prohibit federal courts from enjoining state proceedings. Instead, what the Warren Court did was to adopt a "remedial counterpart" which expanded the federal *writ of habeas corpus* (Cover and Aleinikoff, 1977: 1041). The writ of habeas corpus has had a long and controversial history, especially since the end of the Civil War because it tends to be used as a surrogate for state court appellate review which may have already been exhausted or denied. Habeas corpus relief is similar in effect but not in purpose to appellate review. It provides the opportunity for a defendant to be released from custody by a state prison in order to obtain federal review of state court determinations alleged to have involved the basic denial of due process of law. Unlike injunctive relief, however, it acts not upon the behavior or actions of criminal justice officials but rather on the validity or fairness of the institutional outcome.

Several decisions by the Warren Court eroded the distinction between habeas corpus and appellate relief. In the landmark case of *Brown v. Allen* (1953) the Supreme Court ruled that it could grant certiorari under habeas corpus relief to readjudicate federal claims already fully litigated in state court proceedings. In essence, this allowed a federal habeas corpus proceeding to duplicate the efforts of a state process which otherwise was acknowledged to have been adequate by the Supreme Court.

The Warren Court further extended the federal power of habeas corpus review in *Fay v. Noia* (1963) and *Townsend v. Sain* (1963). *Fay* made it possible for defendants to obtain federal review of state court determinations even if they had failed to exercise their right to exhaust all appellate remedies in state courts. In addition, it protected the defendant from inadvertent decisions by counsel which caused the defendant to forego the use of a federal forum.

Townsend was even more far reaching than *Fay*. What it did was enable a federal district court to reopen and review the adequacy of the fact-finding procedures employed by the state court to reach its decision. Therefore, what the Warren Court had created in effect was a *redundant* framework of checks and balances between federal and state courts. In doing so the Warren Court initiated a novel approach to federalism in which state court prerogatives and independence were subordinated to federal court oversight and enforcement of uniform national policies regulating criminal justice processes. Needless to say, state courts were profoundly unhappy with this state of affairs and eager for the Burger Court to reverse this centralization of judicial power. Nevertheless, the Warren Court's concept of federalism may have produced some irreversible consequences for state court politics and policy which the Burger Court has been unable to influence. As one analysis of the Warren Court jurisdictional reforms astutely observes, they created a "dialectic" between state and federal courts which has become an important vehicle for promoting reform and development of state policy by increasing the possibility of enforcement (Cover and Aleinikoff, 1977: 1047).

The enlargement of federal court jurisdiction through expansion of the writ of habeas corpus came under immediate fire by the National Association of Attorney Generals. Yet their effort to challenge it in federal court (*U.S. v. Hendricks*, 1954) was resoundingly repudiated by the Supreme Court. Over ten years later, in 1966, the Judicial Conference of the United States (composed of state court Chief Justices) mounted a successful effort to amend the Judicial Code which only slightly restricted the habeas corpus jurisdiction of federal courts. The Burger Court simply capitalized on this disaffection in order to gain a more substantial reversal of federal court intervention. For example, in *Younger v. Harris* (1971) the Court held that a federal court could not enjoin a state criminal proceeding unless extraordinary circumstances were involved. In *Picard v. Connor* (1972) the Burger Court interpreted the 1966 amendments to the Judicial Code to modify the *Townsend* (1963) decision by ruling that state court rulings must be presumed to be correct unless specific defects are shown. Finally, the Court's decision in *Schenkloth v. Bustamonte* (1973) set the stage for subsequent decisions consummating the retraction of federal habeas corpus relief. Writing the opinion for the majority, Justice Powell, proclaiming that the original purpose of the writ to prevent unjust imprisonment had been abused, contended that since most prisoners asserting Fourth Amendment claims are not innocent, they should not enjoy the privilege of the writ (McFeeley, 1980).

Next, in its decisions in *Stone v. Powell* (1976) and *Fletcher v. Weir* (1982) the Supreme Court strengthened its attempt to immunize its restrictive post-*Mapp* and *Miranda* policies from additional unfavorable federal court review by removing the possibility of habeas corpus review of state court determination. In *Stone* the Court held that Fourth Amendment claims involving the exclusionary rule could only be readjudicated if the petitioner failed to have a ''full and fair opportunity'' to have his claim considered by the state supreme court. What this means is that once a defendant has been provided state court review of issues involving search and seizure violations, the federal courts cannot review the constitutionality of state policy: that is the state court's sole prerogative. The majority opinion provided the important key to the underlying rationale with Justice Powell's assertion that federal habeas corpus review was premised on the ''mistrust of state courts as fair and competent forums for the adjudication of federal constitutional rights'' (*Stone*, 1976: 493n). Furthermore, the majority acknowledged that state courts now demonstrated ''appropriate sensitivity to constitutional rights.'' However, as one commentator correctly surmised, *Stone* provided the opportunity to contract federal court power while expanding state court jurisdiction (Mays, 1983: 29).

The Politics of State Court Reform

One significant consequence of judicial policies to reform criminal justice processes has been increased efforts by state courts to strengthen their administrative and policy-supervisory authority over trial courts. Although efforts toward court modernization and unification were begun long before the Warren Court era, Supreme Court policy making during the 1960's, combined with LEAA support in the 1970's, provided new opportunities for state courts to reexamine such initiatives. Some state courts see unification and centralization as a way to reclaim the independence and autonomy that had been eroded by federal court intervention during the Warren Court era. Many others have conceived the opportunities more narrowly in management terms. Regardless of these motivations, the significance of state court reform does not appear to reside primarily in its objective accomplishments. Instead, reform efforts have helped to politicize the role of some state courts, increasing their visibility and deepening their influence on state policy making processes.

The growing literature on court reform includes the following principal objectives, among others: (1) consolidation, (2) unification, (3) simplification, (4) professionalization, (5) professional administration, and (6) judicial independence (Baar, 1980). These are described briefly as to their significance for understanding the role of state courts in state policy-making processes.

Consolidation of Court Structure and Jurisdiction

Many states have been plagued by a proliferation of trial courts and overlapping jurisdictions. Moreover, some state courts lacked the power to transfer judges from less crowded to more crowded courts and had little discretion to screen cases brought on appeal. Consequently, several state courts have attempted to undertake state constitutional reforms to reduce the number of trial courts with general and limited jurisdiction, create intermediate appellate courts and institute case screening procedures.

In a comparative analysis of state court structures from 1870 to 1970, Kagan et al. (1978) discovered that changes in case load, brought about in part by the creation of intermediate appellate courts (IAC), had a significant impact on the size of case loads and policy focus of state supreme courts. State courts wrote fewer opinions, but those opinions cited more cases, contained more dissents, decided more constitutional issues, spent more time on criminal and public law cases than commercial or real estate cases and reversed criminal cases more frequently. Moreover, states with IAC's were more likely than non-IAC states to favor criminal defendants. While the authors classify states according to the presence of an IAC as well as changes in state court jurisdiction, it is not altogether clear whether such jurisdictional changes have an independent effect on outcomes.

Other research done by Atkins and Glick (1976) indicates that while the presence or absence of an IAC is significant, socio-economic and political-environmental variables explain a substantial portion of the variance in the distribution of types of legal issues handled by state courts. They found that state courts in rural, politically undifferentiated states decided larger proportions of private litigation than courts in highly industrialized, politically competitive states. Significantly, the study authors suggest that additional studies exploring links between state courts and political subsystems (e.g., criminal justice) would uncover "some of the more subtle relationships between courts and other governmental institutions and environmental conditions" (1976: 114). That, of course, is a central focus of the research upon which this book is based.

Kagan's comparative data also showed that factors affecting the screening of cases before an appeal is heard and the difficulty of the case exercise significant influence on the rate of reversal ("Note," 1978). State courts which exercise greater control over case loads are more likely to have a better opportunity to review cases which enable a more direct expression of their policy preferences. Baum's (1976a) study of the relationship between policy goals and state judicial gatekeeping functions seem to underscore and support these conclusions.

Finally, a time series analysis of the same data again was used to determine whether the addition of an IAC would produce changes in state court case outcomes in terms of opinion style, reversal rate, dissent rate and percentage of cases declared unconstitutional (''Project,'' 1981). Interestingly, this study found no uniform change in these outcome measures as a result of state adoption of an IAC. Some states, such as Michigan, supported the relationship between structure and outcome while others, such as California and Oregon did not.

The most fascinating conclusion to emerge from the Kagan findings, is that ideology, politics and personality appear to confound structural effects on state court decision outcomes. Evidently, structural changes alone facilitate but do not compel judicial activism and innovation (''Project,'' 1981: 961). State courts must have not only the *opportunity* but the willingness to use their powers before adopting an activist posture. It is conceivable (as explored later in Chapters 4 and 5), that a state's political culture establishes a framework within which decision making takes place, thereby determining the politically acceptable boundaries of decision making and state court intervention in specific policy areas.

Unification of Court Administration

Along with court consolidation goes the proposition that state courts must have the authority to administer the state court system. Moreover, a unified court is considered an effective means of protecting state court interests by insuring executive and legislative observance of the separation of powers doctrine.

Glick (1982: 121–125) found some evidence to indicate that centralized judicial management is strongly related to the size and general innovative character of state government. This means that state courts in urban states with specialized governmental institutions are more likely to acquire the political support necessary to get sufficient facility, staff resources and authority to manage the state court system.

But interestingly, the processes involved in the creation and maintenance of state court unification can contribute to new political tensions both within and outside the judiciary. For example, *Hays* (1978) found grudging acceptance by lower court judges and unresolved conflicts between independently elected court clerks and court administrators over authority and responsibility in Florida. Comparative studies show that the success of state courts in achieving reform agendas seems to be determined largely by their effectiveness in cultivating legislative and executive political support (Powell, 1980).

Simplification of Court Procedure

An important element of the reform agenda is the ability of state courts to develop unified rules governing trial court procedures, yet in many states, legislatures either exercise exclusive control in this area or share it with state courts. There is some evidence that state court rule-making authority has been used by some states as a surrogate for reform in the absence of constitutional authority to do so. For example, the Washington state court, was unable to get legislative approval for a constitutional amendment enabling unification. However, it aggressively used its rule making authority to impose a state information system and other uniform administrative requirements on trial courts, obviating the need for legislative approval (Winberry, 1980).

Professionalization of the Judiciary

The replacement of partisan election of judges by merit selection is also an important element of the litany of court reform. Yet few studies are available to support the expectation that merit selection is more likely to increase the caliber and quality of judicial decision making. Glick (1982) discovered that merit selection appeared to be *unrelated* to choices by states to adopt or reject other elements in court reform. In another comparative study of factors shaping the use and outcomes of merit and partisan electoral judicial selection approaches, Dubois (1980) found non-electoral approaches to be somewhat more subject to problematic political influences, with little improvements in accountability.

Professional Administrators

The growth of state and trial court work loads has dictated that professional administrators be employed on a full-time basis to manage case dockets and other administrative functions. However, there are wide variations in the extent of administrators' powers and scope of activities.

A trade off is that judicial involvement as an interest group in the legislative process may actually decrease when liaison activities are delegated to the state court administrator (Baar and Baar, 1981). An unintendend consequence of state court proclivity toward bureaucratization of functions may be to undermine collegiality and informal but effective networks between legislators, judges and executives, essential to achieving the judiciary's policy objectives. Judges are capable of being effective political middlemen if they choose; but reluctance to do so stems in part from perceived constraints originating from the separation of powers doctrine.

Judicial Independence

To be sure, judicial reform of management and structure may not secure the independence of the judiciary from executive and legislative influence. Yet judicial independence can also be defined in terms of state court control over constitutional policy making in the administration of criminal justice.

Threatened by Warren Court federalization of constitutional rights and increased federal court intervention and oversight, state courts have been given new opportunities by the Burger Court decisions to reclaim their independence. New state courts can relax more stringent Warren Court policies in line with less demanding Burger Court policies, attempt to maintain them in the face of potential Supreme Court reversal or advance more extensive civil liberties protections and immunize themselves from appeal by grounding their policies in the state constitution.

Wilkes (1974; 1976) contends that the nation is apt to move in a new direction of federalism in criminal procedure in which state-originated rights of criminal defendants will enlarge in importance as the federal role contracts. One of the more significant consequences is that the use of independent state grounds will illegitimately insulate state courts from effective political review and accountability to other branches of government. Few remedies are available to state decision makers in the face of state court independence other than constitutional revision—a complex, difficult and uncertain task. As I report in Chapter 4, California voters have had some success in limiting the state court's liberal exclusionary rule policies, but the ease of getting constitutional amendments through the initiative process, combined with gubernatorial politics, helped to make that possible.

There may also be strategies available to the Supreme Court to curb state independence but they carry the possibility of escalating political conflict. The Supreme Court could review state court decisions based on independent state grounds but that would precipitate conflicts over jurisdictional issues similar to those raised about federal court injunctive and *habeas corpus* relief. It is also possible that the Supreme Court could assimilate all state constitutional issues under federal law, thus enabling Supreme Court reversal of state court decisions based on the state constitution, but that is an unlikely prospect given the political conflicts involved. Notwithstanding this speculation about potential Supreme Court action however, it seems more likely that the resolution of conflicts over state court decision-making will turn upon the political circumstances unique to each state.

CRIMINAL RECORDS PRIVACY: TECHNOLOGICAL INNOVATIONS AND THE PROBLEM OF CONGRESSIONAL CONTROL

The Growth of Criminal Records

The criminal history record (or "rap sheet," as it is commonly known) consists of a summary of an individual's contacts with the criminal justice system. As such, it contains a record of arrest charges and court disposition or sentencing information. The criminal record is used for a variety of purposes: pre-arrest investigation by police and prosecutors (the most frequent use), arrest and bail decisions (based on seriousness of the crime), plea bargaining (for identification of repeat offenders), court case preparation, witness verification, juror qualification, sentencing (determining the severity of punishment), corrections assignment, and probation and parole decisions (to estimate likelihood of escape).

The criminal record is not limited to these uses. It is also used for employment purposes, licensing of particular professions and security investigations. Almost

20 percent of requests to states for criminal record information come from non-criminal justice organizations. While this constitutes the extent of legal uses, there is also a black market of uncertain proportions for such material (Laudon, 1980; OTA, 1982a).

Criminal history records are maintained in differential proportions between federal, state and local agencies. Of the 216 million records, 21.4 million are held by the FBI and 195 million are held by the more than 64 thousand state and local criminal justice agencies. Of these, 29.2 million are held by state repositories with only 4 million of that number computerized. Approximately 150 million or three fourths of state and local files are held solely by local criminal justice agencies (large police departments) in manual files (Laudon, 1980b: 52).

The introduction of information technology in criminal justice has increased potential risks to individual privacy. Such risks stem principally from the enhanced speed of exchange and dissemination of data enabled by computer technology. The combination of remote terminal access and message switching capabilities (e.g., inquiries to a given location may be routed, through a central switching point to another user) now make it possible to instantaneously disseminate information through multiple ports of entry. What makes that capability damaging is the *slowness* of update processes compared to the rapidity and frequency of dissemination. Factual or contextual inaccuracies in a criminal record may convey an erroneous impression of the data subject's past or present conduct which may result in a false arrest, inappropriate sentencing and so forth.

Improving Information Technological Capacity: Organizational Effects

LEAA attempted to expand the information technological capacity of criminal justice agencies in order to improve the quality of criminal records exchanged and disseminated in the criminal justice process. The success of that effort depended upon LEAA's capacity to influence at least three factors: the processes by which information innovations are diffused; the organizational structures, practices and interorganizational relations involved in the criminal justice process; and intergovernmental relationships. These efforts have had only limited results because of important differences in organizational structures, transactions and informational needs, and the inability to reach agreement on standards for record quality, privacy protection and due process rights.

Computerization has progressed unevenly in criminal justice and has had differential organizational effects (see Table 5). LEAA had a somewhat stronger influence over the development of information technology in law enforcement than in other components of the criminal justice system, but this has resulted in unintended effects. There is some evidence that such applications reinforce "legalistic" approaches to law enforcement, depersonalize patrol activity, and narrow the scope of judgment and discretion, thus magnifying problems of

TABLE 5.

Extent of Utilization of Information Technology in Criminal Justice

Information Systems	Police[a]	Prosecutor[b]	State Courts[c]
Extent of diffusion	Extensive	Moderate	Limited
Integration	Extensive	Limited	Limited
Number of uses	Extensive	Moderate	Moderate
Extent of use in processing	Extensive	Limited	Limited
Efficacy or integrity (e.g., accuracy, completeness, privacy and dissemination safeguards)	Limited to Moderate	Moderate	Limited

[a]Colton, 1978; MITRE, 1977a.

[b]SEARCH Group, 1976; Weimer, 1980.

[c]Hays, 1978; SEARCH Group, 1975.

discrimination resulting from the reliance upon incomplete and inaccurate criminal records (Colton, 1978).

LEAA also sponsored and funded information innovations in offices of prosecution. These initiatives were intended to increase the effectiveness of prosecution by increasing clearance rates, structuring discretion (i.e., plea bargaining) and focusing resources on the trial and conviction of repeat offenders. However, these efforts have had little success because of organizational resistance, inability to reduce complex decision factors to data maintained in criminal records, and the strength of informal collaboration between prosecutors and police in charging and case disposal (Jacoby, 1980; Weimer, 1980).

Attempts to influence state and lower court organizational structures through information innovations have proven to be equally ineffective. The complexity of tasks and court organizational structure, resistance by lower courts to centralization of management, along with separation of power conflicts have made acceptance difficult to achieve (Berkson, Hays, and Carbon, 1977; Hays, 1978; SEARCH Group, 1975).

Enlarging State and Local Participation in the National Crime Information Center (NCIC)

Along with its efforts to influence organizational capacity, LEAA attempted to influence interorganizational exhange processes and the intergovernmental configuration of a national criminal record system. This effort consisted of a two-pronged strategy to upgrade the capabilities of central state repositories and to develop a national network capable of managing record exchanges between federal, state and local systems.

First, LEAA assistance greatly improved and increased state repository record maintenance capabilities. In 1969, when this LEAA assistance commenced, none of the states had established automated name indexes, and none had computerized all criminal history records. By 1982, twenty seven states had fully operational computerized criminal history records with seven having automated name indexes.

Second, LEAA reinforced the fledgling development of the National Crime Information Center (NCIC) through grants to the FBI in order to enable increased participation by states and localities. The NCIC consists principally of two major files: an Identification File (IDENT) and a Computerized Criminal History file (CCH). IDENT consists of arrests, warrants, stolen property and other data. It is considered a "hot" file and used to facilitate investigative and police field work. The CCH consists of records of arrest and convictions submitted by central state repositories.

Compared to NCIC/IDENT, state participation in the CCH component has grown very slowly, largely because of political difficulties discussed below. The maximum number of states who have chosen to participate in the NCIC/CCH has never exceeded thirteen; in 1981, only eight states were participating. An important reason for the limited participation by the states in the NCIC/CCH is the inability of most states to provide complete and accurate records, making utilization of the CCH of limited usefulness to most states and localities.

Federal Court Review and Congressional Policy: An Uncertain Partnership

Federal and state courts have shown a reluctance to intrude upon police discretion in the use of criminal records. Judicial review has been largely confined to issues of identification and record maintenance. Much less attention has been focused upon exchange and dissemination practices, record reporting responsibilities and use of records in case-related decision making contexts. Thus, the scope of court review of criminal records management has differed in significant respects from that involved in the adjudication of civil liberties, due process issues. Moreover, federal and state courts have been unable to agree upon standards which should govern records handling practices, nor have they clearly enunciated where the balance should be struck between the protection of individual privacy, the public right to know and effective law enforcement (SEARCH, 1981).

In many ways, *Menard v. Mitchell* (1971) typifies these difficulties. In its decision, the Federal District Court in Washington, D.C., acknowledged the problems inherent in the dissemination of incomplete and inaccurate records in the conduct of police work. The Federal District Court ruled that an arrest alone did not justify maintenance of fingerprints nor records by either the state repository or the FBI and that the FBI must limit disclosure of such records to law enforcement agencies only (Marchand, 1980: 139).

The *Menard* decision was exceptional in its willingness to question the propriety of commonly accepted record management practices at a time when rapidly expanding computer technology greatly magnified the potential adverse impact of the dissemination of inaccurate and incomplete information. Importantly, in drawing a firm legal distinction between a record of arrest and conviction, the federal court in *Menard* challenged law enforcement conventions which heretofore had drawn no clear distinction.

Significantly, the court found no federal statute which authorized FBI dissemination of arrest records for non-criminal justice purposes (Marchand, 1980: 140). Judge Gezell declared therefore, that the FBI must show a "compelling necessity" to disseminate a record that reveals episodes of doubtful authenticity in a person's life. The determination of "public necessity" however, was considered by the judge to rest not with the executive branch but with the Congress. A case-by-case approach was not considered acceptable and had so far not solved the problem. Rather, the federal court considered that Congress was more properly responsible and uniquely capable (Marchand, 1980: 140).

Interestingly, the *Menard* decision did not result in any controls to *internal* criminal justice use of arrest and conviction records. Thus, the decision did not really challenge the adequacy of procedures available to insure the integrity of record exchange practices. Rather, it concluded that any misuse of criminal records within the criminal justice system could be rectified by the courts. As Chapter 3 indicates, however, the control of dissemination of criminal history record information *within* the criminal justice system has proven to be extraordinarily difficult to achieve, in part, because of the unwillingness of state courts to interfere with law enforcement practices. There have only been two other federal court decisions since *Menard* which have held criminal justice officials legally responsible for the quality of records in the decision-making processes.

In *Tarlton v. Saxbe* (1974) the Court of Appeals in Washington, D.C., further amplified the *Menard* decision by declaring that the FBI was not just a passive recipient of records supplied by state and local agencies but had a duty to prevent the dissemination of inaccurate arrest and conviction records. In addition, federal courts have shown a willingness to review the effects of the utilization of incomplete criminal record information (arrest records) in law enforcement internal decision making processes. Federal courts now cite violations of constitutional rights when incomplete criminal record information was used in setting bail decisions (OTA, 1982a).

Despite these isolated decisions, federal and state courts remain divided as to an appropriate policy response to the problem. A decision by the U.S. Supreme Court has contributed to that indecisiveness. In *Paul v. Davis* 1976) the U.S. Supreme Court held that police have a right to publicize a record of an official act, such as an arrest, without exposing state or federal officials to lawsuits for civil rights violations. Accordingly, the fact that the record may be incomplete does not constitute a prohibition to its dissemination in accord with normal procedures. In its decision, therefore, the Supreme Court clearly had to balance competing rights and chose to weigh First Amendment rights and the public right to know more heavily in the balance.

In the absence of a congressional consensus on a comprehensive approach to criminal records privacy policy, a temporary measure was devised in which LEAA's responsibilities under the Crime Control Act were expanded to include implementation of a privacy mandate. The amendment reads, in part, as follows:

> All criminal history information collected, stored, or disseminated through support under this title shall contain, to the maximum extent feasible, disposition as well as arrest data where arrest data is included therein. The collection, storage and dissemination of such information shall take place under procedures reasonably designed to insure that all such information is kept current therein; the Administration shall insure that . . . the information shall only be used for law enforcement and criminal justice and other lawful purposes. In addition, an individual who believes that criminal history information concerning him contained in an automated system is inaccurate, incomplete or maintained in violation of this title, shall, upon satisfactory verification of his identity, be entitled to review such information and to obtain a copy of it for the purpose of challenges or correction (Omnibus Crime Control and Safe Streets Act of 1968: Section 524B).

The passage of the amendment constituted a limited victory for LEAA and a substantial setback for the FBI in a struggle for control over standards designed to govern the management of state and local criminal records information systems. While the Bureau retains management control over NCIC/CCH it was now subject to LEAA regulations (Title 28). Moreover, both the *Menard* decision and the criminal records privacy mandate provided LEAA with important levers with which to influence the state control and development of information technological reforms it had sponsored and funded.

Competing Proposals for a National CCH: Executive Initiatives and Congressional Default

The exact technical, intergovernmental, administrative configuration and accountability mechanism of the national computerized criminal history record system have been the subject of a protracted policy conflict between LEAA, the FBI and Congress. The debate, discussed in detail elsewhere by Marchand (1980) and Zenk (1979), has directly impinged upon the substance and efficacy of federal regulatory policy.

That debate was begun in 1969 when LEAA sponsored a demonstration project (called Project SEARCH) to test the feasibility of a computerized file for the exchange of criminal records between states. Even though the project was successful, conflicts arose as to what information should be maintained in the system and who should operate it. Although these conflicts were never decisively resolved, in December 1970, Attorney General Mitchell unilaterally decided that the FBI should manage the system (Zenk, 1979).

Since that time, Congress has been unable to reach a consensus on a national policy and comprehensive legislation. Bureaucratic conflicts in the justice department between the FBI and the LEAA over system configuration and regulatory safeguards combined with Congressional and intergovernmental conflicts over governance have contributed to this impasse.

Both the FBI and LEAA have advocated proposals for nation-wide computerized criminal history system which differ in several respects. The most salient differences pertain to record maintenance and control responsibilities, standards governing data quality and privacy, and, importantly, system governance.

Currently, the FBI maintains records of single-state, multi-state and federal offenders of participating states. The FBI proposed system would divest itself of maintenance of all single-state records but retain multi-state offenses in the NCIC central repository. In addition, the FBI would utilize a "pointer" or index system and provide message switching (now handled by the National Law Enforcement Telecommunications System (NLETS), to route inquiries from one state to another for single-state records. Next, the Bureau proposes *voluntary* state and local compliance to privacy, security and other protections for the integrity and quality of criminal history data. Finally, the FBI recommends that its NCIC Policy Advisory Board (currently composed primarily of federal and state law enforcement officials) exercise policy and management control over a national CCH.

Three recent developments with respect to FBI administrative actions are noteworthy with respect to the consequences stemming from the lack of a comprehensive federal policy. First, Congress was officially advised by the FBI in 1980 of a project to test the feasibility of a national index using the Florida central state repository as a message switching point for inquiries to the NCIC files. Congress approved the demonstration (involving the participation of fifteen states) for as long as the FBI did not operate message switching during the demonstration. However, when it was discovered that the Florida computer equipment was unable to handle the widely divergent request formats of participating stages, the FBI operationalized its own message switching capability (OTA, 1982a: 114).

The Congressional Office of Technology Assessment has challenged the FBI's authority to operate message switching even for the purposes of a demonstration (OTA, 1982a: 115–117). Moreover, it is not entirely clear, that the FBI has ceased using the message switching capability. Therefore, it is possible that the FBI may be retrieving criminal history record information from state repository files without the knowledge or permission of state officials. In addition, the FBI has significantly increased the amount of duplication between IDENT and CCH files. For example, the NCIC/CCH records also held in IDENT increased from 44 to 58 percent from 1979 to 1982 (OTA, 1982a: 196). While this duplication between files reflects the FBI's need to develop an automated fingerprint capability, such duplication would also enable the development of a computerized criminal history file technically outside Congressional control, because IDENT is not governed by existing federal regulations.

Finally, the FBI has exploited the lack of a national policy to make incremental expansions in the type of record information stored in its NCIC files. Despite the expression of Congressional concern, the FBI added a "dangerous" persons file ostensibly for the purpose of anticipating potential threats to the President. But recent OTA staff testimony indicated that persons with anti-law enforcement and anti-authority points of view would be likely to end up in the file as well (Committee on the Judiciary, 1983: 71). What is evident from these three related instances of FBI discretionary decisions is that there may be a variety of ways that the Congressional control over the CCH may be circumvented in the absence of policy consensus.

The LEAA-CCH concept has differed substantially from the FBI version. LEAA has insisted that the NCIC maintain criminal records only for federal offenses; central state repositories would maintain both single and multi-state offense records. It has also recommended that the index or "pointer" system be controlled by NLETS. LEAA's contention is that the FBI proposal to operate message switching is tantamount to giving the Bureau the capability to develop a central criminal history repository because of the access it would provide the Bureau to state and local files.

LEAA has also consistently promoted (through SEARCH Group, Inc.) decentralized, state control of the CCH system. In essence, each state would establish an independent commission to develop, monitor and enforce criminal records management and privacy regulations. In addition, each participating state would be represented on a board which would formulate national policy and user standards (SEARCH, 1978). Finally, LEAA has strongly supported the development of a national policy for control of the dissemination and use of criminal records.

Over a ten year period support in the criminal justice system for various technical configurations has shifted markedly from centralized (single-state, multistate) to decentralized, state-focused approaches (national index only). Significantly, while there appears to be a consensus on the national index concept, it pertains only to *technical configuration*. Opinion is still divided on issues pertaining to management, regulation, constitutional rights and governance processes. Moreover, these surveys tell us little about the views and attitudes of governors and state legislators whose opinions rarely get solicited on this issue.

A recent survey of state criminal justice officials conducted by the OTA (1982a) indicates that support for alternative governance configurations has become increasingly divided. That survey indicates that there is extensive variation in support for alternative governance configurations. Moreover, respondents urged that states be given increased policy control and that some other entity such as NLETS or SEARCH Group be given policy and enforcement powers. The Department of Justice survey also found that state law enforcement officials considered an agency other than the FBI to be a more viable governance entity in the long term (OTA, 1982a: 171-172).

POLITICAL CONSTRAINTS TO FEDERAL REGULATION OF STATE AND LOCAL CRIMINAL JUSTICE PROCESSES

The foregoing history of Supreme Court and Congressional policies indicates that there may be some common political constraints to federal regulation of state and local criminal justice processes. The factors described briefly below serve as a convenient referents in our subsequent analysis and explanation of the implementation and outcomes of civil liberties and criminal records privacy policy. These constraints are discussed with reference to criminal justice research in the next few pages:

1. *Constitutional Rights*—the extent of protection of citizens' Fourth and Fifth Amendment rights are essentially contested.
2. *Law Enforcement Practice: Public Safety vs. Discrimination*—there are difficulties in limiting the social costs of investigative practices while maintaining effective law enforcement.
3. *Cross-Cutting Policy: Privacy vs. the Public Right to Know*—there are inherent difficulties in reconciling the tradition of public disclosure with the need for individual privacy protections.
4. *Separation of Powers*—conflicts between executives, legislators and courts over the scope of policy making functions limits support for effective implementation of criminal justice policy.
5. *Federalism*—the establishment of national policies creates jurisdictional conflict between federal, state and local governments and officials.
6. *Governance*—there are basic conflicts over the relative authority and capacity of courts, legislators, and executives to originate criminal justice policy.

Constitutional Rights

The differences between the Warren and Burger Court interpretations of civil liberties policies show that there is little consensus regarding the circumstances under which the Constitution protects citizens' privacy and due process rights. One important source of this conflict stems from the relative generality of the language found in the Fourth and Fifth Amendments to the Constitution. As a former Justice of the Colorado Supreme Court aptly characterized it:

> Defendants' rights are constantly mentioned in the newspapers and elsewhere, but I don't see the word "defendant" in the Constitution. What I see is individual rights, and those rights belong to everybody, regardless of whether they are defendants in a criminal case.

In the absence of clear Constitutional guidance regarding issues of application to criminal justice processes, Courts and the Congress have had to rely upon underlying philosophical proclivities to fashion a doctrine justifying their policy decisions. Thus, differences over Constitutional interpretations stem instead from underlying conceptions of the purpose and functions of the criminal justice system.

The Warren Court viewed defendants' due process rights as a means by which to insure the equity and fairness of the criminal justice process. Thus, an individual should only be deprived of his liberty after being afforded fairness of procedure, the opportunity to present evidence, confront witnesses and exhaust all available appeals. These values are given explicit recognition in the *Mapp* and *Miranda* decisions as well as in subsequent Warren Court decisions.

The Burger Court, on the other hand, has subscribed to a contrasting view of the criminal justice process. Successful law enforcement, from this point of view, turns upon determination of the factual guilt of the accused. Criminal justice involves, therefore, a search for truth as a basis for reasonable and just outcomes. Importantly, an efficient and effective criminal justice system is best attained by minimizing guidelines and maximizing the discretion with which dispositions are reached. This set of priorities is most clearly expressed by the Burger Court decisions in *Bivens*, *Calandra* and *Janis* and reinforced in *Belton*, *Chambers*, *Mosely* and *Leon*.

Similarly, an uncertain Constitutional foundation makes the assertion and application of privacy rights an essentially contested concept. Nowhere in the Constitution is there an explicit recognition of the absolute right to privacy. As Justice Douglas once remarked, the right to privacy can only be inferred from the penumbra of protections flowing from the Fourth and Fourteenth Amendments. This presents a difficult task for Courts to adjudicate statutory privacy rights which lack Constitutional grounding. Nonetheless, the resolution of conflicts between legislatures and courts over the extent to which the privacy of subjects of criminal records should be observed seems to turn upon more basic underlying views about effective law enforcement.

The Courts seem unable to reach agreement as to the relative importance to individual privacy of accurate and complete criminal records compared with public awareness of the individual's contact with the criminal justice process. While the *Menard* decision requires that the disclosure of criminal records be justified by some "compelling public necessity," the *Paul* decision holds that the individual must forego his right to privacy because such invasions are inherent in the criminal justice process. The *Menard* decision invites legislative resolution of the competing issues involved while the Burger Court discourages such intervention. Thus, the Burger Court sees the publicity stemming from criminal justice contacts as a necessary condition whereas *Menard* views it as a contingent condition subject to remedial legislation.

Law Enforcement Practice: Public Safety vs. Discrimination

Another constraint to the implementation of criminal justice regulatory policy is the need to limit the social cost of due process and privacy invasions without jeopardizing effective law enforcement. Many studies of criminal justice process conclude that the successful regulation of law enforcement practices is hindered by the belief that it will hamper effective law enforcement. Some powerful but conflicting arguments, sometimes unsupported by available evidence, are advanced to support or deny the validity of this assertion (Milner, 1971b; Silberman, 1978; Skolnick, 1974; Wilson, 1968). Opponents of police regulation contend that the officer must typically act on split-second judgements, in situations of uncertain risk and danger, involving suspects with criminal backgrounds in the act of committing crimes. However, this stereotype exaggerates the actual nature of police work and presents a somewhat atypical portrayal, at odds with the findings of recent studies.

For example, Wilson's pioneering study of police work (1968) established that there are three substantial variations in departmental styles or approaches to the conduct of law enforcement functions. The "watchman" department acknowledges the impossibility of full enforcement and, thus, places primary emphasis upon discretion and order-maintenance. Here, the seriousness of the offense and public risk dictate the sanctions applied. Police departments driven by a need for uniformity in enforcment of laws, involving prompt apprehension, arrest and charge of offenders, are best characterized as adhering to a "legalistic" style. In comparison to these styles, departments structured by "service" approaches place greater reliance upon non-arrest functions such as conflict resolution and prevention. In a study using Wilson's typology, Talarico and Swanson (1979) determined that most departments characterize themselves in terms of the "service" style.

Wilson (1968) has also contended that most police perceive their occupation as a *craft*. However, Talarico and Swanson (1979) provide evidence that more policemen identified with the professional style than others. Although not a direct comparison to the craft view, it does suggest that the image of professionalization has made some inroads in law enforcement. Although tentative, data such as this would suggest that only a small fraction of police contacts involve the stereotypical conditions described earlier. This conclusion is strengthened by the fact that the vast majority of crimes are never cleared (result in arrest and conviction).

Decisions by both the Warren and Burger Courts have been predicated in part on law enforcement stereotypes. As mentioned earlier, the Warren Court's *Miranda* decision rested in part upon textbook descriptions of interrogation techniques which cannot begin to sustain generalizations about prevailing practice.

The influence of stereotypes is also noticeable in the Burger Court's preoccupation with cases involving "probable cause," accentuating the need to establish "exigent circumstances" obviating issuance of a warrant (*Chambers* and *Robinson*) and its inconsistent and problematic decisions pertaining to searches incident to arrest (*Belton*, *Robbins* and *Ross*).

Similar arguments based upon stereotypical images and specious reasoning have been employed by law enforcement interests to block regulation of the uses of criminal record information, particularly in investigative contexts. Police contend that rapid retrieval, unencumbered exhange and the instantaneous availability of criminal record information to patrolmen is essential for the quick identification and potential apprehension of crime suspects. These encounters are claimed to occur when time is of the essence, the officer is in potential danger, the suspect is possibly wanted for other crimes, and a confession is likely. Under these conditions, the availability of criminal records is believed to considerably reduce the risk and uncertainty to the officer while minimizing the possibility of mistaken identity and false arrest. However, police computer technology has fallen short of its expected benefits of increased response time, apprehension rates and positive identification (Colton, 1978: 285; Hebert, 1978: 154–155). As Murphy (1975) documents, poor record quality in the NCIC/IDENT and CCH files makes those sytems inherently unreliable in establishing "probable cause" for arrest.

There are other problems as well which underscore the social costs of these stereotypes. Studies cited by OTA (1982a: 13) document discriminatory effects involved in police documentation of contacts with black suspects. Accordingly, blacks are more likely than whites to be arrested and, significantly, account for a disproportionate number of releases without charges. Under those circumstances, arrest records may be used as a form of harassment in instances where no actual crime can be documented. Moreover, NCIC records indicate that in 1980 blacks accounted for nearly 29 percent of all records in the CCH file, almost triple the percentage of blacks in the total U.S. population (OTA, 1982a: 141–142). Although this conceivably reflects the fact that blacks commit more crimes, it also suggests that they are more likely to be considered suspects than whites in unsolved crimes.

Beyond these social costs of the unregulated use of criminal records, there are other less visible contexts in which records are employed with more insidious consequences. Criminal records generated as a result of political acts of civil disobedience have also been used to conduct surveillance involving a variety of political groups. In the recent past, many of these records found their way into NCIC/CCH files where they were subsequently flagged by the FBI for investigative uses. Although the FBI has reassured Congress that these practices have ceased, the Bureau continues to find new justifications for intelligence and investigative uses of criminal history record files. Although police generally consider investigative information exempt from public access and regulation, the ACLU has had some limited success in Seattle and Los Angeles in lawsuits resulting in the imposition of regulatory restraints on police collection and use of intelligence information. A national policy addressing the intelligence and investigative uses of records found in the NCIC/CCH would further threaten police control over existing intelligence networks.

Cross-Cutting Policy: Privacy vs. the Public Right to Know

The implementation of civil liberties and privacy policy also creates dilemmas for the continued observance of the public right to be informed of the workings of its government.

This dilemma is exemplified in the vacillation by the Supreme Court with respect to defining the circumstances under which an individual has a "reasonable expectation of privacy" or when statements made in custody can be used to incriminate or impeach his testimony at trial. In search and seizure policy, the Burger Court has consistently used a lower threshold for privacy invasions of the home than for searches involving vehicles and the personal effects of the individual. Yet the line is never clear when the threshold has been crossed between privacy and public knowledge and precisely when exceptions to the "warrant requirement" apply. Consequently, there continues to be multiple and conflicting legal bases for which state courts can formulate policy. The Burger Court post-*Miranda* decisions also present similar policy dilemmas. In its decisions in *Calandra*, *Janis* and *Michigan v. Tucker*, the Supreme Court has wrestled somewhat indecisively with the circumstances under which a suspect or defendant's communications are privileged and when a request for post-arrest silence must be observed barring subsequent use of statements at trial.

The dilemma involved in balancing privacy and the public right to know is perhaps best exemplified in the use of criminal records. The press and private employers constitute two significant interests in the support of unrestricted access to criminal history records. Policies for the protection of privacy rights with respect to information systems and other areas have been preceded by at least a decade of federal policies designed to greatly enlarge the accessibility of governmental records. Therefore, it is not surprising that efforts to limit certain information made accessible to the public by prior policy would be controversial. Given policies with cross-cutting objectives such as these, the conditions of implementation are uncertain and policy success is problematic (O'Brien, 1980).

First, federal and state public disclosure laws generally provide little guidance about determining which criminal justice records are public records. Moreover, the exemption of police intelligence and investigative information under public record guidelines has seriously limited subsequent efforts to include them under criminal record regulations.

Second, given conflicting signals from the Supreme Court in *Paul* and Congress through LEAA, it is not altogether clear at what point in the process and what type of records may be obtained by the press. By the Supreme Court's reckoning, few restrictions to press access are acknowledged while LEAA has limited access to arrest records if they fail to contain complete dispositions.

In addition to these problems, a third difficulty resides in determining when a ''compelling'' or legitimate need is established for non-criminal justice access to criminal records. Ever since the concept was first used, but not defined, in *Menard* there has been almost no effort by the courts and only limited guidance by LEAA with respect in determining agencies with legitimate access to criminal records. Consequently, there are substantial variations in state policies regarding record dissemination guidelines.

Finally, while the courts and Congress appear to have reached some agreement on designating criminal justice agency responsibility for record quality, police have generally shifted these burdens to the record subject. In addition, underutilization of record monitoring and audit procedures and lax enforcement (as discussed in Chapter 3) limit efforts to improve record quality to only those instances involving specific challenges of record content.

Separation of Powers

Besides these policy-based limitations to national policies, conflicts between executives, legislators and courts over the constitutional limits of their policy making roles have constrained the implementation of criminal justice regulatory policy.

The initial adverse reaction by Congress to the *Miranda* decision and continuing conflicts between courts and legislatures over the exclusionary rule are indicative of the extent to which underlying conflicts over the separation of powers impede the implementation of national criminal justice policy. To some members of Congress *Miranda* appeared to usurp their policy-making prerogatives by prescribing positive and specific guidelines better left to statutory resolution. Consequently, an amendment was added to the Crime Control Act of 1968 expressing Congressional concerns in a gesture of more symbolic than practical consequence. The Burger Court has helped exacerbate institutional conflict by underscoring the fact, as it did in *Michigan v. Tucker*, that *Miranda* constitutes an ''interpretive rule'' not a *right*.

Similar conflicts surround the implementation of the exclusionary rule. Criminal justice officials, including trial court judges, do not consider *Mapp* to have imposed an absolute constitutional test but rather to provide one regulatory strategy among several. Thus, officials are free to pursue other approaches short of the replacement of *Mapp* by legislative policy. The increased disenchantment shown by some states (including Colorado as discussed in Chapter 4) has been expressed by the passage of statutory guidelines establishing ''good faith'' exceptions to the exclusionary rule limitations. Actions such as this simply deepen the political conflicts between state courts and legislators with respect to jurisdictional control over procedural and substantive policy matters.

The functional interdependence of the criminal justice system has not been sufficient thus far to overcome resistance to executive erosion of judicial power posed by criminal records regulations. Although court functions are integrally related to the maintenance of complete criminal records, and thus make some overlapping power nearly unavoidable, executive regulation poses a threat to court autonomy. This problem is endemic to all such regulatory policies because courts have thus far been better able than executives and bureaucrats to resist encroachment by using constitutional arguments to deflect the burdens of compliance.

Federalism

The formulation and implementation of federal policy typically invites conflict over the balance of authority between federal, state and local governments.

Tradition dictates that the criminal justice system is highly decentralized both in political and functional terms. Like education, law enforcement and the administration of criminal justice is considered a matter of local control; leadership of most of the major elements of local criminal justice (e.g., police, prosectuors and courts) is selected through general elections. Thus, criminal justice officials represent diverse and overlapping constituencies. The relative political independence of each component sustains and reinforces differences in perspectives on appropriate policy responses to crime, and thus limits the efficacy of federal policy intervention.

The Warren Court employed the doctrine of "selective incorporation" to apply the Fourth, Fifth and Sixth Amendments to the states in the *Mapp* and *Miranda* decisions. This doctrine has used the Fourteenth Amendment due process clause to incorporate or subsume the states under these constitutional protections. This has been controversial for it seemingly conflicts with the constitutional rights of the states to independently exercise all powers not expressly reserved to the national government. Ironically, the Bill of Rights was specifically advanced by anti-federalist, states-rights interests to limit the potential abuse of power by the federal government (Storing, 1981: 64–65). Such arguments continue to underly challenges of Supreme Court use of the "selective incorporation" doctrine.

The emergence of differences between Warren and Burger Courts over the role and jurisdiction of federal courts, especially with respect to civil liberties issues, indicates that the boundary between federal and state court power is fluid and shaped by differing philosophies of federalism. Some state courts have reacted to such jurisdictional disputes by increased reliance upon independent state grounds, in order to strengthen their authority and enforcement effort. Others have limited the applicability of federal policy as a way to minimize state court interference in police conduct. But there seems little consensus as to how far Supreme Court authority extends relative to state court prerogatives.

The attempt to develop a national CCH regulated by uniform criminal records privacy policy has been besieged by similar problems. A national CCH implies a centralization of regulatory authority of state and local law enforcement and other criminal justice agencies which heretofore has not existed. Federal, state and local law enforcement interests are often divided on policy issues which require consensus on governance and management because of strong differences over functional responsibilities, roles, jurisdiction and so forth.

Also, the development of a national criminal information exchange system necessitates increased state authority and/or enforcement of policy which presents some novelty for most states. Only four states now exercise any regulatory control over criminal justice activities including information system processes (Skoler, 1977). It is not entirely clear what role state and local *elected* officials should assume under a national CCH and what agency or agencies should assume an enforcement or oversight role. Moreover, it is not self evident how uniform policy might take shape under conditions of decentralization of criminal justice leadership. For, unlike the relationship between federal and state courts, criminal justice agencies are not clearly linked in either a formal or informal hierarchical structure. Thus, the configuration of the criminal justice system and power conflicts pose important constraints to the implementation and enforcement of a national CCH.

Any national CCH system must necessarily include guidelines for record management processes by users, limits to file size and content, standards for record quality and oversight provisions for audit purposes. Such guidelines are essential to ensure the integrity, security and privacy of a criminal history record information. There is little uniformity across criminal agencies with respect to record management practice. Consequently, the interstate transmission of criminal record information involves potentially wide variations in the care and restrictiveness with which information is maintained and utilized.

The inability to reach agreement among federal, state and local interests as to the size and content of a national criminal history record file also constrains the development of a national policy. Generally, the larger the size of national files, the greater the likelihood of problems of record quality (i.e., inaccuracy and incompleteness) and the potential for surveillance abuses. Technical issues such as these necessarily involve unresolved political issues. For this reason, civil liberties and minority group interests have generally opposed enlarging the NCIC along the lines of a national repository or utilization of an FBI-controlled message-switching service between the states.

System audit mechanisms are also necessary but, again, political factors limit consideration of approaches which insure adequate control. The Government Accounting Office has most recently been proposed by the OTA for nation-wide audit responsibility, but criminal justice interests contend that outside auditors lack expertise, necessitate security clearances and are unable to guarantee confidentiality of findings.

Governance

One final constraint which must be overcome to effectively regulate criminal justice processes is the resolution of conflicts over system governance. This pertains to the *authority* and *capacity* that courts, legislators and executives claim to originate public policy in criminal justice.

Differences between the Warren and Burger courts have created new *dilemmas* in the justification and legitimation of the exercise of judicial authority. The Burger Court's pursuit of a *minimum* rather than *maximum* constitutional floor for the protection of civil liberties and due process rights has increased the latitude and discretion of state courts. In decisions intended to limit the scope of federal court interference the Burger Court has invited state courts to develop approaches best suited to prevailing state and local circumstances. But the capacity of state courts to implement and enforce their own judicial policies depends to some extent upon their legitimate authority to do so. While there is some evidence that differences in state court supervisory power and case outcomes are related to differences in state court structure, little is known about the political circumstances which support or inhibit the assertion of state court authority to originate and enforce criminal justice policy.

Similar questions of legitimacy have been posed with the attempted development of a national CCH and creation of uniform criminal records regulations. The availability of technical capacity alone has not compensated for the lack of legislative authority underpinning federal and state systems. Because the FBI has demonstrated its technical capacity to operate and manage a national CCH, it already exercises a *de facto* authority to govern the NCIC/CCH. Nevertheless, state and local law enforcement interests do not acknowledge FBI authority to regulate state or local criminal justice processes. Moreover, the capacity of state central repositories has improved, facilitating potential enlargement of state law enforcement management and regulatory capacity. LEAA has expressed support for state governance options running contrary to either FBI or state law enforcement preferences. Acquisition of regulatory control, combined with new federalism rationales, has enabled the implementation of a criminal records privacy policy at odds with law enforcement organizational prerogatives and prevailing public record philosophies. Thus, differences in approach to criminal records privacy undermine the potential for reaching a consensus on questions of authority central to the ongoing struggle for control over the direction of the national CCH.

3

National Patterns of State Policy

This chapter is intended to determine state responses and performance under civil liberties and criminal records privacy policy. This will involve an effort to organize existing studies, identifying their limits as well as raising issues and questions in need of additional analysis. The data presented in this chapter portrays nationwide patterns and then compares performance in four states (California, Colorado, Washington and Massachusetts) selected for more detailed analysis in Chapters 4 and 5. A preliminary attempt is made to assess some contrasting explanations of policy outcomes, leaving for Chapter 6 a more thorough explanation of performance and consequences of the policies we have chosen to study.

IMPLEMENTING *MAPP* AND *MIRANDA*

The Expectations and Realities of Change.

Initial responses by criminal justice officials to the *Mapp* and *Miranda* decisions are striking in their common expectation that if implemented, they would result in extensive, adverse change in the conduct and outcome of the criminal justice process. The observance of defendants' rights was expected to constrain law enforcement investigative functions, impede effective prosecution and produce judicial outcomes contrary to the findings of factual guilt. Subsequent studies suggest, however, that these beliefs or perceptions were greatly exaggerated: the actual effects of the policies have varied substantially from initial expectations. And there is some evidence to suggest that *Mapp* has actually resulted in greater change than *Miranda*.

Although the response by the criminal justice community was largely negative and consistent with public opinion, neither decision was unexpected by criminal justice officials. Twenty-two state courts had already adopted some form of the exclusionary rule prior to *Mapp*. Moreover federal courts had been operating under the rule since *Weeks* in 1914. Yet, police in states operating under the exclusionary rule prior to *Mapp* perceived greater disruption of existing practice (M. Murphy, 1966). Pre-*Mapp* states also showed a greater likelihood of rejection than post-*Mapp* states, although implementation would be unlikely to involve much policy change for the former states.

The *Miranda* decision simply consolidated the several incremental steps the Court had already taken to insure adequate and uniform due process protections in the states. In fact, the decision seems to have been better anticipated by police than *Escobedo* decided in 1964 (Wasby, 1970; 1974–1975). Yet once the complete panoply of defendants' rights was specified and embodied in a concrete procedure, anxieties about change intensified.

Studies of the impact of *Miranda* generally suggest that expected effects were greatly overdrawn. Changes have occurred but not necessarily in either intended or anticipated directions. Adoption of the policy does not carry the onerous consequences expected by police and prosecutors, nor do the decisions appear to close avenues available to bypass or evade implementation (Baum, 1979; Wasby, 1970). The issuance of *Miranda* warnings, for example, has not endangered the likelihood of conviction (Seeburger and Wettick, 1967; Wald et al., 1967). And both decisions have generally revealed the resilience, adaptiveness and pervasiveness of informal practices (e.g., plea bargaining) which limit policies designed to formalize procedures and structure discretion (Horowitz, 1977). In this regard, the *Miranda* decision, more so than *Mapp*, lends itself to perfunctory response.

In comparison to the findings on *Miranda*, studies of *Mapp* are more sharply divided as to the effects of the decision on police behavior. Part of the disparity stems from the multiple and ambiguous measures used to evaluate performance as discussed in Chapter 1. It is difficult to establish a precise causal relationship between changes in any measures and outcomes of the *Mapp* ruling. By two of the possible measures, arrest and conviction rates, for example, Oaks (1970) found that the exclusionary rule had little effect on altering police behavior. In contrast, Canon (1974a) found a less clearcut relationship between the rule and ratios of arrests to convictions. Moreover, he discovered a substantial increase in search warrants and extensive police adoption of departmental procedures to implement *Mapp*, thus supporting the conclusion that behavior had changed in the direction of acceptance. Therefore, Canon counsels against a "precipitous" conclusion regarding the efficacy of *Mapp* because of the difficulty or even impossibility of supporting a conclusion for or against police deterrence. But by any account, police may be finding it difficult to absorb the *Mapp* requirements into existing practice.

Responses of two district attorneys from Washington and Colorado illustrate the problematic effects of *Mapp* compared to *Miranda* on ongoing practices. A Washington prosecutor had this recollection:

Q. How do your expectations about Mapp *and* Miranda *compare then and now?* It was sort of an act of resignation mixed with anxiousness and opposition. But *Miranda* didn't have the effect we thought it would have. Very few defendants have refused to confess. In fact, it has not really burdened our criminal justice trial procedures. But in *Mapp*, given a constitutional application to trial procedure, most of us including myself would like to see it go or be modified by a "good faith" rule. It is ridiculous for a defendant to go free because of a mistake in collecting evidence.

A former district attorney from Colorado had this to say:

Q. Given your experience with both policies, how do Mapp *and* Miranda *compare?* *Miranda* is less of a problem because you are dealing with a narrower area. It may require further definition of "custody" perhaps, but it really is clear. It's not a big problem, although initially it was. . . . *Miranda* ran its course years ago. We know what the parameters of the effects of the decision are now but we don't really know what they are in *Mapp*. We are many years from having enough circumstances to know where we are in search and seizure. . . .
The exclusionary rule is more problematic. Even judges have shown their inability to consistently apply it when confronted with actual situations. It's gotten to the point of being so sophisicated that even people making the law can't apply it. The "good faith" exception is necessary to cover situations when violations come to light subsequent to an arrest and search. It wouldn't affect anyone's rights because it is an attempt to get at the truth.

The complexity of procedural issues and uncertainty of consequences has made perfunctory acceptance of *Mapp* a less viable police response. The admissibility of evidence bears a more direct relationship to the possibility of conviction for certain crimes than do circumstances surrounding the questioning of suspects. Therefore, if the objective of police is to secure convictions, then obtaining warrants and following other procedures is essential. Yet even when police have accepted these changes they have no assurance that evidence obtained from warrant-based searches will be admissible in court. As LaFave (1965: 412) notes, judges often issue warrants with little attention as to whether there are adequate grounds for doing so. Consequently, police use of warrants to seize evidence may still result in successful motions to suppress evidence at trial.

These findings underscore the limited behavioral change required to adopt unambiguous policy yet dramatize the differences in outcomes which appear to stem from variations in clarity. Interestingly, *Mapp* appears to have come much closer than *Miranda* toward effectuating changes in the administration of criminal justice.

Procedural Clarity and Perfunctory Behavior

One of the novel attributes of the Supreme Court civil liberties decisions, contributing no doubt to the general image of profound policy change, was the attempt to specify police and trial court behavior in detailed terms. In this regard, the *Miranda* decision constituted a model of clarity and precision, atypical of most court decisions as well as legislative policy. In addition, *Miranda* was intended both to minimize the variations in state court criminal defendant guidelines and to limit the leverage lower-level implementers might have to either evade, avoid or fail to comply with the policy.

Studies of the impact of these court-originated policies suggest, however, that there may be an inverse relationship between the extent of policy concreteness and implementation. Policies limited to procedural objectives may increase the probability of perfunctory behavior and thus limit actual performance and change.

Studies of the *Mapp* and *Miranda* policies suggest that *Miranda* has resulted in patterns of literal and perfunctory adoption while the less precise *Mapp* ruling has produced differential acceptance and greater behavioral and organizational change (Baum, 1979). While the majority of police may now be using the *Miranda* warnings, they have developed a variety of subtle, informal methods by which to adapt to *Miranda* and avoid its consequences. The tight focus of the decision on a discrete point in the investigative process has invited exploitation of marginal situations in which custody is ambiguous.

In contrast, the exclusionary rule, given the absence of procedural prescription, has produced far more uncertainty among police and others about whether behavior inconsistent with *Mapp* will go unnoticed or unchallenged. Acceptance of *Mapp* therefore seems dictated largely by the nature of the case and the importance of obtaining a conviction (Canon, 1974a). The observations of a Massachusetts public defender are instructive as to the relationship between clarity and change and the differential nature of the problems police and prosecutors are likely to face with *Mapp* compared to *Miranda*:

> *Q. How do the* Mapp *and* Miranda *decisions compare with respect to clarity of guidelines?* All *Miranda* really does is provide a set of words to repeat. It's simple, I frankly don't think there is much compliance to *Miranda*. Depending on what level of court you are involved with 95% of all cases are disposed of by guilty pleas. Only gross injustices are corrected—that is by people taking cases on appeal but that number is very small with the chances of success very, very small.
>
> But with search and seizure cases police have to deal with two categories which aren't clear: If there is a warrant, it may be shown defective; if no warrant was obtained then the burden is on the prosectuor to show that police satisfied exceptions. But exceptions to *Mapp* like "exigent circumstances" are much vaguer than "consent" is to *Miranda*, . . . such as whether instructions were given, did the subject understand them and what was the defendant's reaction.
>
> *Q. What about prosecutors, do they supervise police at all?* Very little, but it does vary. It depends on relations with local police. Most minor cases are dealt out—are disposed of by some kind of guilty plea. Therefore the procedural problems go with them. If you consider the number of cases that go to appeal it is miniscule.

When response to the civil liberties decisions is enlarged to include the prosecutorial stage, implementation is more problematic. The pervasive practice of plea bargaining means that the overwhelming majority of cases are disposed of through guilty pleas. This, along with the variety of ways prosecutors may use to deal with problems of evidence, makes the likelihood that a case will go to trial, involve a successful motion to suppress evidence *and* lead to sanctions of police practices rather slim (Horowtiz, 1977).

In addition to these problems, unambiguous Supreme Court policy mandates have not produced uniform state court rulings either. In some instances state courts have chosen to qualify, limit or even expand Supreme Court civil liberties policies in ways that cannot be clearly categorized as in conformance or not (Kramer and Riga, 1982). The specificity of the *Miranda* decision has, for example, produced state court responses which clearly divide along ideological lines (Romans, 1974) and show wide variations in the behavior defined to fall inside or outside interrogation guidelines (Cimino, 1973). Moreover, apparent violations by state courts appear related less to clarity and substance of policy than to the protection of long-standing state practices which they perceive to be threatened (Tarr, 1977).

Finally, the communication of these court policies has undergone some distortion in their transmission from superiors to subordinates. It is not evident, however, that policy clarity contributes to more effective transmission processes. Clear policies are just as vulnerable to distortion as unclear ones, particularly if they are controversial as in *Miranda*. Press reports of the *Miranda* rules greatly oversimplified the policy and often failed to report how it affected the interrogation process (Wasby, 1973). Moreover, how *Miranda* was understood by police depends primarily upon the source interpreting it. Milner (1971a) discovered that departmental sources were more likely to involve greater distortions than those outside the department.

Despite these sources of distortion, the continuous coverage and favorable portrayal by the media of the *Miranda* decision in the context of police conduct has evidently had a long term positive impact on increasing public support. McClosky and Brill report in their national survey that 79 percent of the public agrees that the right to remain silent ''is necessary to a fair system of law enforcement'' (1983: 159). In addition, support for the principle is even greater among community leaders and the legal elite with 89 percent endorsing it. Conversely, given more complex issues pertaining to the exclusionary rule and more critical media coverage, only 11 percent of the public showed a willingness to approve acquital of defendants based on legal technicalities of evidence (1983: 163). In addition, two-thirds of the sample of legal elites felt that acquital was an improper response. Significantly, the public perceived problems of evidence as stemming primarily from judicial oversensitivity to police conduct which the public thought constrained effective crime control.

Differential Support by Elites

State court justices are potentially important intermediaries in determining the way that Supreme Court decisions are implemented at the state and local level.

Most state courts now have authority to supervise trial court behavior through adoption of rules and through development of guidelines resulting from review of trial court cases. State court opinions may be used to express support or opposition to policies implied by Supreme Court decisions and such decisions may help commence a process by which additional state policies emerge. Although studies have not established a direct causal relationship between state court decisions and directions of local response, they do provide evidence of the importance of state and trial court support for Supreme Court policy.

State courts participated in the widespread controversy among national, state and local elected officials provoked by *Mapp* and *Miranda*. Canon (1974b) discovered that ''organizational contumacy'' was widespread. This consists of attempts to express defiance, disobedience or resistance to court policy through tactics which include adoption of strained interpretations, expressions of confusion and other means of delaying implementation.

Significantly, the most frequently expressed criticism of both decisions pertained to their adverse implications for effective law enforcement. State courts showed considerable sympathy for police and strongly sided with law enforcement values. As Canon observes:

> Those taking this approach seemed to identify less with values ascribed to the courts in determining constitutional policy than with values held by those outside the judiciary (1974b: 61).

Thus, state court contumacy may provide an important source of political symbolism in state politics. Given the negative public reaction to *Mapp* and *Miranda*, perhaps state courts found it necessary to shield themselves from the political repercussions likely to ensue from acceptance of the decisions of their judicial superiors. Such cues express attitudes to prosecutors and police that Supreme Court policy is being implemented under protest and that actual enforcement may be unlikely. State courts may also influence the direction of response of lower level implementers through ancillary decisions which attempt to square Supreme Court policy with contrasting state court ideological predispositions and practices.

Yet once federal standards have been adopted by state courts, it appears to have been difficult to persuade them to relax or withdraw the standard in face of Supreme Court invitations to do so. Studies by Wilkes (1974; 1976) and Gruhl and Spohn (1981) show that Burger Court efforts since 1971 to relax the *Miranda* standards have neither resulted in similar decisions by state courts nor produced increased attempts by local prosecutors to evade the ruling. Interestingly, prosecutors, who have been overwhelmingly critical of the policy (Katz, 1966), still uphold the doctrine in their day-to-day decisions.

In addition, there is some evidence that police also look primarly for direction from local trial courts. While local trial courts sometimes demonstrate little familiarity with state court decisions, where local courts do comply with instructions from state courts, police practices are likely to be more consistent with state court policy (LaFave, 1965).

The foregoing analysis suggests that where police and prosecutors' attitudes and styles are similar, where state and trial court judges share a common hostility to Supreme Court policy, where judicial willingness to supervise police investigative activity is minimal and where prosecutorial case screening is unsystematic, police resistance is likely to flourish. Where such conditions prevail, the unintended consequences of civil liberties decisions may result, as Horowitz (1977) contends, in reinforcing rather than weakening an informal and, at times, arbitrary set of institutional practices.

The Underenforcement of Supreme Court Decisions

The foregoing discussion has shown that most state courts have complied with the Supreme Court civil liberties decisions despite initial criticism (Baum, 1979; Tarr, 1977), *and* trial courts and local prosecutors are generally willing to accept state policies. Therefore, it would be reasonable to expect increased police observance of defendants' due process rights and substantial reform in police investigative practices. But the available evidence fails to support these expectations. Instead police conduct continues to be governed primarily by local custom and practice. Moreover, extensive variations in police performance often persist even within states governed by clear and consistent policies expressing the unequivocal protection of defendants' due process rights (Canon, 1973; Manwaring, 1972; Porter and Tarr, 1982).

Two arguments help explain the enforcement gap between federal and state policy and local performance: (1) State courts do not directly intervene in police conduct and therefore are unable to enforce decisions. And (2) there are important ideological, political, intergovernmental and organizational constraints which limit the aggressiveness with which state courts enforce Supreme Court mandates.

Inability to Enforce Decisions

While it is true that there are important limitations in the capacity of courts to supervise police behavior, state courts do have the power to supervise lower court behavior and, thus, may impose sanctions on both trial courts and prosecutors. Yet studies of state court implementation of *Mapp* indicate that while state courts have been more willing to overturn police methods conflicting with the exclusionary rule, they have been unwilling to impose actual sanctions on offending departments and individual officers. Moreover, there is evidence to suggest that some state courts show less willingness to apply *Mapp* guidelines to lower court procedure than to police conduct. A reanalysis of Canon's (1973) attempt to categorize state court rulings on procedural issues left unresolved by the Supreme Court shows a greater willingness by state courts to provide guidelines for police conduct than to supervise lower court trial decisions. This is consistent with more general practice wherein state courts are more likely to side with trial courts than intermediate appellate courts. State courts reversed intermediate court cases upholding the trial courts 38.6 percent of the time while reversing those cases reversed by the intermediate courts 52.5 percent of the time ("Note," 1978: 1202).

In addition, Manwaring's (1972) analysis of state court responses to *Mapp* shows that state courts have been unwilling to apply the *Mapp* standards to determine what constitutes a reasonable search and seizure and "probable cause" for arrest. Manwaring discovered that state courts have developed a number of inventive ways to pursue restrictive interpretations of *Mapp* regarding those issues affecting the acceptability of police conduct. Morever statements by police officials in states such as New York, where the exclusionary rule existed prior to *Mapp*, also tended to confirm weaknesses in state enforcement. For example, Police Commissioner Murphy (1966) singled out the *Mapp* decision for its devastating effects on law enforcement procedure, specifically citing the need to reevaluate procedures put in place to implement state court policy subsequent to the *Mapp* decision. Yet if New York police were already in compliance with state court policy on the exclusionary rule, why would such an extensive impact be expected and why would police procedures necessitate change in light of *Mapp*?

Evidence of this kind suggests that there have been, in fact, significant state court policy variations in the interpretations of the federal exclusionary rule and that state court policies frequently lack aggressive enforcement.

Ideological, Political, Intergovernmental, and Organizational Constraints

State court rulings after the *Miranda* decision presented a very difficult profile of policy responses than those following *Mapp*. What is more, one study seems to imply that the more clear and specific the policy, the greater the likelihood of state court compliance. Romans (1974) discovered there was a greater tendency among state courts to comply with the *Miranda* ruling rather than the less clear *Escobedo* decision. He also found that conservative state courts—those having less restrictive requirements governing the admissibility of confessions before *Escobedo*—tended to give a more *liberal* interpretation of both the *Escobedo* and *Miranda* decisions than liberal courts.

Romans explains this seemingly contradictory result this way: The specificity of the decision provided little opportunity for state courts to rule on issues other than those "peripheral" to the ruling such as retroactivity, the collateral use of evidence collected when *Miranda* warnings were inadequate and extension of the ruling beyond felony trials. Thus, the *Miranda* decision, unlike *Mapp*, provided little leverage to state courts to match expressions of contumacy with actual decisions which minimized or altered its impact on law enforcement. To be sure, state court responses to both *Escobedo* and *Miranda* hardly constituted a massive display of approval for either decision. For in both cases, the majority of state courts ruled conservatively by restricting their applicability on the basis of factual distinctions. Nonetheless, Romans found that favorable responses to *Miranda* occurred most frequently among the unanimously conservative courts.

Based on a reanalysis of Romans' data, Tarr (1982) challenges the significance of the seemingly contradictory relationship between clarity of court decisions, ideological predisposition and favorable rulings. Tarr contends that when the Supreme Court specified rights and guidelines in more detail, it reduced the ability of conservative state courts to evade the decision. When confronted with the choice between their policy preferences and national policy, state judges chose adoption, in part, because they did not have an alternative policy that they were trying to protect.

Tarr contends that this analysis supports what he terms the "state impact hypothesis." This hypothesis suggests that judges will fail to implement Supreme Court decisions only when important state practices are threatened which have been in operation for a relatively long period. In other words, state court judges are predisposed to avoid implementing policies expected to produce substantial disruption in state policy or practice (Tarr, 1977: 105).

Manwaring's (1972) study of selected state court rulings in the wake of *Mapp* seems to contradict Tarr's thesis. Manwaring found that state courts which had adopted an exclusionary rule comparable but prior to *Mapp*, showed a greater likelihood towards non-compliance in the face of *Mapp*. C. Johnson and Canon (1984: 68) find this irreconcilable, but it might be explained two ways. This finding appears to contradict the "state impact hypothesis," since we would not expect much of a burden for states with similar policies already to observe *Mapp*. However, it might simply suggest that these states saw no need to invalidate existing state policies since they were considered equivalent to *Mapp*. Alternatively, the adoption of the *Mapp* rule by pre-*Mapp* states, while not inconsistent with state policy, would be disruptive nevertheless. It would challenge the authority of ancillary state court rulings already developed by pre-*Mapp* states and/or substitute federal court enforcement for state court authority.

There are perhaps good reasons to prefer the second explanation of state court response for it appears better able to reconcile differences in accounts of state court behiavor. It places more emphasis on avoiding potential conflict between state courts, lower courts and police and potential disruption of prevailing political culture. State courts which had adopted their own exclusionary rule before *Mapp* were less likely to adopt that decision because acceptance of the federal rule would preempt state policy and enforcement.

By the time *Miranda* was decided in 1966, criticism of federal district court preemption of state court supervisory, policy making and enforcement power was widespread (as discussed in Chapter 2). One important recurring state court complaint about the civil liberties rulings was that they energized federal court intervention of state court proceedings. This put state and lower courts in an awkward and unwanted position of being second guessed. Therefore, potential federal replacement of state enforcement mechanisms constituted a threat for the pre-*Mapp* and imposed rule states alike.

A former Justice of the Colorado state court, active in the National Judicial Conference, recalled the widespread concern with federal court intervention, when asked about issues considered important to state court justices during those years:

One of the functions of the judicial conferences over the last few years has been to protect the interests of the state court system. One of the issues of extreme importance to us was how to establish better rapport with the federal courts. Chief Justice Burger was terrific in this area by working out the differences in keeping the federal judiciary out of our hair. The problem was a lot of federal judges got the idea that the mantle of the lord was on their shoulders. When they took the bench they suddenly got a new set of brains. Some even presided over cases which they had originated as state court judges and reversed them after realizing what terrible things they had done.

Q. Was this a result of the Warren Court decisions? Yes, as a result of the *Townsend v. Sain* ruling, the Supreme Court ruled that it was a duty of the federal judge to reexamine what had been done in the state court system. So you had cases coming out of trial court going through the state court and then reaching federal court through a writ of habeas corpus. . . . You know, no one objects to a federal court interpreting legal principles but they would make rulings based on different interpretations of facts. They don't do this anymore. There was a lot of abrasiveness because of the practice but this problem has receded a lot in the last few years. Burger has had a lot to do with that, by ending the abrasiveness between federal and state court systems.

Evidence of this kind suggests that conflicts over federal court review introduced an important intergovernmental dimension into the state courts' reckoning of civil liberties issues. The Warren Court years marked a high water period of intergovernmental conflict. However, as chapters 4 and 5 will show, that conflict has not been eliminated simply by the removal of federal court review of state court decisions. Instead, the roles and ideological positions of Supreme Court and state courts have been reversed. Therefore, the conflict has been recast in terms of state court independence from potential reversal by a more conservative Supreme Court.

Analysis of State Court Response: The Four State Context

State court policy making by California, Colorado, Washington and Massachusetts from 1966 through 1982 was analyzed to see if any discernible patterns emerged which might help adjudicate between competing theories of the relationship between state court response and local performance. State court case summaries found in the *Dicennial Digest* were grouped according to whether they addressed issues pertaining to search and seizure or confessions. In addition, they were distinguished according to whether they were made during the Warren or Burger court periods. Finally, as a way to separate the rulings according to ideological or philosophical leanings, the cases were categorized in terms of whether they adopted *elaborative*, *independent* or *restrictive* policies implementing the Supreme Court decisions. Decisions were considered *elaborative* if the state court provided a more expansive or innovative interpretation of civil liberties issues than the Supreme Court. Decisions in which the state court ruled more narrowly than the Supreme Court were designed as *restrictive*. Finally, the term *independent* was used to characterize those decisions in which the *state constitution* was used to justify its decisions. (It should be noted that the state constitution is frequently used to show *concurrence* in a case in which a federal constitutional issue is involved. In these instances, further analysis must be conducted to examine underlying factual or procedural issues in order to determine whether the ruling resulted in a more expansive interpretation of constitutional protections).

The overall results of this analysis are presented in Table 6. An interesting pattern emerges challenging the greater significance of clarity and ideological differences compared to intergovernmental ones. Surprisingly, in spite of the predominantly restrictive or narrow interpretations in state court responses to Warren Court decisions, they did not maintain this approach in response to the Burger Court. If clarity were a significant factor then we would not expect an increase in the number of state court decisions *elaborating* on *Miranda*. Yet in California and Colorado the majority of the confessions policy rulings were elaborative after 1970, and in Washington and Massachusetts the change from exclusively restrictive decisions to a more even proportion of restrictive and elaborative rulings was significant.

The state courts in our sample of decisions showed a greater willingness to enlarge protections against illegal searches and seizures after 1970. While some variation was expected, the citation of independent grounds grew to significant proportions during these years. While the conservatism of the Burger Court civil liberties decisions constitutes an important impetus to state court evasion, it does not fully explain increased state court use of independent grounds. Of course, independent state grounds affords an immunity from Supreme Court reversal which is no doubt an important incentive. But this seems a rather excessive way to distance state courts philosophically from their judicial superiors.

State court motives seem to lie elsewhere, perhaps for reasons embedded deeper in political culture. What appears to be at stake in state court assertion of policy independence is the legitimacy of its authority to develop policy based on the interpretation of the state constitution and ability to enforce it. Thus, the efforts to get federal court oversight, intervention and enforcement withdrawn did not simply reflect ideological differences with the Supreme Court but marked the attempt by some state courts to increase their own policy-making powers compared to state executives and legislative rivals (Bice, 1972).

STATE CRIMINAL RECORDS POLICY AND PERFORMANCE

Although spare in detail, the 1973 amendment to the Crime Control Act provided LEAA the opportunity to impose a national policy on the states through

TABLE 6.

State Court Rulings on Civil Liberties Policies, 1966-1982

		Total No. of Decisions	Interpretation		
			Restrictive	Independent	Elaborative
Search and Seizure Rulings					
California	1966-69	30	17	2	11
	1970-82	69	12	21	36
Colorado	1966-69	12	5	4	3
	1970-82	46	1	20	25
Washington	1966-69	13	10	0	3
	1970-82	32	2	12	18
Massachusetts	1966-69	10	7	0	3
	1970-82	31	13	2	16
Interrogation and Confessions Rulings					
California	1966-69	42	32	0	10
	1970-82	39	10	3	26
Colorado	1966-69	9	8	0	1
	1970-82	25	10	0	15
Washington	1966-69	9	9	0	0
	1970-82	8	4	1	3
Massachusetts	1966-69	7	7	0	0
	1970-82	25	16	0	9

Note: Compiled from *Dicennial Digest* listings, 1966-1982.

regulation of criminal justice information systems. The Title 28 LEAA regulations subsequently set in motion a state planning process by which state policies could emerge. The guideline development process was prolonged, with extensive revisions in 1975, 1976 and 1977, primarily because it gave contending political interests an opportunity to further influence national policy. State policies initiated during this period of unsettled federal law provide an important basis for understanding subsequent state performance.

LEAA officials expected the regulations to result in substantial change in state records management practices, improvement in the integrity and quality of criminal records, and, importantly, the establishment of uniform state policies limiting the dissemination of criminal history record information (Marchand, 1980: 204–205; Zenk, 1979). The profile which emerges, however, shows extensive procedural adoption and strengthened controls over public access yet little evidence of change in record management processes or improvement in record quality. State enforcement is lax with great variability in local practice.

This section examines state performance and policy responses to federal guidelines in order to establish a national context for our four state sample. In addition, other available studies of national criminal records policy are assessed in order to identify factors shaping outcomes.

Defining Criminal History Record Information: From Clarity to Ambiguity

LEAA's 1974 draft regulations drew heaviest fire from criminal justice interests with respect to the definition of criminal history information. The significance of this controversy was that an overly broad definition might hamper effective law enforcement while a narrow one might make dissemination controls inadequate.

In 1974, LEAA defined criminal history information to include that information collected for the purpose of identifying individual criminal offenders and *alleged* offenders. This implied that the use and dissemination of investigative information pertaining to suspects would be subject to regulation. The Director of the Michigan State Police expressed incredulity at this prospect by commenting:

> I cannot believe that you truly wish to provide the criminal or organized crime individuals with access to information regarding them that involves ongoing investigation into their criminal activities (U.S. Department of Justice, 1974a: 33).

LEAA's final version of the Title 28 regulations, published in 1975, reflected concessions to these criticisms by limiting criminal information resulting from actual arrests or convictions. The definition included criminal record information contained in "rap sheets" or other arrest reports, but specifically excluded intelligence and investigative information. The states included in our four state sample all adopted definitions consistent with LEAA regulations, as did most other states.

But subsequent problems have arisen in interpreting what the definition means. For example, problems arose with respect to determining whether court records fell under the definition. Washington resolved this issue by exempting court records from dissemination controls but allowing court access to law enforcement criminal record information. In contrast, California and Colorado have not experienced these difficulties, in part because of significant differences in state policy and organizational relationships.

Dissemination Policy: Challenging the Prevailing Public Philosophy

LEAA's attempt to establish limits on the dissemination of criminal history record information was fraught with controversy. Part of the difficulty stemmed from LEAA's overly broad definition of criminal record information. This problem was corrected in part by permitting the dissemination of arrest information lacking final disposition for up to one year.

Revisions put forward in the 1975 version of the privacy regulations showed both a softening of LEAA's position with respect to dissemination and greater clarity about which records would fall under dissemination restrictions. Nonetheless, LEAA regulation writers failed to define the term dissemination. In its 1976 planning instructions, LEAA acknowledged this oversight with the following definition:

> Although dissemination is a key concept in the regulations, regulations do not define the term. However, it can be interpreted to apply to the release or transmission of criminal history record information by an agency to another agency or another individual (U.S. Department of Justice, 1976c: 14).

Clearly, the term dissemination was intended to include exchange of information from one criminal justice agency to another. This had important regulatory consequences for both local agencies and the central state repository. It required every criminal justice agency (with certain exceptions) to obtain the most current and complete disposition information from the CSR prior to release of arrest record information. Also, the disseminating agency as well as the CSR were to maintain a log of each dissemination, recording the name of the record subject, type of record involved, date and receiving agency. These restrictions also applied to arrest records used for investigative purposes.

Needless to say, law enforcement was not happy with these restrictions. One comment submitted by the Phoenix Police Department is illustrative of these widely shared concerns:

> Our investigators work on a daily basis with other criminal justice agencies in our normal duties and are constantly discussing criminal history information on suspects, prisoners, etc., and the logging of this dissemination would be ludicrous and impossible to control. The dissemination of criminal history information is inherent within the criminal justice system, it cannot be contained or curtailed without a corresponding decline in effective law enforcement (U.S. Department of Justice, 1976a: 10).

Most central state repositories, including those involved in our four state sample, maintain dissemination logs, but there is extensive variation in the frequency with which dissemination logs are monitored. Only Massachusetts conducts annual reviews while the other three states either do so when an abuse occurs or not at all.

In addition to these difficulties, LEAA had not made it clear initially that factual information regarding criminal justice processes (e.g., status of investigations, apprehension, arrest, release, prosecution, correctional status) was publicly available. Thus, a rule was added that information ''which is reasonably contemporaneous with the events to which the information relates'' could be disseminated without restriction (U.S. Department of Justice, 1975: SEC 20.33[c]). While this rule provided a bit more clarity as to when criminal record information could be legally disseminated, it did not placate concerns of the press.

Importantly, the press considered itself to have a special responsibility and freedom to convey information about the criminal justice system without restriction. That right and responsibility was asserted to be predicated on the public right to know:

> The American Newspaper Association's position on the proposed rules of law is one of outright opposition. We applaud the intent of these rules to afford greater protection of privacy to individuals. However, insofar as these proposed rules would infringe upon the right of the press to gather and disseminate information relating to criminal justice we do seriously object. The danger it seems to us, is that LEAA's effort to protect one right, i.e., the right of privacy, it is proposing to make that right supercede the public's right to know (U.S. Department of Justice, 1974a: 31).

Given this pressure, the vague standard of ''contemporaneousness'' gave way to operational distinctions in police files. LEAA guidelines adopted in 1976 were now based on common police administrative practices which distinguished between chronological records of arrest, maintained in active police blotters and permanent files kept in alphabetical order. Only files maintained in a chronological order and not identifiable by person would be accessible to the public.

LEAA had also proposed in 1974 that neither arrest nor conviction information be disseminated for non-criminal justice purposes unless provided by statute or executive order. But by 1975, LEAA regulations permitted criminal justice agencies to release criminal records if state statutes or executive orders made the absence of a criminal record a precondition for employment or licensing.

Evidently these changes did not concede sufficient ground to private sector employers who, by 1975, had become increasingly concerned about the adverse effect of these regulations on their access to criminal records. For example, written responses to the 1974 regulations included only two comments from private employers. In comparison, when the 1975 regulations were published, 33 of the 74 comments submitted to LEAA came from private sector firms and associations. Most of these comments expressed strong opposition to limitations on dissemination to non-criminal justice agencies (U.S. Department of Justice, 1974a; 1976a).

Consequently, under pressure to further relax what had initially been a very restrictive policy, LEAA made further concessions. First, it defined a new category of criminal history information to consist of ''non-conviction data.'' This information pertains to an arrest which has not resulted in a disposition either favorable or unfavorable to the data subject at least one year after the arrest. Thus, limitations on dissemination now applied only to non-conviction information (i.e., arrests).

Second, LEAA made two more revisions in dissemination requirements which all but capitulated to the pressure of state and local public and private interests. First, a 1976 revision permitted state and local discretion in the interpretation of statutes permitting access to non-conviction data. Second, the 1977 revisions no longer required expressed statutory authority for access to such data (U.S. Department of Justice, 1976d; 1977: Sec 20.21[b][2]).

Indeed, given substantial discretion by LEAA to do so, states showed extensive differences with respect to both the *form* and policy *content* of dissemination guidelines, as shown in Table 7.

However, these variations in the form and content of policy do not compromise the generalizability of my explanation presented in Chapter 6. Most states (over half) did pass comprehensive dissemination policies similar to LEAA recommendations, including the four states in my sample. Three fourths of the states acknowledged some distinction between arrest and conviction records, with only a few rejecting the distinction upon which the LEAA policy was based. Moreover, dissemination policy was only one of several regulatory requirements that states were required to implement, with requirements pertaining to accuracy and completeness having substantial significance for the overall enforcement effort. Also, the sample states I selected reflect the dimensions along which states reflect the greatest variation with respect to state agency roles, policies, enforcement mechanisms, etc.

Court Records and the Separation of Powers Doctrine

LEAA's attempt to make its 1974 draft regulations apply to court proceedings proved equally unpopular. LEAA's initial broad definition of criminal history records included records of court proceedings which heretofore had been publicly accessible. This was proposed not only for policy reasons but because LEAA recognized that court participation was essential to achieving the goals of completeness and accuracy.

The National Center for State Courts submitted a strongly worded challenge to provisions including the courts under LEAA's 1975 regulations. These statements not only questioned LEAA's authority to promulgate regulations regarding state court activities, but challenged the *constitutionality* of executive regulation of the judiciary. The National Center contended that LEAA's actions "marked a clear departure from its often stated policy of not imposing federal regulation on states, and, more particularly state courts, that utilize LEAA funds" (National Center for State Courts, 1974:4). The courts felt that LEAA had exceeded its administrative authority. The National Center pointed out that all the original privacy amendment to the Crime Control Act required was that information

TABLE 7.

Variations in State Dissemination Policy and Management, by Year of Adoption

I. States with Laws Resembling Changing LEAA Title 28 Regulations:

A. State Laws Comparable to Title 28 in 1974		B. State Laws Comparable to Title 28 in 1975		C. State Laws Comparable to Title 28 in 1976	
Alaska[a]	1972	California	1973	Washington	1977
Massachusetts[a,e]	1972	Iowa	1973	Hawaii	1978
Georgia[b]	1976	Alabama[b]	1975	Kansas[b]	1978
Illinois[a]	1976	Oregon	1976	Louisiana	1978
Maryland[d]	1976	Connecticut	1977	Montana	1978
Colorado	1977	Virginia	1977	Nevada	1978
Nebraska	1978	Washington[a,e]	1977	North Dakota	1978
		Maine	1978	Oklahoma	1978
				Pennsylvania	1978

II. States with Dissemination Policy which Applies only to the Central State Repository:

A. CSR Statute Only		B. CSR Policy Only		C. CSR Administrative Procedure	
Kentucky	1974	Arkansas[c]	1975	Michigan	1975
Missouri	1975	Delaware	1975	Rhode Island	1976
New Mexico	1975	Mississippi	1975	Minnesota	1977
South Dakota	1976	New Hampshire	1976		
Vermont[b]	1976	North Carolina	1976		
Arizona	1977	South Carolina	1976		
Indiana	1977	Wisconsin	1976		
Idaho	1978				

III. States with Other Approaches

A. State Open Records Law		B. Executive Order		C. Employment Practice	
Texas	1975	Tennessee	1975	New York	1976
Utah	1975	New Jersey	1976		
Ohio[c]	1977				
West Virginia	1977				
Wyoming	1977				
Florida[b]	1978				

Note: Compiled from U.S. Department of Justice, 1978b; 1979.

[a]Regulatory authority in independent commission.

[b]Advisory commission with no regulatory authority, management by state law enforcement agency.

[c]Management by personal information system board.

[d]Management by state law enforcement agency in all states without superscripts.

[e]Regulatory authority transferred to state law enforcement agency in 1979.

stored in criminal justice information systems be accurate and complete. This did not imply some additional state regulatory authority.

Clearly the National Center was troubled by the ambiguities and the lingering implications they left for further encroachment of executive control over courts:

> Thus, the regulations appear to give LEAA wide discretion in determining the extent to which the judiciary will be bound by its regulations and what must be done by a state judicial system to comply with the regulations. Such discretion in a federal agency over actions of the state judicial branch of government poses serious problems from both the standpoint of the limits of federal authority and judicial independence (National Center for State Courts, 1974: 4).

As a result of widespread dissatisfaction with the attempt to include the courts under Title 28 a successful lobbying campaign was mounted by state court judges and administrators to exempt the courts from coverage. Consequently, the 1976 version of Title 28 specifically exempted court records.

That exemption and its underlying doctrine has created some enormous difficulties for many states in satisfying federal mandates for improved record quality (accuracy and completeness). State courts have generally interpreted the exemption to mean that the separation of powers also prevents mandatory court reporting of disposition information to either local law enforcement or to the central state repository. In many instances, the exemption is asserted despite policies explicitly requiring court participation.

In light of these difficulties, it should not be surprising that poor record quality is the most serious weakness of central state repositories. Record incompleteness varies from 15 to as much as 42 percent of total files (OTA, 1982a: 93–94). Substantial differences between the number of arrests and dispositions reported on the CSR dramatize the problem of incomplete records. In most instances, as Table 8 indicates reported arrests far outstrip available dispositions.

However, in Massachusetts the reverse is the case for reasons explored in Chapter 5. And significantly, only Massachusetts in our four state sample appears to be above the national average with respect to its level of court disposition reporting.

State Record Management and Enforcement

Ever since the publication of the SEARCH model regulations in 1972, LEAA strongly recommended that states create an independent agency or commission to administer and implement the criminal records privacy regulations. However, perhaps realizing that it would be inconsistent with the New Federalism, LEAA declined to specify agency responsibility for state administration of federal guidelines. Instead, it delegated the responsibility to the governors.

Few states have actually followed LEAA's preferred alternative of establishing an independent commission. States with an independent commission included

TABLE 8.

Court Disposition Reporting

	50 State Pattern	4 State Sample	
Court disposition reporting system			
formal statute	20.8%	WA	
formal agreement	14.6%	MA	
informal practice	12.5%	CO	
none varies	52.1%	CA	
Court disposition information linkage			
unique tracking number	14.6%	CO	
number plus fingerprints	31.3%	WA,	MA
number, name, fingerprints, other	50.0%	CA	
Court disposition monitoring procedures			
automated review	35.4%	CA,	CO
manual review	12.5%	MA	
inquiry sometimes	14.6%	--	
none	35.4%	WA	
Court disposition reporting			
percent	59.2%	CA CO WA MA	59.2%, 10% 94.3% (60%)* 98%
Arrest reporting			
percent	74.1%	CA CO WA MA	-- 98% (95)* 40%

SOURCE: Laudon, 1980b.

*From 1982 interview by the author.

Massachusetts and Washington. Five other states established advisory commissions with little actual regulatory authority. But the remaining vast majority of states (84%) designated the state law enforcement agency (either State Patrol, State Police or Department of Public Safety) to assume management and regulatory responsibility (Laudon, 1980b). The state of California has pursued this latter alternative, in which the Department of Justice, under the Attorney General in California administers the privacy regulations. The Colorado Bureau of Identification (which has CSR authority) has almost no involvement in administration of privacy regulations because of court assumption of a quasi-administrative role described in Chapter 4.

Confusion still lingers among state and local criminal justice officials, as to the scope of state agency administrative authority. Most officials (including state agency representatives) view that role as passive and limited to technical assistance, while some see it as one of active enforcement (MITRE, 1977b: 71).

Whatever the reason, there appears to be a nearly universal lack of aggressive enforcement of state policy. Few states, including those in our four state sample, had ever conducted routine accuracy checks or audits of CSR records by 1977, as Table 9 indicates, even though most states have the capability to do so. Instead, most states, including our four state sample do make a comprehensive set of procedures available for the individual to inspect his record file and correct and/or challenge inaccuracies. For the most part therefore, the burden for maintenance of accurate and complete records falls primarily upon the record subject.

Some Analyses of Criminal Records Privacy Outcomes

Several studies have been completed recently to account for the failure to achieve a uniform national policy for the management and control of criminal records. A significant deficiency of these studies is their preoccupation with the politics of *national* policy making which tends to downplay the importance of factors in shaping *state* responses and performance. Nonetheless, a brief review of three alternative acounts will serve to identify the kinds of explanations that have been suggested to date. Studies by MITRE (1977a; 1977b) and OTA (1982a; 1982b) share the presupposition that a clear, uniform, effectively communicated and technically optimal policy constitutes the key to creation of a national CCH capable of vast improvements in record quality and use while effectively protecting individual privacy.

Significantly, in nearly every instance in which MITRE found deficiences in procedural compliance, a connection was established to ambiguities originating in the Title 28 regulations. The MITRE survey suggests that state and local officials sought a "correct" interpretation rather than one which best fit local conditions and policy orientations (1977b: 6).

In its conclusions, MITRE stressed that greater progress in state and local compliance depended upon three principal elements: (1) Congressional amendments to clarify the Title 28 regulations, particularly on dissemination policy,

TABLE 9.

Audits and Accuracy Checks of CCH Records

	50 State Pattern	4 State Sample
Routine use of accuracy checks		
yes	43.8%	CO
no	56.3%	CA, WA, MA
CSR audit (ever?)		
yes	25%	CO
no	75%	CA, WA, MA
Annual audit capability foreseen		
yes	60.4%	
no	18.8%	CA, CO, WA
already available	20.8%	MA
Systematic audit capability foreseen		
yes	68.8%	WA
no	8.3%	CO
already available	22.9%	CA, MA
Extent of procedures in place for individual access		
individual access or challenge only	4.2%	--
plus appeal	4.2%	--
plus ability to correct	18.8%	CA
plus public right to access	66.7%	CO, WA, MA
Source of procedures for individual access		
statutes for all criminal justice agencies	29.2%	CO
CSR statute	22.9%	CA
custom, tradition, administrative policy	37.5%	WA, MA

SOURCE: Laudon, 1980b.

specifying a more precise role for the central state repository; (2) passage of comprehensive state legislation; and (3) increased federal enforcement and technical assistance to help state and local agencies interpret and properly implement required procedures (MITRE, 1977a: 24–25).

OTA contends that the absence of a political consensus between law enforcement and civil liberties groups about the technical configuration of a CCH and adequate protections against privacy invasions and surveillance abuses has primarily blocked implementation of national legislation thus far. Consequently, OTA has recommended that a two-pronged approach be undertaken by Congress to resolve the policy difficulties. One element consists of strengthening state and local criminal justice information technological capacity and enforcement. The other involves passage of comprehensive legislation which reconciles differences over governance, oversight, privacy protection and record quality standards. According to OTA, the relative effectiveness of civil liberties and privacy protections is assumed to vary according to the technical configuration of the CCH. Therefore, the most significant benefits to be realized from an optimal system would consist of a more equitable and effective use of criminal records in the criminal justice process combined with enhanced civil liberties protections.

Both the MITRE and OTA reports present some interesting assumptions which could be tested in the context of our four state analysis. The Massachusetts experience in particular casts serious doubt on the OTA assumption that agreement on technical issues is sufficient to achieve the consensus required for successful policy.

Finally, Marchand (1980) advances a more scholarly argument familiar to students of organizational behavior and collective action. Marchand attributes the failure to achieve a comprehensive national policy and adequate state efforts to the ability of criminal justice organizations to define and dominate the politics of technology and social costs associated with the development of criminal justice information systems.

First, the nature of privacy issues and its publics have not been sufficient to reach the critical mass necessary for effective collective action. Criminal records privacy involves publics which are characterized by low visibility and intensity and by diffuseness. The number of criminal records subjects is rather small and are not likely to attract attention to that fact. Instead, the issue is of concern only to a small minority of traditional civil liberties groups, the press and employers. Moreover, the need to identify ex-offenders because of the risk they are presumed to pose to their communities vastly outweighs the intensity of concern for privacy violations.

Second, federal, state and local law enforcement agencies have been able to dominate policy by capitalizing on the amorphousness and weakness of privacy interests. Civil liberties-oriented policy considerations have never been able to advance very far or effectively, according to this view, because of law enforcement-bureaucratic control over information system technologies. Even Congress, as Marchand points out, has been unable to loosen that control or hold accountable federal or state law enforcement agencies through oversight fuctions. Consequently, instead of urging more national legislation which only increases centralized law enforcement control, Marchand favors a decentralized, federated approach, similar to that sponsored by SEARCH and LEAA discussed in Chapter 2 (Marchand, 1980: 312).

While commendable, Marchand's solution seems greatly inferior to the dimensions of his diagnosis. If the source of the problem lies in the characteristics of the issues and interests involved, then deeper changes in national and local political culture must occur in order for political action to emerge and be successful. And if organizational hegemony of law enforcement organizations persists, then that suggests that state and local officials have not been effective in exercising oversight to ensure accountability.

PRELUDE TO ADDITIONAL INQUIRY

The studies of state and local performance under the policies reviewed here tentatively sustain three important conclusions: (1) There is evidence of uniform but incomplete procedural adoption and some behavioral change. (2) Overall weaknesses in performance nationwide could be attributed to ambiguities in the statutes or court rulings and the threat of change. (3) Significant differences between judicial and legislative policy-making and the differential effects of their political environments account for variations in the capacity to influence the clarity of policy and the extent of public support and implementation. While plausible, these conclusions are premature because each raised additional considerations which invite further investigation.

The upshot of these qualifications is that a common point in the policy process needs to be examined where institutional actions and policy decisions intersect. This would afford a greater opportunity to weigh the relative significance of all potential factors shaping outcomes. Therefore, the next two chapters will focus on state policy and guideline development as a potentially fruitful avenue by which to explore additional factors shaping state executive, court and legislative responses to federal policy. This comparative analysis focuses on state courts, legislatures and bureaucratic policy-makers because they are the intermediate recipients of intergovernmental policy and have common responsibility for supplementary rule-making functions. The way in which state officials respond to policy enunciated by their federal superiors in the intergovernmental system may have important consequences for the way that policy is understood and interpreted, transmitted, communicated, overseen and enforced, and received and reacted to by lower level implementers.

There are several reasons why the national context of performance presented here must be further interpreted through a deeper examination of selected state experiences. First of all, it is not self-evident that change in performance has been either uniform or substantial. Indeed, the extent of change appears to be a function of the policy chosen. For example, the *Miranda* and criminal records policies exhibit evidence of substantial procedural adoption and change in behavior and practice. Yet strangely, *Mapp* doesn't appear to share these uniformities, in presenting a more ambiguous picture. We know more about perceived impact of the exclusionary rule than we do about actual performance or change. It is conceiveable that the relative ambiguity of *Mapp* may account for this difference but we need to find out more about the extent of change that has actually occurred relative to the other two policies to corroborate that conclusion.

There are other variations in performance which introduce additional uncertainty in developing an adequate interpretation. For example, available data and the limited studies of criminal records privacy tell us much about public reaction to the policy but little about the responses and perceptions of impact by state and local criminal justice officials. Consequently, it is uncertain as to whether performance is to be primarily explained by negative public responses *or* by resistance originating from conflict within the criminal justice system. In addition, the discrepancies between procedural adoption and perfunctory use of procedures, in the case of *Miranda* and criminal records privacy, strongly contradict the presumptive relationship between clarity and policy success. This invites additional analysis of the significance of enforceability as a potential intervening factor.

Despite these difficulties in establishing an adequate explanation of outcomes, it could still be argued, as has been the case in other policy studies reviewed so far, that fundamental differences in institutional practices and capacities and the greater significance of political environment for legislative than court-originated policy account for the discrepancies in performance. Impressive evidence indeed can be martialed to support this explanation. As noted in Chapter 1, it has become popular in many academic quarters to attribute differences in the effectiveness of court and legislative policy to underlying differences in institutional structure (e.g. "sanction" and "inducement" systems). The profile of implementation and performance under the three policies would appear to underscore the signficance of these differences.

The Crime Control act and the LEAA block grant program provided substantial inducements to decision makers at all levels of government to accept as well as abuse regulatory conditions of aid in exchange for federal funds. The efficacy of these incentives in influencing state organizational behavior is best demonstrated in studies by Feeley and Sarat (1980) and Gray and Williams (1980). They find that Congressional regulatory policy is most likely to work when agencies are given wide latitude to make policy and program innovations without the fear of reprisal in the loss of funds. On the other hand, a frequent consequence of excessive bureaucratic influence over policy implementation processes is the substitution of *de facto* policy making by administrative elites for the legitimate authority and accountability of elected officials (Nieman and Lovell, 1981). The causes of such organizational consequences are amibiguous federal laws, loosely monitored funds and excessively delegated discretion (Feeley and Sarat, 1980; Lowi, 1979).

The state implementation and outcome of the federal criminal records privacy mandate appears to fit these theoretical expectations precisely. It is an example, *par excellence*, of politics of bureaucratic dominance and dilution of a federal agenda. While the available data lends credence to this view, it misses information with which to judge how legislative inducements affect the preferences, responses and actions of state elected officials, (e.g., legislators and state court justices) as well as state and local criminal justice officials. If federal intergovernmental programs effectively bypass state officials through insidious bureaucratic processes, then we need to know whether this occurs *because* of or *despite* the involvement of state officials. The way this issue is resolved can make a substantial difference in determining the significance of factors leading toward particular state outcomes.

Given the absence of implementing bureaucracies and provided with only the power to sanction non-compliant behavior, courts must rely principally upon communication processes to influence the implementation of policy (Wasby, 1973; 1974–1975). It seems that this dependency is no more apparent than in the case of the civil liberties decisions. Where the Supreme Court decision is clear and state court rulings few and limited in scope, as they were with *Miranda* compared to *Mapp*, then adoption is likely. The *Mapp* decision seemingly confirmed the courts' institutional limitations in influencing implementation by creating the possibility of endless interpretation and uncertainty. In fact, differences in the intensity of attitudes of state decision makers toward the two policies seem to turn primarily upon differences in clarity, for *Mapp* rather than *Miranda* continues to be problematic and stubbornly and actively resisted. But an important question remains unanswered: Why do institutional conflicts persist with *Mapp* while they have subsided with *Miranda*?

Moreover, additional doubts remain about the indispensibility of clarity and effective communication for implementation. It seems unreasonable to assume that effective communication alone is capable of overcoming substantial resistance to a policy; an unpopular policy is not going to be made any more palatable by faithful transmission through the judicial hierarchy and/or through the lower regions of the criminal justice system. Besides, there are numerous points at which the communication process can break down over which the state and lower courts have little influence. Moreover, state courts rarely issue unanimous decisions so there is plenty of opportunity for dissenting opinions to be exploited by disappointed criminal justice officials. Beyond these problems though, little is known about factors shaping state court responses to Supreme Court decisions such as the avenues available to formulate and enforce state policy interpretations and the impact of state and local interests and practices on these policy decisions. Information of this kind would help put theories about the significance of institutional limitations in sharper focus.

Investigation of these questions would be particularly insightful as they bear upon what many commentators consider to be the key difference between judicial and legislative policy—*the significance of the political environment*. Baum (1981) argues that the environmental perspective associated with legislative implementation processes is somewhat misleading when applied to courts. Judicial behavior is thought to be primarily the product of personal preferences of judges whereas legislative policies reflect the application of interest group pressure and public opinion. Baum cites the *Mapp* and *Miranda* decisions as examples of judicial policy made in the seemingly unfavorable climate of public opinion. Yet if the political environment has differential consequences for the results of court and legislative policy then we should not have expected Congress to have passed a criminal records privacy policy in the absence of a substantial consensus for the development of a national CCH. Indeed, the fact that interest group politics happens to be more visible in legislative policy-formulation and rule-making processes may only exaggerate the influence that public opinion actually exerts on the implementation of criminal justice policy, while obscuring political factors *internal* to the criminal justice system likely to dictate outcomes, regardless of the policy origin.

4

California and Colorado: Contrasting Styles of Populism

California and Colorado are a study in contrasting political cultures. California had a population of almost 22.5 million and spent 2.6 billion dollars on criminal justice (state and local) in 1979 (Laudon, 1980b). The population is highly concentrated in urban centers along the coast with a huge agri-business industry in the central valleys. The large diversity in age groups, occupations and lifestyles finds expression in populist politics of ideological extremism. Political leaders take pride in their national leadership and tradition of innovation, seemingly regardless of political direction.

Colorado also has a history of political populism, but its demographic characteristics and public philosophy of local accountability make for a far more consensual political culture than California. Colorado had a population just under three million and spent 250 million dollars on criminal justice (state and local) in 1979 (Laudon, 1980b). The dominance of rural-agricultural interests over that of the Denver metro area, makes for a more predictable politics of interest group conflict and compromise.

These differences in political culture are manifested in state institutional structures and political practices. California has a forward looking state constitution which incorporates guarantees against unreasonable search comparable to the Fourth Amendment and privacy protections added by voter initiative in 1972. The state legislature has been dominated by liberal Democrats for the last twenty years through the successive leadership of Jesse Unruh and Willy Brown as speakers of the House and by Representative David Roberti, the originator of many criminal justice reforms including criminal records privacy legislation in 1972.

The office of governor of California has been an important conduit for entrance into national politics. Earl Warren, a hard-driving Alameda County (Oakland) district attorney and a three-term governor (1942–1952), emerged as a presidential contender in 1952. In exchange for his support of Eisenhower in the campaign, Warren was appointed Chief Justice of the U.S. Supreme Court in 1953. The rest is history. Reagan's rise to the Presidency from California politics epitomizes the political extremism of contending elites which typify the California political culture. Moreover, there is some philosophical continuity between the Reagan and Jerry Brown administrations. Reagan's assault on liberal programs was matched by Brown's austerity and retreat from the liberal philosophy of government intervention. By the time Brown was confronted with Proposition 13, he had already established a fiscally conservative managerialism, consistent with emergent public opinion.

Perhaps no other state elective office is as important to upward mobility in California political life as that of the office of attorney general. First, the structure and powers of the office are substantial. By law, the attorney general has independent investigatory powers and policy authority over local district attorneys, and can remove local sheriffs or chiefs on the basis of malfeasance, corruption or abuse of discretion. Importantly, he is the administrative head of the state Department of Justice, which houses state law enforcement, a statistical activity center, including the central state repository, and the civil and criminal divisions of the attorney general's office.

Beyond these formal powers, however, the role of attorney general in the implementation of criminal justice policy has been an important element in the political equation of California electoral politics. For example, in the late 1950's Pat Brown used the office as a springboard to governor by taking a no-nonsense, aggressive approach to law enforcement. Even Jerry Brown, while never attorney general, used the powers of Secretary of State in the early 1970's to aggressively enforce campaign laws in a way reminiscent of his father's career as attorney general. Evelle Younger, Republican attorney general from 1968 through 1978 also used the office not only to guide the state implementation of the early LEAA program, but to promote an unsuccessful race for governor against Jerry Brown in 1978. Younger's term as attorney general was characterized by his continuous opposition to the Warren Court civil liberties decisions and state Supreme Court liberalism. Finally, George Deukmejian, now Republican governor of the state, increased, his political capital as attorney general by publicly attacking Governor Brown's appointees to the state Supreme Court and their liberal policy making.

If California is best characterized by elite conflicts and populist extremism, then Colorado would best conform to the description of a centrist populism. The political and philosophical themes of open government, accountability and decentralization animate the political culture of Colorado. Such a government is thought to be incorruptible and able to justify its decisions to the people. The theme of accountability includes decisions by the state Supreme Court. One former Chief Justice held weekly (deep background) briefings for the press to apprise them of decisions in exchange for information from the press about forthcoming legislative and executive actions.

Governor Richard Lamm, a Democrat now in his third term, also illustrates this public philosophy with his leadership in the so-called "sagebrush rebellion." For example, Lamm's outspoken criticism of natural resource policy from the pulpit of the National Governors' Conference constitutes a rejection of federal programs and their regulatory intrusiveness. Such intervention is condemned because it is inconsistent with the need to keep the government close and accountable to the people.

The state Supreme Court has helped to maintain political traditions while dealing with the realities of the ever-growing federal presence. On the one hand, the state court system has undergone significant organizational changes involving merit selection, centralized budget and rule-making powers and administrative reforms. This has put the court well ahead of its institutional rivals in terms of organizational capacity, such as the attorney general and state law enforcement. But its increasingly liberal policies on civil liberties issues has put it on a collision course with a profoundly conservative state legislature. As a former executive director of the District Attorneys Association noted, even though the state Supreme Court has primary responsibility for procedural matters and the legislature for substantive matters, the dividing line has begun to dissolve.

The state legislature, on the other hand, has traditionally been the focal point for a decentralized interest group politics. As a consequence, criminal justice policy is originated by well organized and influential professional associations—specifically the District Attorneys and the Sheriffs and Chiefs Associations. These advocates have continually found a sympathetic ear for an aggressive criminal justice policy, given a dominant Republican majority in the state legislature.

The governor and attorney general appear to have an indirect rather than direct influence on public policy in Colorado. The governor's role is limited partly for reasons rooted in the constitutional structure. For example, Governor Lamm's most frequent complaint has been his inability to appoint more than just a handful of middle level managers to run the state bureaucracy. This prompted Lamm to observe that: "The Governor of Colorado has the responsibility but not the authority to run the state government" (Simmons, 1984: 76). A constitutional amendment put before the voters in 1976 which would have substantially enlarged his appointive powers was resoundingly rejected because it was perceived as a patronage measure.

Another reason for Governor Lamm's weakness in policy leadership is the enduring control of the legislature by an aggressive Republican majority. Governor Lamm's liberal credentials, which include his voluntary support for ACLU activities, tend to be liabilities in the legislative process. He has consequently opted to take a low profile by declining to support particular reform policies, fearing that it will guarantee their rejection in the legislature (Simmons, 1984: 78).

Thus, Lamm's influence has been most strongly felt in a party brokerage role with his appointments to the state Supreme Court. He has appointed six of seven current court justices in the last ten years, all reflecting strong liberal philosophies.

This expression of loyalty to liberal Democratic doctrine has generally disarmed interest groups such as the ACLU, who rarely state a position on civil liberties issues to the left of Lamm's liberal political philosophy.

This ground rule of mutual respect and studied caution was apparent in the state's reaction to the LEAA program. Realizing that Governor Lamm was no fan of federal conditions of aid, the ACLU and other reform minded groups struck a path toward compliance with criminal records privacy which avoided making concessions to federal policy.

Compared to the govenor's office, the office of attorney general has not been an active force in criminal justice policy. This largely uninfluential role stems from its statutory structure. Lacking the ability to investigate or prosecute local officials, the attorney general's role is limited to technical assistance to local district attorneys and to representing the state in appeals before the state Supreme Court. Ironically, an attempt by the attorney general to expand the powers of the office in 1975, by citing an ancient and forgotten statute, culminated in a losing effort in which the statutory provision was withdrawn and the limited role of the attorney general reinforced even more explicitly.

The success of this effort was due to an enormously well organized and powerful District Attorneys Association. What gives the Association clout is that they are a public entity by law with the ability to regulate their affairs and coordinate informational relations between county offices through a technologically advanced case management system called PROMIS, an innovation initiated by LEAA. This clout carries over into legislative policy. According to a former head of the District Attorneys Association, the legislature generally defers to the Association on matters of consequence to criminal justice policy. If anything, the Association has had to restrain the "lock them up" legislature from assigning too much power to prosecution in areas already well regulated by the U.S. Constitution and the U.S. Supreme Court.

In contrast to the District Attorneys Association, state law enforcement shares many of the weaknesses of the attorney general's office. State law enforcement functions have traditionally been fragmented between patrol functions, training, technical services and investigative/information systems which include the central state repository. Although many of these functions are now being consolidated, the central state repository and investigative systems are not included, forcing them to continue to occupy a position on the periphery of state executive power.

This brief comparison of state political cultures reveals that California and Colorado differ substantially in institutional relationships and policy making practices. State elites have varying degrees of institutional power, aptitude, aspirations and the resources upon which to draw to shape policy outcomes. Significant differences in political culture appear to account for important variations in the ways in which state executives influence public policy. While California politics seems to thrive on the externalization of political conflict in the electoral process, conflict over institutional policy making processes has been more subdued: interest group conflicts are internalized and contained within institutional parameters. These differences in political culture establish an important context in which to understand state responses to the U.S. Supreme Court civil liberties policies.

CIVIL LIBERTIES POLICY: THE ELECTORAL IMPLICATIONS OF STATE COURT ACTIVISM

California State Court Civil Liberties Policies: From Pragmatism to Absolutism

The California state Supreme Court anticipated the *Mapp* decision by several years in 1955. Yet, as with any innovation, substantial differences emerged between state policy and Supreme Court doctrine, especially in the area of "probable cause" and grounds for the issuance of search warrants. In fact, for most of the Warren court years, the California court insisted on distinguishing its policies from the U.S. Supreme Court regarding both search and seizure and interrogation policy. But towards the end of the 1960's, California tentatively began to examine whether state constitutional guarantees afforded greater protection of defendants' due process rights. With the decisions in *People v. Brisendine* (1975) and *People v. Pettingill* (1978) the state court moved from pragmatism to substantive liberalism.

By pragmatism I mean a style of legal and policy reasoning which bases judgements on common law and the attempt to strike a balance between constitutional principles and societal needs and values. A pragmatic policy making style will generally reflect prevailing societal norms and the balance of political forces instead of exhibiting a commitment to a coherent ideological doctrine. In contrast, a substantive style looks to the constitution or a political philosophy as a source of guidance about absolute principles by which to guide decision making. The substantive style tends to be result-oriented, that is, it attempts to prescribe specific rules or strategies by which to achieve preferred outcomes. Such a policy orientation will express a disposition toward strong liberal or conservative political philosophies.

Predictably, however, state court decisions of the 1970's in California ignited political forces determined to abrogate policies predicated on more liberal civil liberties guarantees. The ultimate success of this challenge accentuates the polarity of California politics indicative of its political culture. This challenge of state court policy making casts doubt upon the viability of this latest stage of new federalism for state court independence and legitimacy.

Policy Development

The importance of *People v. Cahan* (1955) resided not so much in its holding of automatic standing of defendants to challenge the admissibility of evidence but as an expression of the majority will to maintain its independence from some U.S. Supreme Court rulings. Although the state court acknowledged that common police practices were of questionable legality, it warned that the decision was a limited one. Justice Traynor, in citing the state constitution, established these limits by distancing the Court from potential future requirements by the U.S. Supreme Court:

> In developing a rule of evidence applicable to the state courts, this Court is not bound by the decisions that have applied to federal rule (*Weeks*, 1914) and if it appears that those decisions have developed needless refinements and distinctions, this Court need not follow them. Similarly, if the federal cases indicate needless limitations on the right conduct of reasonable searches and seizures or to secure warrants, this Court is free to reject them (*Cahan*, 1955: 915).

When *Mapp* was finally decided, the California Supreme Court reiterated its steadfastness in this promise. It asserted in *People v. Parham* (1963) for example, that erroneously admitted evidence later ruled inadmissable did not constitute a penalty for illegal police conduct but rather for the prosecutor. In essence, the California exclusionary rule was intended not so much to regulate police conduct as to supervise trial court proceedings (Manwaring, 1972).

Because of this and other rulings, a discernable shift began to occur in the state court cases in the late 1960's. With decisions in *People v. Edwards* (1969) and *People v. Krivda* (1971) the court made an effort to distinguish the legality of places searched in citing parallel provisions in state and federal constitutions. Since it was not clear whether the state court was asserting the superiority of the state constitution to support its judgment, the U.S. Supreme Court remanded the cases for clarification.

During this period, the state court still showed occasional relapses to a hands-off attitude towards police in instances in which a "good faith" search occurred such as in *People v. Chimel* (1968) and *People v. McGrew* (1969). But with *Chimel*, the U.S. Supreme Court was not countenancing independence and reversed (*Chimel v. California*, 1969). Yet after 1970, the state court followed a pattern of elaborative and independent policy making, ruling that the state constitution required warrants be issued to justify "probable cause" in *People v. Medina* (1972) while lashing out at the "plain view" doctrine of the Burger Court in *Guidi v. Superior Court* (1973) that visible objects in auto searches are legally seizable.

Finally, in *Brisendine* (1975), the California Supreme Court ended its equivocation about its policy independence by holding that the state constitution provided greater protection against unreasonable searches and seizures than the federal constitution. In its decision, specifically rejecting *U.S. vs. Robinson*, the state court held that searches incident to custodial arrest must be guided by rules involving specificity of items sought, consideration of safety of persons involved and limitation on the duration of the conduct of the search.

Since 1975, the state court has asserted its independence using state constitutional grounds to establish criteria for warrantless searches and to outline limits to the intrusiveness justified by warrants while acknowledging privacy rights of subjects of bank records and other holdings. In an address designed as much to justify as to explain the new federalism and criminal procedure in California and other states, Justice Stanley Mosk specifically cited dissention within the Burger Court as a primary cause (Mosk, 1978). In support of state use of independent grounds, he cites U.S. Supreme Court Justice Brennan's article (1977) inviting states to rely upon non-federal grounds to protect civil liberties gains in the Warren era.

Consistent with the approach taken by other liberal state courts by the U.S. Supreme Court *Miranda* decisions, California chose to emphasize the salience of the earlier *Johnson* (1938) *Escobedo* (1964) "voluntariness" test in the development of state court policy (Romans, 1974). Subsequently, however, some of the most innovative decisions have resulted from that emphasis in such areas as what constitutes a "detention," a "confession," a "rational intellect" and so forth.

The California Supreme Court anticipated a U.S. Supreme Court decision in *Edwards v. Arizona* (1981) with its ruling in *People v. Disbrow* (1976). It acknowledged that a suspect's "right to counsel" while making a confession was deemed crucial to its "voluntariness." Yet, with equal suddenness, in two companion cases in 1978 (*Pettingill* and *People v. Jimenez*), the state court finally anchored its interrogation and confession policy in the state constitution. In taking aim at the police use of improper influences and duress prior to giving *Miranda* warnings to extract statements, the state court declared that under the state constitution such tactics constituted unnecessary delay in speedy arraignment before a magistrate for specific charges. Since these decisions, the state court has added further clarification in situations surrounding pre- and post-custody policy conduct. *People v. Braeseke* (1980) is a particularly good example of the court's willingness to innovate. For it anticipates the Supreme Court ruling in *Edwards v. Arizona* (1981).

Implementation and Reaction

The difficulty involved with disentangling interpretations from perceived policy consequence cited in Chapter 1 is further compounded, as the California cases suggest, by underlying beliefs regarding the legitimacy of the originating institutions. Policy implementers had to deal not only with Warren and Burger court civil liberties policy, but had to respond also to growth in independent state court policy. It is conceivable that policy originated by multiple sources may result in "cognitive dissonance," for implementers must predicate their responses on the perceived authority of the policy source. Yet separate beliefs about legitimacy of policy originators can create difficulties in reconciling inconsistencies between beliefs and behavior.

Confronted with conflicting policy sources, each of whom is invested with beliefs supporting legitimacy, implementers are likely to experience divided loyalties. Consequently, as this case suggests, implementers may have to sacrifice some consistency by accepting state court policies at odds with the Supreme Court in order to retain identification with the state political culture. Therefore, state policy responses to federal policy may be conditioned in important respects by the attempt to reconcile conflicts over legitimacy.

The substance of the *Mapp* and *Miranda* decisions drew mixed reactions from California criminal justice officials. Extensive state court elaboration on *both* of these rulings may have accentuated their impact. When asked to evaluate the nature of the policies and their expected effects, one district attorney from the Central Coast had the following comments:

I think both civil liberties decisions are pretty specific and clear, although the appropriate time to give the *Miranda* warnings can be pretty technical as well as the determination of the waiver of rights. The rule is simple but the application is difficult. There are hundreds of different circumstances under which it can occur.
Q. What did you expect the impact of the civil liberties decisions to be? I wasn't pleased with them from my point of view at all. I felt they would have an adverse impact. I think they are unrealistic. The courts are like medieval monks in talking about technicalities that have no place in society and police work.
Q. Could you specify the adverse effects of these policies and how they have changed over time? It's difficult to say. There are a lot of problems with cases that can only be solved by confessions, usually more serious ones like murder. . . . Most people involved in murder will not talk to police. Therefore, the solution rate to murder has been dropping since the early 1960's as well as the conviction rate too—less than a 50% conviction rate.
Q. Has there also been a drop in narcotics convictions because of Mapp? No. I can't see that at all. Personally, I think *Miranda* had a bigger impact than *Mapp*. We need confessions to get convictions. When the exclusionary rule was initiated it eliminated some outrageous activities but with continual expansion it has gone too far.

A northern California Superior Court judge suggested that, while *Miranda* may have been necessary, *Mapp* ended up compounding the burdens of law enforcement. He suggested that policy makers choose between the two policies as rules of criminal procdure:

The exclusionary rule was valid until *Miranda*, although it has been difficult to enforce. The exclusionary rule will always have its critics. *Miranda* is just not controversial, except for the detention issue. We lived with *Miranda* for decades, we have become accustomed to it. It doesn't fly in the face of reality or common sense. But the complexity of the exclusionary rule around physical evidence bore no relationship to that skepticism. The rule deals with things that are inherently more reliable than confessions, which are obtained under stressful situations. If you don't like confessions or admissions then you better be more liberal about permitting the introduction of physical evidence. If you don't like one, you need more leeway in the other. I think excluding physical evidence is distasteful in terms of common sense.
You know, conversely, it was once thought that confessions were good for the soul. Much police practice today is aimed at producing a confession. Perhaps we have hand-

icapped this process of rehabilitation by not working harder to produce confessions at an earlier stage of the criminal justice process.

Unhappiness with the U.S. Supreme Court civil liberties decisions was connected with the state court interpretations of those policies. Proposition 8, a constitutional amendment, (described below), passed in 1982 as a "Victims' Bill of Rights" epitomized the struggle for control over the direction of criminal justice policy in the state. The authority of the state Supreme Court is now being directly challenged by state officials and local criminal justice decision makers.

The success of Proposition 8 was in no small way due to the on-going conflict between the attorney general and state court. While Attorney General, Governor George Deukmejian made his assault on liberal state court decisions the primary focal point of his campaign for governor in 1982. His cause was given impetus by a controversy involving state court decision making practices in 1978.

In 1977 Governor Brown appointed Rose Bird, his Secretary of the state Department of Agriculture to be Chief Justice of the California Supreme Court, to fill the last year of an unexpired term of her predecessor. In June 1979 charges were investigated that Justices Bird and Tobriner had intentionally withheld final decisions on four cases involving controversial criminal justice policies until after a special election in 1978, so that it would not jeopardize Bird's chance of remaining on the court. Evidently, Justice William C. Clark (later Reagan's Secretary of the Interior) was the only Justice to publicly testify that the opinions were deliberately withheld. Although no formal charges were ever filed, and Bird narrowly survived the election, the inquiry was a severe blow to the prestige and authority of the state Supreme Court. The inquiry conducted by a special commission on judicial performance was enlarged to include almost every facet of court administration and collegial relationships. It continues to provide gossipy grist for books either condemning (Stolz, 1981) or supporting (Medsger, 1983) Bird's actions and the role of the Court.

Deukmejian, riding the wave of this unfavorable publicity, escalated his attack on the state court. In a 1979 article in the *Hastings Constitutional Law Qaurterly*, Deukmejian complained of the historic reallocation of power from the state legislature to state courts resulting from the use of independent state grounds to promote a result-oriented jurisprudence. He claimed that citation of the state constitution had enabled the California state Supreme Court to evade U.S. Supreme Court rulings and accused the state court of violating several principles of federalism. Consequently, he argued for a uniform federal policy.

Next, Deukmejian joined the successful initiative movement for Proposition 8 (coordinated by Paul Gann of Proposition 13 fame). Deukmejian offered the voters his analysis of why this initiative was needed:

> Crime has increased to an absolutely intolerable level. . . . Yet, higher courts of this state have created additional rights of the criminally accused and placed more restrictions on law enforcement officers. The proposition will overcome some of the adverse decisions of our higher courts (California Voters' Guide, 1982: 34).

The "truth in evidence" section of Proposition 8 limits the rules regarding admissibility of evidence to minimum federal standards, therefore abrogating state court policy based on the state constitution. It has presented new opportunities and difficulties for judicial and other criminal justice officials in the state. Criminal justice officials are now faced squarely by a problematic choice: either cite Proposition 8 and scramble to find U.S. Supreme Court decisions that support your case, or continue to cite more familiar but tenuous, state court precedents. It is not an easy choice, as some respondents indicated, especially if the authority of the policy originator is under challenge.

When asked about the focal point of his interpretation of civil liberties policy, a central California district attorney responded:

> We look at Supreme Court decisions first. There is a lot of interpretation required to implement those decisions. That process starts with the attorney general's office providing a breakdown of how to interpret them. There is also extensive sharing of information between local district attorneys and the use of special instructional tapes from Alameda County.

But when asked about post-Proposition 8 policy, and whether there was any conflict in their minds between state court and U.S. Supreme Court policy, there was some equivocation:

> Up until Proposition 8 we followed the state court. If the state court used independent state grounds, it has been our responsibility to follow it. But now, with Proposition 8 things are somewhat up in the air. We are . . . not changing what we have done in the past. Although we do cite the state courts sometimes, we argue that federal rules should be followed. The judges appear to be buying it. But we'd rather be safe than sorry. If Proposition 8 goes so do our cases. . . . It hasn't been decided yet (by the Supreme Court). So we are taking a wait and see attitude. . . . We're still advising police to follow California state court rules until otherwise advised.

A Supreme Court judge also showed some ambivalence about state court policy following Proposition 8 revealing as well beliefs about state court legitimacy:

> If the state Supreme Court requires something that the U.S. Supreme Court doesn't, then I'm bound by the decisions of the United States Supreme Court. . . . After Proposition 8, if state courts could support their interpretation of the exclusionary rule by showing U.S. Supreme Court decisions would support it, then they are doing their functions. They are now unable to use pre-Proposition 8 decisions. But there is a practical problem. I don't have any copies of the United States Supreme Court decisions in my office. The logistics of the state law business were built up around state court decisions. Some of the Burger Court decisions present really radical changes in standing in California. . . . Proposition 8 freed police from warrant requirements and technical constraints which is increasingly in the direction of common sense. Thus "probable cause" has become a central focal point of our decisions.

The politics surrounding Proposition 8 continue to be controversial and fluid. In 1982, for example, the state Supreme Court had an opportunity to rule on the constitutionality of Proposition 8. In *Brosnahan v. Brown* (1982), the petitioners contended, among other things, that the proposition violated the "single subject" rule which requires that the contents of a proposition shall pertain to a single and unified subject matter to facilitate voter understanding and prevent unintended statutory or constitutional changes.

The majority, sidestepping the dilemma of legitimacy that the proposition posed in challenging state court authority, upheld the constitutionality of Proposition 8 in concluding that it embraced a single-subject matter pertaining to public dissatisfaction with previous judicial decisions in the area of criminal law. Ironically, the judges cited Deukmejian's ballot argument as further support for their conclusion. In addition, the majority acknowledged the undesirable consequences of intervention in the expression of popular sovereignty by the people in asserting that:

> While we might disagree with both the accuracy of this premise (Deukmejian's ballot assertion) and overall wisdom of the initiative measure, nonetheless, it is not our function to pass judgment on the propriety or soundness of Proposition 8. In our democratic society in the absence of some compelling, overriding or constitutional imperative, we should not prohibit the sovereign people from expressing or implementing their own will on matters of such direct and immediate importance as their own perceived safety (*Brosnahan*, 1982: 36).

Significantly, Chief Justice Bird wrote a spirited dissent (joined by Justice Mosk) attacking Proposition 8 for its incoherence and inability to present a unified theme. She cited numerous unanticipated and unintended consequences of the constitutional amendment, in capitalizing on the difficulties Proposition 8 posed for a constitutional separation of powers:

> Finally, by depriving the people of this state of their paramount role in approving or rejecting changes in their constitution and by impermissably transferring power from the people to the legislature, the draftsmen of Proposition 8 have attempted to alter the fundamental distribution of power between the people and their elected representatives. They have violated the prohibition against constitutional revision by initiative (*Brosnahan*, 1982: 68).

Colorado's Populist Consensualism: The Silent Transition from Pragmatism to Proceduralism

Although the Colorado Supreme Court did not anticipate the U.S. Supreme Court civil liberties decisions with its own policies, it has gradually advanced innovative policies sharply at odds with the Burger Court. In the Warren years, the Colorado court struck a very pragmatic course in its interpretation of the Warren Court civil liberties policies, showing caution in the attempt to balance defendants' rights against a need for effective law enforcement. More often than not, however, the state court deferred to the overriding interest of law enforcement.

During the 1960's and early 1970's the Colorado state court system underwent a substantial reform in judicial selection and in procedures, administration, organization and funding. Although in the midst of achieving a unified court system which conferring broad new powers on it, the state court seemed undecided about how to develop a uniform state civil liberties policy.

However, given a large turnover of justices on the court and replacement by appointees of Governor Lamm in the mid-1970's, the state court found the constitution an important tool in developing a technical, procedural doctrine which enlarged the protections of defendants' rights. This new procedural approach has not gone unchallenged. The U.S. Supreme Court has challenged its policy initiatives by attempting to deter this innovativeness by exercising its power to reverse its judgments. Criminal justice critics have also construed Burger's new federalism as an invitation to challenge state court policy through the legislative process. Thus the Colorado state court has discovered that its assumption of policy leadership in criminal justice procedure is fraught with risks. The state court has discovered that policy independence from the U.S. Supreme Court is not sufficient to immunize it from challenges to its legitimacy by criminal justice officials and a determined legislature.

Policy Development

The Colorado state court decisions under the Warren Court and early Burger Court rulings adopted a view that the state constitution was not a tool of reform but one that enabled the court to justify a *selection* of which U.S. Supreme Court decisions it would follow. This has produced some noticeable inconsistency in the use of the state constitution to justify policies seemingly at odds in terms of the protection of defendants' rights.

But this surface inconsistency, perhaps a boon to the court's critics, can be explained by an abrupt change in its philosophical pragmatism towards technical proceduralism. By proceduralism I mean a policy making style which sees the role of legal and policy processes in terms of making appropriate rules available to regulate disputes among competing interests. Proceduralism is more concerned with controlling discretion and insuring the fairness of the process than the exact nature of the outcomes. There is consequently a tendency toward specificity and rigor of technical guidelines, sometimes perceived as constraints to achievement of either liberal or conservative substantive agendas, depending upon whom the burdens fall.

The *Stewart v. People* (1967) decision exemplifies the state court's initial philosophy of pragmatism. Following their interpretation of the Fourth Amendment, the Colorado Supreme Court argued that the state constitution did not require a more restrictive standard with respect to automobile searches. That is, everything in an automobile is fair game for a warrantless search as long as it was incident to a legal arrest. When questioned about the rationale for the decision, a former Justice provided the following perspective:

> The citation of independent state grounds is just fluff because we were deciding (*Stewart*) on the basis of particular U.S. Supreme Court decisions. What we said in *Stewart* was that if we applied one U.S. Supreme Court decision in *Cooper*, we would have to say that the search was illegal. But since *Cooper* had not overruled *Pratt*, we were going to follow *Pratt*. The case would have turned out the same way whether we cited the state constitution or not. It's just fluff, language, rhetoric.
> *Q. Well, then, are independent state grounds irrelevant*? The state constitution is just an ancillary device—it was then and it is now. Our state was making distinctions between two constitutional provisions. They are using the state constitution. It gets a little complicated . . . because the court wants to say that we're not going to follow the U.S. Supreme Court decisions in this area, but instead interpreting our own constitution in order to bolster our use of cases where the U.S. Supreme Court has pulled back.
>
> Justice Brennan was telling us (in his 1977 article) that the U.S. Supreme Court was no longer protecting the rights of people, so it was up to us to do it, under our state constitution. So now you're getting some decisions that, no matter what the Feds say, our constitution interprets it differently.

According to this account the state constitution can become a flexible tool justifying a pragmatic approach to state policy making. The doctrine is workable as long as there is some underlying consistency in how the state constitution is applied. The former Justice also provides some insights as to the difficulties attendant to a sudden change of judicial philosophy, precipitated no doubt by Governor Lamm's appointments to the state court:

> What is involved in this change are particular philosophies of judges. Either you are going to decide a case in terms of strict adherence to precedents, or the basis of societal needs, or according to what you want it to be as a judge. You have a lot of judges today, especially the younger ones, who haven't had that kind of strict discipline of following precedent. Rather, they have the power now and declare it the way they'd like it to be. If there is a group that doesn't agree with the majority of the U.S. Supreme Court they'll use the state constitution to gain their independence. There is now really a feeling of independence. But the law should move more slowly, inexorably coinciding with common law and with what people need, want and demand. If it's done according to the desires of the judge that makes him a legislator.

Indeed, by the mid-1970's, the state court membership began to reflect significant changes in philosophy, conspicuously focused upon the relationship between the "warrant requirement" and "probable cause." In *People v. Thompson* (1974) and *People v. Haggart* (1975) the state court reversed an earlier decision in *People v. Lujan* (1970) by unequivocally declaring that the state and federal constitutions made warrantless searches presumptively illegal.

Unlike the federal rule, which requires a "reasonableness" test for issuance of warrants, Colorado requires an affidavit in writing regardless of the evidence or circumstances in which it is encountered. Thus, ''probable cause'' becomes a critical issue with respect to the admissibility of evidence. Moreover, not content to permit lingering ambiguity about circumstances involving warrantless searches, in *People v. Burns* (1980) the state court declared that the state constitution also applied standards to those situations as well. The state court continued to extend this doctrine in *McCall v. People* (1981) by saying that no distinctions could be drawn between entry for search and entry for arrest; thus a warrant would be required in searches incident to arrest.

The Colorado court expressed its irritation with the Burger Court in *People v. Counterman* (1976), labelling as ''academic'' the attempt to develop a continuum of conditions under which an ''expectation of privacy'' was ''reasonable.'' The state court reinforced its opposition to this policy in *People v. Casias* (1977) by arguing that steel containers cannot be searched regardless of where they are found. Significantly, this decision preceded a contrasting one spelled out by the U.S. Supreme Court in *Belton* (1981), and, along with the others put the Colorado state court on a direct collision course with U.S. Supreme Court policy.

Unlike the search and seizure area, Colorado, as most other states, has taken a more restrictive path regarding interrogation and confession policy. The state court initially openly rejected the *Miranda* requirements in favor of a ''voluntariness'' test. However, later on it did reject the Supreme Court's ruling in *Michigan v. Mosley* (1975). More recently in *People v. Quintana* (1979) they rejected the use of pre-warning, in-custody statements to impeach a defendant's testimony at trial. But they also followed the Supreme Court's lead in *Edwards v. Arizona* (1981) which strengthened the effect of the *Miranda* warnings by holding that a request for counsel requires a termination of an interrogation.

The differing approaches on civil liberties taken by the Colorado state court have contributed toward a differential response by criminal justice officials. The following dialogue with a federal district attorney, formerly head of the Colorado District Attorneys Association, examines the reasons for these differences:

Q. How do the Mapp *and* Miranda *decisions compare with respect to clarity and specificity?* The exclusionary rule is more problematic. Even judges have shown their inability to consistently apply it when confronted with actual situations. Its gotten to the point of being so sophisticated that even people making the law can't apply it. The good faith exception is necessary to cover police violations come to light. It would affect everyone's rights because it is an attempt to get at the truth.

Q. What about the state court's approach to Miranda *and the exclusionary rule—how do they affect you?* Whereas *Miranda* ran its course years ago nationally, we still really don't know what the parameters of *Mapp* are. We are many years away from having enough circumstances to know where we are in search and seizure. What makes it even worse is that although the U.S. Supreme Court has taken pleasure in limiting the civil liberties decisions, our own state court has taken the opposite view.

Q. Is it because the state court is more liberal now or just a victim of unclear Supreme Court rulings? It's both. On the one hand you have a membership of a court which is

> extremely liberal. On the other, that philosophy necessitates that the court solve all problems. This is what happens when the approach becomes more mechanical, technical and procedural. The whole trend of the court of Colorado is more punitive. Most recently the state court has argued that the prosecutor may be held liable for aiding police in securing illegal warrants.

Two of the state court's more recent decisions constitute a culmination of their application of a new doctrine of hard minded proceduralism to search and confession areas. But now they have had to contend with an increasingly hostile U.S. Supreme Court, and increasingly unhappy state and local criminal justice officials.

The *People v. Bannister* (1980) decision which attempted to expand the mandatory warrant rule to include evidence found in "plain view" was a culmination of this evolving conflict. The state court cited *Coolidge* (1971) in arguing that evidence in plain view could not be seized until after a lawful search was in progress. The U.S. Supreme Court, however, took this as an opportunity to reverse the Colorado state court in citing *Carroll* (1925) and *Chambers* (1975) which declared that immediate on-the-scene searches of automobiles are permissible under the "probable cause" doctrine (see *Colorado v. Bannister* (1980)).

Similar differences in the application of principles to specific circumstances occurred with respect to confessions. In *Quintana* (1979) the Colorado court used *Doyle v. Ohio* (1976) to prohibit the use of post-arrest silence to impeach the testimony of the defendant, finding *Fletcher v. Weir* (1982) inapplicable because the *Miranda* warnings had already been given prior to the resumption of the interrogation. Although now on appeal to the U.S. Supreme Court, if *Bannister* is any indication, the Supreme Court is likely to reverse.

Implementation and Reaction

Given a profoundly conservative legislature and a strong District Attorneys Association unified in their opposition to liberal state Supreme Court rulings, it was inevitable that some political action would be taken to relax the technical straight-jacket of the mandatory warrant requirement. Even when warrants were obtained, it was argued that evidence is frequently thrown out because of legal problems in the issuance of the warrant. Therefore, legislation was introduced and passed in 1981 to provide for a "good faith" exception.

A former head of the District Attorneys Association, active in passage of the legislation stressed that this new policy had its origins in the Burger Court doctrine of federalism. When asked about state responses to the Burger Court limitation of civil liberties policy he acknowledged:

> I'm sure Burger was surprised that some states would not accept his invitation for further narrowing of civil liberties policy. But remember, the Burger Court did not just invite state courts but also the states and their legislatures to do so too. Colorado is a good example of a dichotomy in action with the state court going further and further down the path of seizing more freedom and power and trying to out-liberal the liberals. But the legislature has concluded that something constructive can be done. So they passed the

"good faith" exception. So we've really responded to the Burger Court invitation in opposite ways.

An important catch in the legislation, however, prompted one observer to conclude that the legislation was of dubious constitutionality (Stross, 1982). The language used to define a "good faith mistake" means that, in spite of the absence of "probable cause," evidence will be admissible if an officer made a reasonable error of judgment about the existence of facts, which if true, would constitute "probable cause." The effect of this definition is to justify an arrest of an individual through the introduction of evidence obtained *prior* to having legal and sufficient grounds to do so. It also threatens to override a series of decisions undertaken by the Colorado state court regarding the mandatory warrant requirement, thus setting the stage for a conflict over the separation of powers.

CRIMINAL RECORDS POLICY: THE ATTORNEY GENERAL AND STATE COURT IN LEADERSHIP ROLES

California: Anticipating Federal Intervention with a Managerial Response

Policy Development

In many respects, national initiatives for the development of a computerized criminal history system and policy regulation of the use of criminal records originated in California. SEARCH Group Incorporated, based in Sacramento, was long active as a consultant to California officials and LEAA on privacy matters and originated a committee representative of the fifty states which has been actively involved in lobbying for a national policy with decentralized state control (Zenk, 1979). In addition, California was one of the earliest participants in a demonstration test of the feasibility of the CCH. In addition, Congressman Don Edwards (D) and Senator John Tunney (D) began extensive hearings in the early 1970's to investigate criminal records abuses and determine the best path towards the development of a national policy.

But the California political leadership of the early 1970's was not favorably disposed to solutions advanced by liberals. The proposed national legislation was particularly distasteful because of its criticism of an attempt to control FBI investigative practices. As one California Department of Justice official acknowledged, it is just not that easy to dissuade police from their traditional practices in the use of criminal records. He observed that the police understand secrecy but not privacy. Moreover, Governor Reagan had already indicated his lack of active support for Governor Sargent's petition in 1973 requesting states not to participate in the FBI's NCIC/CCH program, discussed in Chapter 5. In addition, Evell Younger then Republican attorney general, and former employee of the FBI, was suspicious of both national and state legislative proposals.

Potential state legislative action was particularly imminent, however, and threatening. Representative Roberti, a long time Democrat civil liberties activist, had introduced a bill with far reaching controls (incidentally in line with policies recommended by SEARCH). Also, leading newspapers such as the *Los Angeles Times* and *Sacramento Bee* continually publicized records abuses and various lawsuits brought against the attorney general.

One of the problems that prompted legislation was the collection, use and dissemination of intelligence and investigative files for subjects with no apparent criminal records. The practice began in earnest with the creation of a special committee on un-American activities in the late 1950's in California, and apparently failed to cease once the McCarthy era had passed. Attorney General Younger was concerned that these kinds of abuses had to stop. This was so not only because it would diffuse precipitous actions by the legislature, but undermine good record management practices and obstruct the development of uniform records standards necessary for the development of a state computerized system. Therefore, the legislative proposals which appeared in the early 1970's in the California legislature provided a perfect opportunity for the attorney general to seize the initiative from them.

Appointed to chair Reagan's Governor's Committee to oversee the early LEAA program in 1968, Attorney General Younger was in a particularly strong position to influence state legislation. When the state legislature acted on the attorney general's proposal in 1972, LEAA had not yet added the privacy amendment to the Crime Control Act, so it had little influence in the legislative session. But LEAA did influence Younger's approach to centralizing the records in the state repository and the development of uniform records management practices. Younger was very supportive of these measures, thus enabling the development of a statewide statistical activity center, the first in the nation.

Enabling Legislation

The eventual statute reflected this management emphasis. The attorney general was given administrative control and responsibility for issuing regulations and conducting audits. The legislation specified that criminal history information include only summary information of the subject's contacts in the criminal justice system. It required that all criminal justice agencies, including courts, submit records of arrest and dispositions to the central state repository. In addition, criminal justice agencies were required to submit data to the statistical activities center that would permit tracking of an offender's criminal history from arrest to eventual release.

One element of the legislation particularly important to Attorney General Younger was the record purging policy. A scale of seriousness of crimes and prescribed length of retention of respective records was developed along with other criteria to remove a great number of unnecessary records. One state Department of Justice official estimated that over three million records were purged from the state files in a four year period.

Liberal interests registered a strong victory in dissemination policy. The policy anticipated subsequent LEAA policy recommendations by enabling the release of criminal records for non-criminal justice purposes only if provided for on the basis of a specific statutory exclusion. It was not until after the LEAA regulations were published that additional record subject rights were added to the law.

Implementation and Reaction

The timing of the LEAA regulations for California was not very good. Jerry Brown had been elected Governor the year before and was no fan of the LEAA program. By 1975, he was in the midst of implementing his program of governmental austerity. The LEAA funded state planning office offered a convenient target to exemplify his electoral promises of a reduced federal presence.

Other commentaries (Navasky, 1976) have suggested that Brown eliminated the LEAA program early in its administration, as witnessed by his return of millions of dollars of federal crime funds. However, according to a former director of the Office of Criminal Justice Planning (OCJP) in the mid 1970's, Brown actually institutionalized the concept in the state, so that the state could administer its own program:

> I recommended to Brown that the state assume policy and budgetary responsibility in a number of federal areas including the privacy one. Therefore we could cite our own state laws as conferring prior jurisdiction in response to LEAA. LEAA officials were resistant to this idea but they finally agreed.

Also, a local district attorney concurred with this view:

> Most of the LEAA programs have been institutionalized in the state with general fund support. When Brown came into office he had a very critical view of LEAA. He accused them of being an overstaffed pretzel factory. This was a good political opportunity, it made a good political target. But after two years in office, Brown lost interest in the criminal justice area.

The LEAA mandate for privacy protection did present some special difficulties for the Brown strategy. While the state already had a law administered by the attorney general, state policy was deficient with respect to federal guidelines. Moreover, only the governor had the authority (by federal law) to establish policy or recommend legislative action. Brown responded by establishing a special study committee of criminal justice and civil liberties groups including the attorney general, to determine whether revisions in state law were necessary and to provide an estimate of the fiscal cost of compliance.

The director of OCJP under Brown thought the most politically astute approach would be to defer to the attorney general:

> Since the state law was administered by the attorney general, who had been under Republican control, Brown thought that the LEAA regs would be more acceptable to the

law enforcement community if they came from the attorney general. It's the politics of the situation. It basically took out the attorney general as a potential source of criticism of the LEAA requirements.

The committee made two somewhat conflicting recommendations. One was to incorporate federal requirements for record subject access provisions. The other was that satisfying other federal requirements aimed at improving the accuracy and completeness of criminal records was too expensive. Brown concurred with both sets of recommendations and in the process both pleased and irritated LEAA officials.

The California criminal records privacy law got its first significant review and constitutional test by the state Supreme Court four years after enactment. Indeed it is strange that the state Supreme Court, which had been so uncompromising in the use of the state constitution in the development of civil liberties policy, would be reluctant to do so in the area of criminal records privacy. Yet, the state court ruled in *Loder v. San Diego* (1976) the retention and dissemination of arrest records did not violate the record subject's right to privacy, and that the state criminal record statute provided adequate safeguards against improper dissemination to the public. This case and the assumptions underpinning its analysis reveal an emphasis on the greater need for law enforcement records in the criminal justice process compared to the potential for abuse. The case is an important one to examine in more detail because it may have established the limits of judicial involvement in this policy area possibly for years to come.

The state court ruled in *Loder* that arrest records need not be erased just because they failed to result in the filing of formal charges or a final disposition either favorable or unfavorable to the defendant. Three reasons were given.

First, the state court contended that the privacy amendment to the state constitution was not absolute but must be weighed against other important governmental and public interests. The compelling governmental interest justifying retention of arrest records, the court added, was "the promotion of efficient law enforcement and criminal justice; more specifically, the statute's purpose is to protect the public from recidivist offenders" (*Loder*, 1976: 628). Yet, nowhere does the state court find a common law basis for legal precedents to justify why recidivism should outweigh privacy interests.

Second, the court went on to elaborate how arrest records are important in each stage of the decision making process in criminal justice. Such uses included investigation, determination of "probable cause" for arrest, bail, sentencing, probation and parole. Yet not once did the state court acknowledge the problematic and adverse consequences of the internal use of arrest records which are not complete. Several state and federal court cases including *Menard* and *Tarlton* have documented these problems.

Finally, the California Supreme Court elaborated extensively on the additional criminal record privacy protections made available by recent legislation. In it, the court specifically cited the limitations which had been placed on dissemination of arrest records to the public and non-criminal justice agencies. At the time of the case, these restrictions were substantial, although subsequent state legislation has considerably relaxed these limitations. Yet, in *McCall v. Oroville Mercury Co.* (1983), the state court ruled that a right to confidentiality of criminal records does not extend to public figures, even though a "rap sheet" was purchased by the press in violation of state statute. Although acknowledging that illegally obtaining criminal records is a misdemeanor, the court held that the press was intended to be exempted from such guidelines.

Moreover, additional non-legislative intergovernmental changes in state participation in the NCIC/CCH cast doubt on the viability of existing state protections in this area and the willingness of the courts to intervene. As Chapter 2 has indicated, the Congress has been unable to keep up with the frequent changes in the configuration of the NCIC/CCH system. One consequence of the FBI development of the national index is potential dissemination of criminal records inconsistent with state law. This is especially likely to occur in instances of security clearances for federal employment, because federal agencies are often ineligible under state statutes to gain access to criminal history record information. The California Department of Justice had already begun to relax previous legislative restrictions on dissemination before participation in the national index began. Yet this program provided an added impetus for expansion of agencies eligible to receive California arrest and conviction information. The Department of Justice has proceeded to effectuate these changes through regulatory revision rather than statutory amendment by holding that agencies may be provided access to such information on the showing of "compelling need." A "compelling need" is defined in the Department of Justice memorandum in the following way:

> A compelling need is established when the agency or individual needs the information in the course of their duties and there is no other practical way they can obtain it. Examples of compelling need include the subject is in custody, is a party to a criminal or security investigation, is seeking employment, is seeking a license or certificate (California Department of Justice, 1983: 1).

An official in the Department of Justice characterized an important rationale for this change in these terms:

> Now, as you may know, the national index concept must allow us to control the dissemination of our own records and I think they observe this need. This is what brought California and New York back into the NCIC. What we did was to simplify our regulations so they are consistent with the federal regulations regarding non-criminal justice access. We now just make federal agencies go through us.

Interestingly, the California list of authorized agenices includes almost every federal agency. Thus, the California case suggests that significant technologically induced changes in intergovernmental relations involved in the development of the NCIC/CCH can occur with little or no state court, state executive or legislative oversight. As long as the FBI maintains the appearances of deference to state policy, the state executives cannot be expected to resist those changes, especially where the principal effect of the change involves the use of records for the *internal* administration of criminal justice and governmental decisions.

Colorado: Showing LEAA a Different Approach

In what were otherwise a set of farsighted, comprehensive regulations and recommendations, LEAA failed to anticipate two important constraints to successful achievement of a uniform national criminal history policy. One oversight by LEAA was its failure to see the pervasiveness of prior state policy commitments to public disclosure. The other was its inability to influence the relative weight that states would give to multiple statutory and regulatory goals. Both factors played an important role in explaining Colorado's policy response to the federal regulations.

The unique elements of Colorado's political culture and elite-interest group relationships established a framework within which these factors became an important catalyst to state response. The Colorado experience also demonstrates that the institutional limits to change can be converted to supports if state sovereigns must absorb policy impacts in order to limit the erosion of their power.

Policy Development

Perhaps no other factor is as important to understanding Colorado's approach to implementing federal criminal records policy than the political culture of accountability. One Denver district attorney characterized its importance this way:

> Colorado has always been a populist oriented state. The privacy philosophy was really overridden by the ideal of public accountability. Accordingly, public officials must always justify why public records should not be accessible to the public. This was really more important than individual liberty. Further, we had already had the public records law ten years before criminal records privacy came along. Thus, the provisions and sanctions in the legislation were very much dictated by the principles of openness, more so than the goals of accuracy and completeness.

At the time of the Crime Control Amendment in 1973, the biggest problem in Colorado was not uncontrolled dissemination but the absence of effective exchange of criminal records between criminal justice agencies. Colorado state officials faced a feudalistic criminal justice system incapable of accurately and uniformly documenting the nature of its contracts and dispositions of cases processed through the system. Unlike most other states, Colorado had not developed a central state repository nor promulgated policies for the collection and submission of criminal record information. Therefore, a top state priority involved the development of a uniform record management policy necessary for the exchange of criminal records. As one participant (a district attorney) in the state policy development indicated, *accountability* not *privacy* was sought:

> Our notion was that in order for judges or police to justify their decisions, they had to document their contacts with the subject. One benefit of this exercise was to identify those points in the criminal justice process which should be documented for the purposes of assembling a criminal record. We took a different approach than requested by LEAA. We contended officials must be held accountable for each decision in which they were involved and that it would be made available for public scrutiny.

In fact, there is evidence to suggest an overriding desire by state and local criminal justice agencies to increase the accessibility of criminal records, which helped minimize elite conflict over state implementation of federal guidelines. One official responsible for administration of the state criminal records policy indicated that police saw the Title 28 regulations as the "logical progression or consequence of the need to develop automated criminal records systems."

Governor Lamm, evidently eager to dispose of his responsibility under the Title 28 regulations in a perfunctory manner, appointed a committee headed by the SPA director to establish a state policy response. Although broadly representative of various interests (i.e., ACLU, the press, employers, criminal justice officials and private security forces), the Governor's Committee involved many individuals with interests inconsistent with the objectives of federal policy. A representative of the ACLU complained that:

> Most of the people of the committee were trying to do the least they could to satisfy or get by the federal regulations. What they really wanted was to keep the records as open as possible. But given this seeming consensus of the committee on that point, we reached the best possible compromise. Although we really didn't deal with the LEAA regulations, I was thankful that there was a mandate as an impetus to state policy development.

Perhaps the one member of the committee most influential in dictating its agenda and doctrinal approach was Samuel Archibald. He had been one of the authors of the federal Freedom of Information Act. A journalism professor and representative of the state Newspaper Association, Archibald was extremely effective in advancing the press' right to access to criminal records. A veritable arsenal of arguments were used including the First Amendment, prior restraint and censorship as policy grounds to prevent limitations on dissemination.

This forceful combination of interests seeking unlimited access made strange political bedfellows of the ACLU and police. The concern of the ACLU that some kinds of criminal record material be legitimately restricted (i.e., arrests resulting in acquittals) combined with police concerns that access be limited to intelligence and investigative information made some restrictions possible. Nonetheless, the ACLU's dissatisfaction with its inability to limit access and dissemination of criminal records surfaced in the legislative process, where suppressed conflicts between the police, the ACLU and the press began to emerge.

Governor Lamm was non-committal if not indifferent about the committee's work. Their recommendations pertained only to the limited area of agreement and generally provided little guidance as to the form of legislation. Both the committee and Governor were also silent as to a state agency responsible for continuing administration and regulatory enforcement. Perhaps this was predicated on the belief that the law would be self-executing just as public disclosure had been.

The legislation that resulted could hardly be considered to satisfy even minimum federal guidelines. There was no mention of nor provisions for the improvement in the accuracy and completeness of criminal history records. In fact, the burden for record quality generally fell on the record subject himself. No state agency was designated to exercise continuing responsibility for record management and oversight, although the courts have had to assume that responsibility with respect to sealing procedures. While the legislation did require automatic reporting of police arrest records to the central state repository, it failed to mandate court disposition reporting. And, finally, the state policy for limitations on dissemination generally fell below LEAA's minimum requirements by making arrest and conviction records publicly available with certain exceptions. Most of these deficiencies, of course, can be attributed to the strength of the press as an interest group in the legislative process.

In spite of these deficiencies the legislation involved one of the most far reaching provisions for the sealing of records of any state. Ironically, the sealing provisions (and recent legislative amendments developed to formalize an administrative and appellate process for that purpose) have given the courts more direct administrative and oversight responsibilities for criminal records privacy, than other states.

There are several reasons for this unlikely situation. First, the ACLU guessed correctly that a more viable strategy for protection of record subjects' rights (given the emphasis upon openness and accountability) would be one that established a statutory limitation on the dissemination of criminal records. The upshot of these provisions was that the use of an arrest record which failed to show a disposition after two years could be eliminated from criminal justice use upon the request of the record subject.

Second, a separation of powers issue was at stake in the legislative passage of the sealing measure. The courts strenuously argued that sealing was solely their prerogative. However, the legislature was persuaded by the ACLU that the enforcement of this right required a special, administrative procedure, distinct from the cumbersome ways that complaints are normally handled through the courts. The state courts finally acquiesced because, as one participant observed, it was the only way the state court could legitimize their inherent power to seal records.

Beyond the separation of powers issues, the state court had already established an underlying policy basis for the sealing provisions. In *Davidson v. Dill* (1972) the state court ruled that the state and federal constitutions mandated the purging of any arrest record that resulted in acquittal, unless the state could show a compelling interest in its retention. The rationale advanced in its ruling was consistent with the philosophical pragmatism it had shown in civil liberties policy:

> A court should expunge an arrest record or order its return, when the harm to the individual's right of privacy or dangers of unwarranted adverse consequences outweigh the public interest in retaining the record or police files (1972: 161).

Language identical to that found in *Davidson* reappears as the test that courts must apply in determining whether a criminal record will be sealed.

A final reason for a formalized procedure (under 1982 legislative revisions) stemmed from the need of the prosecutors to justify their decisions and make them stick. The procedures consist of the submission of a written petition to the court identifying record information to be sealed; a review and rebuttal by the originating district attorney; and judicial decision and enforcement in which all record holders are to be notified to seal their records within a 120 day period.

Shortly after passage of the state law in 1977, the executive of the District Attorneys Association and state court administrator conducted a ''roadshow'' to train criminal justice officials. They found that the presumption of disclosure underlying the law was not sufficient in those instances where the district attorney and court had to justify denial of requests for limitations to access or for permanent sealing of records. They found that a cogent reason was frequently not provided to deny a request, therefore failing to satisfy the balance test established by the legislation. A district attorney involved in the training process observed that there had been mixed results from state and federal court review resulting from appeals to the sealing determinations:

> There had been a number of decisions specifically acknowledging the types of adverse consequences which subjects contend are involved in the dissemination of arrest and conviction records. But I think the decisions by and large uphold the trial court decisions on sealing.

The Colorado response to federal policy is both *ironic* and *significant* in that a law consciously designed to be self executing has failed to eliminate the need for administrative oversight. The irony is that the courts have been drawn ever deeper into a quasi-administrative role that the California courts have been able to avoid. What is significant is that sealing may provide a viable alternative to address the consequences of dissemination of inaccurate and incomplete records. Criminal justice officials may find it more difficult than expected to justify how dissemination of inaccurate and incomplete records *within* the criminal justice process outweighs the harm to individual privacy.

5

Washington and Massachusetts: The Politics of Ambivalence and Activism

Unlike the contrasting states of California and Colorado, the political cultures of Washington and Massachusetts exhibit many similarities which outweigh minor differences in demographic profile and criminal justice policy making.

Washington experienced a multi-year period of rapid growth beginning in 1974, after the end of a Boeing-related recession, to reach a population of four million in 1979 (Laudon, 1980b). This new growth brought in not only engineers but a diversity of young professionals in business and government. Recent diversification of Boeing and Weyerhaeuser into eastern Washington corporation farming and increased growth and conflict over the nuclear power industry have helped reduce political and philosophical differences between rural and urban political interests. A resulting receptivity to progressive reforms has been manifested in state executive reorganization in which fragmented agencies have been consolidated, new centralized policy planning and budgeting approaches adopted and proliferation of boards and commissions reversed. This progressivism has also been reflected in the legislature which now conducts annual sessions and has greatly expanded its professional staff.

Massachusetts, with a population exceeding Washington's by only two million people, has not experienced dramatic population growth. However, its economic profile has undergone a significant if not wrenching change from an industrial one to a research-oriented, technologically based economy. Nowhere is this change more evident than in the Boston area where an academic research and technology development complex borders the Route 128 beltway.

Unlike Washington, Massachusetts has had a tradition of both liberalism and professionalism. The Kennedy School of Government at Harvard has had a direct influence on the policy proclivities of national as well as Massachusetts state executives. Beyond this, given historical dominance of the Democratic party and geographic close proximity of state elites, political and policy making relationships are underpinned by a stabilizing political consensus. One example of this consensus is Governor Dukakis's utilization of an Anti-Crime Council (consisting of over fifty members) to develop criminal justice policy for the state. One member of the Council described it as a clever way to reach agreement on criminal justice policy priorities, by requiring each policy proponent to justify his proposals (including costs) to the others. Once a proposal gets past the Council it is likely to be enacted by the legislature.

The politics of reform and progressivism has fairly deep roots in Washington. But that politics found its most recent and perhaps most enduring expression in the state leadership which emerged in the early 1960s. Dan Evans (Governor from 1965 to 1977), Slade Gorton (Attorney General from 1970 to 1980, when he defeated Warren Magnuson for Senate), Bruce Chapman (Secretary of State for two terms during the 1970's) and several others formed the core of a liberal, Republican legislative caucus, who eventually assumed roles as state executives. Together, they provided the state with a blend of pragmatism, and an ethic of honest and clean government. Their success was interlocking and interdependent. And it depended in no small way upon the continuation of the political culture they had helped to create as progressive legislators.

That consensus was violated in form but not in content when Governor Dixie Lee Ray replaced the Evans dynasty in 1977. Although locked into conflict with the press and environmental interests over nuclear power, Ray's policies simply reflected a different strategy towards the same end: making government efficient by reducing rather than increasing its size and scope. Yet her first year legislative accomplishments in criminal justice were indeed surprising and inconsistent with a conservative philosophy. By the end of her first year, for example, she signed more criminal justice reform legislation than Evans and Gorton were able to accomplish in the preceding twelve years.

The office of attorney general in Washington has none of the extensive powers of the California attorney general. Yet, Gorton used its limited powers to make it an informal and leading source of criminal justice policy. One of the roles Gorton assumed during his tenure as attorney general, no doubt contributing to a successful bid for the Senate in 1980, was the chairmanship of the Governor's Committee on Law and Justice throughout most of the 1970's. In that role, Gorton's political career flourished primarily because of his control over the distribution of LEAA funds. Consequently, compliance with criminal records privacy mandates, like so many other conditions of aid, presented only a negligible concession for the opportunity to preside over such a large political bonanza.

When the Evans empire began to fold, the state legislature began to assert itself, especially in criminal justice policy. A coalition of liberal Democratic reformers acquired the power to produce a plethora of criminal justice reforms (in juvenile justice, criminal records and sentencing) in the 1977 and 1978 legislative session. State and local law enforcement interests, only newly organized (funded in part by LEAA grants), did not have the organization, unity or clout to influence the direction of these reforms. Besides, the legislators were listening more to reform-minded civil libertarian groups. It would take several defeats, including passage of criminal records privacy legislation, to galvanize law enforcement into a more powerful political force.

But perhaps no branch of government underwent more dramatic change than the Supreme Court. The mid and late 1970's were watershed years for the state court with respect to organizational rather than policy reforms. The key to change lay in the acquisition of an aggressive state court administrator, who was nearly successful in unifying the state court through a constitutional amendment in 1976 (Powell, 1980).

This and other efforts to increase state court visibility as a governmental lobby were rewarded. The state court acquired many of the powers it sought short of administrative unification, including such things as centralized rule making, jurisdictional simplification, rules for judicial qualification and a unified information system. Also in 1978 it assumed a greatly strengthened role in the state LEAA program as well as becoming increasingly active in the National Judicial Conference.

State court policy making reflected this increased assertiveness in judicial decisions regarding civil liberties. Since 1980, the state constitution has been used to express its independence from U.S. Supreme Court policy. These policy changes have marked a dramatic departure from the philosophy of pragmatism to substantive liberalism, thus cutting the state court off from its political-cultural moorings. Therefore, state court activism has begun to undermine the stabilizing consensus among state executives which has persisted for nearly twenty years.

Governor Sargent was an oddity in Massachusetts state politics. With a background as a state bureaucrat (Secretary of Public Works for several years), Sargent's first elective office was as Lieutenant Governor in the Volpe administration in 1966. When Volpe left in 1969 to become Nixon's Secretary of Transportation, Sargent stepped in as acting Governor, and won reelection in 1970 against Boston's Mayor Kevin White. Sargent, who showed no particular fondness nor aptitude for his administrative duties as governor, as one commentator noted, adopted a strong issue-oriented style to maintain his visibility and ensure his reelection (Weinberg, 1977: 18–19). Issues such as privacy rights were therefore ripe for exploitation by young liberal staff eager to find a policy focus to establish their reform credentials.

But Sargent's substantive focus has long since been replaced by one favoring a hard nosed managerialism characterized by Democratic Governor Dukakis' two administrations (1974–1978 and 1980–). In many respects, Dukakis, like Jerry Brown, has simply capitalized on an anti-government theme popularized during the Carter and Reagan presidencies. This focus not only helped Dukakis defeat Sargent for his alleged management ineptitude, but has long been ascendant in the transformation of Massachusetts' political culture (Litt, 1965).

By managerialism I mean a style of policy-making which puts a premium on the efficiency and effectiveness of policy-making and implementation processes. There is less concern with both procedural technicalities and abstract principles than with ways to best improve the administration of ongoing programs. There is some affinity with pragmatism in this regard, but managerialism differs with respect to its willingness to innovate in ways which may lack public support. Thus, a managerial style does not necessarily imply obeisance to the status quo. However, deference to organizational solutions makes bureaucratizaton an ever present tendency. Nowadays it is not inconsistent for an official adopting a managerial style (e.g., governors Dukakis or Brown) to subscribe to a liberal social philosophy. This is so because organizational reforms which result in the reduction of government services to various marginal populations are now being justified on the basis of an overall improvement in general social welfare (e.g., reduction of inflationary pressure, costly regulations or ineffective programs).

There is some irony, however, to Governor Dukakis' political success. The area suffering from the greatest neglect happened to be criminal justice information systems. Dukakis attributed the continued inability to develop a computerized central state repository to burdensome privacy regulations. Yet it was also clear that his predecessor, Republican Governor King, had shown a disinterest in resolving institutional conflicts which have blocked CSR development. Dukakis' 1980 campaign therefore promised to correct these festering technological problems. However, Dukakis has been unable to resolve the underlying persistence of institutional conflicts which have prevented resolution of the technological and managerial issues necessary for the development of a statewide computerized system.

As in Washington, the office of attorney general in Massachusetts provides few formal powers but an excellent position from which to influence criminal justice policy. Over the last ten years, Francis X. Bellotti has exerted a strong liberal commitment to civil liberties issues from that office while maintaining leadership of the state Democratic party. Bellotti is no newcomer to state politics, for he had run unsuccessfully for governor against John Volpe in the mid-1960's. Since then, he has become a very respected leader in state politics and an important reason for Dukakis' electoral success in 1982. Bellotti's active involvement in the implementation of privacy policy following Sargent's departure from office was instrumental in reconciling serious differences between executives and the state court that could have easily undermined the viability of the fledgling state policy. Unlike the Washington attorney general, Bellotti had little control over LEAA financial largesse but used his staff to put his personal stamp on LEAA funded programs. Some of his most capable staff were assigned to handle LEAA projects and were used to staff the state's Criminal History System Board and Security and Privacy Council. Yet his persistent electoral ambitions explain a more recent shift to political pragmatism in adjusting to a changing public mood.

State law enforcement as a political interest group, like that in Washington, has been slow to develop. This has been due, in part, to gubernatorial indifference in the appointments of the state Commissioner of Public Safety. Until recently the commissioners have often been unrepresentative of law enforcement interests, at times exhibiting a somewhat surprising and idiosyncratic liberalism. An important peculiarity of the Executive Office of Public Safety is its lack of control over its central state repository. Responsibilities for the collection of arrest and disposition data are divided between it and the Office of Probation, which is an administrative division of the state court. Consequently, there has been little cooperation and coordination between the two offices with respect to unified collection of police and court records. Although the passage of the state Criminal Offender Record Information Act now gives administrative authority for the central state repository to the Criminal History System Board, that authority has yet to be exercised to create an operationalized state repository.

As the administrative arm of the state court system, the Commissioner of Probation has been an important political figure in criminal justice policy. The conservatism of recent commissioners has put them at odds with the more liberal state legislature on criminal justice issues. The influence of the probation commissioner has also exacerbated conflicts over the separation of powers.

Finally, in contrast to the state's historic tradition and rather innovative liberal policies with respect to freedom of speech, press and substantive due process, the Supreme Judicial Court of Massachusetts has been conservative regarding rights of criminal defendants. The court has been cautious and circumspect in relying on the state constitution to resolve civil liberties policy issues and reluctant to upset national policy uniformity established by the U.S. Supreme Court (Wilkins, 1980: 890–921).

By and large, despite occasional skirmishes there is a tradition of mutual respect between political institutions and a kind of rationalistic consensualism in Massachusetts politics. New policy is most likely to occur only when there appears to be strong elite consensus; policy proposals which fail to acknowledge these political and cultural limits are unlikely to survive.

CIVIL LIBERTIES POLICY: THE INCIPIENT CONSEQUENCES OF STATE COURT INACTION

Washington: The Belated Assertion of Constitutional Independence

It is somewhat surprising that the Washington Supreme Court was one of the earliest states to adopt the exclusionary rule because the court was not particularly innovative during the interim. Since its first use of independent state grounds in a 1962 case involving the issue of standing, it has, by its own admission in *State v. Ringer* (1983), suffered from a form of doctrinal amnesia. The transition from the Warren years to the Burger Court produced an acquiescence to a pragmatic approach to interpreting and implementing U.S. Supreme Court policies that all but abandoned the 1962 doctrine.

From the late 1960's through the 1970's the Washington state court seemed to be honestly struggling to find a consistent way to apply the frequently inconsistent, ever shifting U.S. Supreme Court policy on search and seizure to Washington cases. But the court never found a satisfactory way of reconciling the Burger Court's test of "reasonable expectation of privacy" with the need to find a determinant guideline for issuance of warrants. Moreover, the state court has had difficulty in establishing the circumstances under which the fruits of a "plain view" search could be used and how evidence bears on confessions. Thus, the post-*Mapp* rulings and to some extent decisions following *Miranda*, did not provide a satisfactory way to reconcile the three-fold problems of: scope of legal searches, search incident to arrest and "probable cause."

It was not until the early 1980's, when the state court regained doctrinal consciousness that it began to move swiftly and surely in establishing a coherent and substantively grounded policy in these areas. With this rediscovery the state court proceeded to abrogate a number of earlier state court decisions by asserting the supremacy of state constitutional protections pertaining to search and seizure policy.

The state court's attempt to rejuvenate a doctrine threatened with extinction through indifference has not been well received by either the U.S. Supreme Court or by state and local criminal justice officials. Perhaps anticipating criticism and increduality by implementers and legislators, the state court in *Ringer* offered an elaborate argument based on a reading of the intentions of the authors of the state constitution. But such justifications may only further exacerbate resentment, threatening to put the Washington court, like its neighbor to the south, in a legitimation crisis.

Policy Development

State v. Gibbons (1922) was not an extraordinary decision; it simply accepted the *Weeks* ruling regarding the exclusionary rule at face value but restricted its applicability. It was not until *State v. Michaels* (1962) that the Washington state court held that the state constitution confers automatic standing on defendants charged with an offense in which admission of physical evidence is involved. That is, the defendant has a right to challenge the legality of evidence admitted to trial. Yet, as stated earlier, it was a doctrine in search of reinforcing applications for nearly twenty years. Aside from the citation of the state constitution in *State v. Canaday* (1971) and *State v. Patterson* (1973), where the state court actually sided with the Burger Court on the "reasonableness" test, nine of the twelve cases using independent state grounds occurred on or after the watershed year of 1980.

The years between 1962 and 1980 show an unexceptionable pattern of state court response to *Miranda*. Like other states, the court stressed during the Warren years that no absolute standard was available to test the "voluntariness" of confessions; it depended on the "totality of facts and circumstances" surrounding the case. In one idiosyncratic application of *Miranda*, however, in *State v. Adams* (1969), the state court contended that a suspect could determine which questions to answer in an interrogation, as long as it was voluntary. In the only significant recent case regarding confessions (*Dutil v. the State*, 1980), the court ruled that under the state constitution, parents could not be considered surrogate attorneys and therefore a waiver cannot be considered valid when obtained with their consent.

In contrast to the rather limited issues presented by *Miranda*, the state's post-*Mapp* policy was more vexing and complex. The state court initially found their approach to *Miranda* equally serviceable to that used with *Mapp* by insisting there was no absolute test available to determine whether warrants must be issued. Yet it also struggled to put some parameters on the timing of the search by insisting that it be "contemporaneous with an incident to a lawful arrest" (*State v. Wilson*, 1967).

With its decision in *State v. Gluck* (1974), using the Burger Court "reasonableness" standard as its point of departure, the state court argued that the "reasonable expectation of privacy" for searches of homes differed from that of automobiles. It also ruled in a few cases from 1976 to 1979 that what constituted "exigent circumstances" must also be made clear in order that warrants be properly exempted.

Finally, clearly unsatisfied with the U.S. Supreme Court's "sliding scale of privacy expectation" the state court undertook a different strategy of defining the conditions of a proper search. In *State v. Thompson* (1979) the court ruled that an officer must form a reasonable suspicion which must be "individualized" before a determination of "probable cause" could be reached.

Clearly, police responses to the U.S. Supreme Court civil liberties decisions turn upon how state and lower courts chose to interpret and communicate those decisions to law enforcement officials. One deputy sheriff in a western Washington city illustrated the difficulties involved when the law is ambiguous and there are conflicting interpretations:

> *Q. What difference does the source of policy make to your response and implementation? How does the source of the policy affect its credibility*? Well, the police officer doesn't make these distinctions. We're not really directly affected by federal law. We don't pay that much attention to Supreme Court decisions until they come through our state court. We pay attention almost exclusively to our state court rules and decisions they make. We hear about state court decisions from our local courts who rule on facts of specific cases. . . . However, there is basic lack of communication. The rules change so quickly as well. That's why we're upset by *Mapp*, especially when an officer acted on "good faith," under reasonable expectations—and then gets suppressed on the basis of rules we never heard about. That is why you get officers overreacting to a system which is falling apart. It's a tool that takes us out of the ballgame. But I don't mind *Miranda*. . . . It doesn't bother me at all.

Prosecutors, unlike police, are not only more apt to distinguish between sources of policy, but quick to perceive philosophical differences in state court variations from Supreme Court policy. The following dialogue with an eastern Washington prosecutor is instructive as to the policy conflicts prosecutors face when confronted with competing policy sources:

Q. How have the state court interpretations of U.S. Supreme Court civil liberties policies affected their clarity for implementation? I think the U.S. Supreme Court decisions have been very clear, especially in enunciating a "bright line" distinction on the seizure of evidence. But the state court has muddied the waters. It's not clear what law enforcement can do especially in automobile searches.
Q. Given a divided policy situation like this which court do you follow? I prefer to go by the U.S. Supreme Court decisions but I don't have a choice. We are bound by the decisions of the Washington state Supreme Court. The Burger Court has said, however, that states can interpret their own constitutions. So we see little hope that we can appeal to the U.S. Supreme Court to overturn our state court's decisions.
Q. How much direction have you gotten from the state court in civil liberties matters and has it been helpful? The state court has given us a lot of direction. But it usually takes nine or ten decisions to figure out what they want. Clarity is never a one shot deal because of the nature of the court as an institution. Clarity or greater ambiguity occurs over time. With each additional fact new issues arise to test old principles. That is why the Burger Court has created the "bright line" rules, to cover many different factual situations. Our state court has developed a lot of ancillary decisions which are not as clear as we would like them to be.

It is not entirely clear why the Washington state Supreme Court decided to wrap itself in the mantle of its own state constitution starting with *State v. Simpson* (1980). Nonetheless, there were some incipient signs, besides twenty years in case law that showed indications of strain from a balance that could not be successfully struck between an increasingly restrictive U.S. Supreme Court and the reality of the need to safeguard individual rights. The state court had undertaken a partially successful effort to unify state courts through expanded use of rule-making powers. A state court information system was implemented and the justices and local judges had taken over leadership of the Governor's Committee on Law and Justice in 1978, to assume control of the state LEAA program. These were signs that the state court was on the move. Surprisingly, all of this happened with little change in the composition of state Supreme Court.

The importance of *Simpson* like that of *Brisendine* in California, lies in the state court's declaration of the power to interpret state constitutional provisions as more protective of individual rights than parallel provisions of the U.S. Constitution:

Such independent interpretation of state constitutional provisions is particularly appropriate when the language of state provisions differs from the federal provisions and the legislative history of the state constitution reveals that the difference was intended by the framers (1980: 1200).

The state court contended that the state constitution differed from the Fourth Amendment by clearly recognizing an individual's right to privacy with no expressed limitations: "No person shall be disturbed in his private affairs, or his home invaded, without authority of law" (Constitutional Article I and VII). Notwithstanding the fact that *Simpson* involved a search of an automobile, the court held that the defendant has automatic standing to challenge a search or seizure if the offense with which he is charged involves possession as an essential element of the offense. In making the decision, the majority specifically took exception to the U.S. Supreme Court decision in *Salvucci* (1980) in which they abolished the automatic standing rule first enunciated in *Jones* (1958). The Washington state court speculated that the U.S. Supreme Court had overturned *Jones* in an effort to subsume such principles within the broader doctrine of the "expectation of privacy rule." With this parting shot, the state court finally ended its unsuccessful struggle in trying to reconcile the Burger Court doctrine with the necessity for some modicum of protection of individual rights. Yet the dissent written in *Simpson* was equally unforgiving of the majority decision, sounding much like Governor Deukmejian's condemnation of the California Supreme Court for evading U.S. Supreme Court policy through an unprincipled use of result-oriented decision-making.

In another 1980 case (*State v. Chrisman*) the Washington state court was not so successful in getting past U.S. Supreme Court scrutiny. The state court ruled that the case involved an illegal search incident to arrest, citing *Jones* and *Coolidge* (1971). However, the U.S. Supreme Court reversed (*Washington v. Chrisman*, 1982), contending that the "plain view" doctrine applied instead, citing *Pennsylvania v. Mimms* (1977) and *Belton* (1981) to justify this ruling.

Perhaps realizing the vulnerability of controversial decisions to U.S. Supreme Court reversal when unprotected by state constitutional grounding, the state court in *Ringer* (1983) strengthened its assertion of state policy control. The principle was now unambiguous: the state constitution posed a *bar* to warrantless searches and seizures with very limited exceptions. The state court provided an intriguing analysis of why they must return to the principles enunciated in *Michaels* over twenty years before. The U.S. Supreme Court and, through its complicity, the state court had nearly allowed the exceptions in the use of warrants to swallow the original intentions in *Weeks* (1914) and *Mapp* (1961). The majority found a statement by Justice Frankfurter in *Rabinowitz* (1950) lamenting this process of erosion which was initiated by the premise that an arrest creates a right to search. The distortion was simply extended to justify the right to seize evidence in "plain view" and to search the place where an arrest occurs. In other words, a new concept of routine law enforcement conduct had been advanced to which the state court could not subscribe.

Implementation and Reaction

There is a great deal of uncertainty regarding the impact of *Simpson* and *Ringer*. Obviously, neither police nor prosecutors are happy with the decisions. The state Sheriffs and Chiefs Association has concluded that the decisions eliminate exceptions to warrants such as "exigent circumstances" (surely an exaggeration) and the ''plain view'' doctrine vindicated by the U.S. Supreme Court decision in *Chrisman*. They are now actively organizing an initiative drive to get a constitutional change on the November 1985 ballot. Prosecutors are issuing dire warnings that warrants will be more difficult to get in a timely way for the purpose of auto searches and that citizens can expect to be detained for longer periods of time until a legal search can be conducted.

Significant as these problems are for implementation and potential further abuse of individual rights, a dialogue with a chief prosecutor in eastern Washington is revealing about the underlying issues the decisions raise for the legitimacy of state court policy-making.

Q. How will you respond to Ringer? When we try to decide what ''exigent circumstances mean'' we are going to cite the U.S. Supreme Court and hope we can make it stick.
Q. Why did the state court elaborate at length in Simpson *and* Ringer *on the state constitution*? What they are saying is that they can make their own body of law. The state court used *Simpson* for this purpose. But it's ludicrous to assume that the framers of the state constitution meant that it applied to auto searches when there weren't any cars.
Q. How have the state prosecutors reacted to the decisions? The Association is now conducting a series of meetings to formulate a response. We may have to try to amend the state constitution so it reads the same as the federal constitution. The *Simpson* and *Ringer* decisions have thrown out a great deal of case law and procedure developed by the U.S. Supreme Court so it is of great concern to us what happens next.

While there is no denying that judges respond to *legal* as well as political considerations in pursuit of state constitutional activism, what is problematic is how to clearly *separate* their influence. Washington state Court Justice Utter's recent law review article (1984) provides a good example of this. The significance of the article lies in its admission that it is simply not sufficient to merely predicate state judicial policy on state constitutional grounds (as the Colorado court has done frequently). In addition, the court must justify the state constitution's relevance to a policy argument by demonstrating that the policy satisfies the intent of the founders. Utter demonstrates that this will require historical research into the political culture, immediate problems, and citizen concerns which gave rise to particular constitutional provisions protecting citizens' rights. Moreover, this strategy is significant because it is designed to *legitimate* policies considerably to the left of the Burger Court, in the face of considerable opposition by law enforcement and other interests. Interestingly, while a strategy such as this is not necessary to immunize state policy from U.S. Supreme Court reversal, it anticipates that possibility in the future. Also, it acknowledges that one of the most pressing immediate needs of activist state courts is to secure the *authority* necessary to legitimize their policies. What this suggests is that legitimation is not just a problem of legal interpretation; it is a political issue as well.

Massachusetts: Maintaining Liberal Appearances Through Pragmatism and Proceduralism

Like California, Massachusetts has a national reputation for policy innovation. But also it has exhibited greater political stability than California, given a unified political philosophy of classical, New Deal liberalism which crosses party lines. Yet strangely, Massachusetts has not been particularly innovative nor attempted to adopt civil liberties policies to the left of the U.S. Supreme Court. While the state court observed in-custody rights of the accused long before *Miranda*, the state court has failed, until recently, to satisfy the intent of the Warren Court. Instead of providing leadership it has exercised caution, exhibiting the intermingling styles of pragmatism and proceduralism. Such overlapping styles insulates the court from criticism while maximizing its leverage over state policy.

The Massachusetts Supreme Judicial Court has shown a willingness to be innovative in search and seizure as long as it is not inconsistent with the underlying philosophical basis of Supreme Court decision making. Such state court innovations must be clearly authorized by past precedent and embodied in common state practice. The state court has also shown no strong inclination or willingness to use the state constitution as a tool to either promote new policies or ratify existing ones.

The state court's most recent cases involving civil liberties issues, however, have contributed to a dilemma. As the U.S. Supreme Court continues its relaxation of civil liberties protections by continuing to lower the minimum standards for state practice, the state court is confronted by the problem of determining where the boundary is to be drawn between the Massachusetts and the Supreme Court policy. To continue in this tenuous mode, the court must read prevailing state practice astutely while continuing to conceal its underlying but long suppressed ideological preferences.

Policy Development

The state court's decisions regarding in-custody, pre-interrogation rights of suspects typifies the idiosyncratic and conservative nature of state policy. Having predated the Warren Court, Massachusetts' interrogation policy conformed more closely to *Johnson v. Zerbst* and *Escobedo* than *Miranda*. Therefore, the state court stressed "voluntariness" rather than the importance of understanding or effectively using the defendant's rights. As a consequence, the important policy issues in Massachusetts turned not upon the effectiveness with which defendants' rights are exercised but rather on the *impeccability* of procedures to insure the "voluntariness" of the suspect's participation in the interrogation process. This policy distinction was clearly enunciated in *Commonwealth v. Femino* (1967) and *Commonwealth v. Morrissey* (1967) with the state court holding that questions of whether a confession is obtained in violation of constitutional guarantees and whether it is voluntary are distinct *substantive* and *procedural* issues.

This doctrine has been carried forward nearly unchallenged into the Burger

Court era. For example, the state court ruled that an oral waiver of rights is a sufficient test of whether they were understood (*Commonwealth v. Bettencourt*, 1972); that police failure to advise or assist a defendant in making a telephone call is no bar to the legality of an ensuing interrogation (*Commonwealth v. Daniels*, 1975); that an illegal arrest does not compromise the legality of a subsequent confession (*Commonwealth v. Sylvia*, 1980); and that lack of clarity of pre-interrogation warnings is no bar to admissibility of a confession (*Commonwealth v. Zukoski*, 1976). Only recently has the state court (in *Commonwealth v. Meehan*, 1979) seen fit to reverse *Daniels* by characterizing the inability to make an in-custody telephone call as a form of "duress."

The upshot of these policies pertaining to in-custody rights seems to be that police procedural error by itself does not constitute an automatic bar to the fruits of the interrogation process. The practical result for police practice is the encouragement of a formalistic and perfunctory compliance with the *Miranda* protections.

The state court generally has advanced a restrictive (albeit incoherent) policy in the area of search and seizure. It has had recent opportunities to find greater protections of defendants' rights against privacy invasions of police searches (e.g., in *Commonwealth v. Reynolds*, (1977) and *Commonwealth v. Ortiz* (1978)) but has declined to do so. Although careful to avoid the more ambiguous policy of the Burger Court regarding "reasonableness," it has asserted but not clarified the difference in standing regarding home and auto searches by declaring that the "place" determines the "reasonableness" of the search (*Commonwealth v. Campbell*, 1967; *Commonwealth v. Thomas*, 1971; *Board of Selectmen v. Boston*, 1977; *Commonwealth v. Ortiz*, 1978; *Commonwealth v. Sylvia*, 1980). It has vacillated by ruling that consent does not affect scope (*Commonwealth v. Walker*, 1976) and that the scope of the search provided by consent is dictated by specific rules (*Commonwealth v. Cantalupo*, 1980). However, the state court has held that the police may exercise reasonable caution as to whether some limitation was intended. And while consent must not be defined as simple acquiescence to authority (*Commonwealth v. Harmond*, 1978), consent does not require that a precise statement be made to authorize a search.

Finally, with the exceptions of some early cases (*Commonwealth v. Bowlen*, 1967; *Commonwealth v. Garreffi*, 1969) which determine that warrants are not required for searches incident to arrest involving "plain view" seizures, the state court has provided no policy direction at all with respect to warrants until two 1983 cases. This oversight has had important consequences for local practice and the future direction of state court policy-making.

One Superior Court judge from a suburban town outside Boston complained that the state court provided no guidance with respect to issuance of warrants even though most of his cases involved "probable cause" searches involving alleged "exigent circumstances." He said that the police used "good faith" rationales most often as a way to have illegal practices excused, even though unsupported by any official state court policy.

Three recent decisions by the state court help explain this apparent ambiguity in policy by forcing the court's philosophical leanings to the surface. These decisions also suggest that the court is reaching the limits of its silence about its ideological leanings and inaction on the search and seizure guidelines. In *Commonwealth v. Sheppard* (1982), subsequently reversed on appeal to the U.S. Supreme Court in *Massachusetts v. Sheppard* (1984), the state court specifically acknowledged that although police acted in "good faith" by obtaining evidence through a warrant issued for "probable cause," the evidence was inadmissable because the warrant was technically defective in failing to correctly describe the things to be seized. There is a twofold significance of the case for understanding state court policy.

First, the majority used the case to renew their criticism of the exclusionary rule and obvious displeasure at having to let a technicality force them to reverse an original conviction. In citing a litany of Burger Court cases to support their concerns, the justices contended that cases like this prove that the rule was unworkable and that instead of deterring illegal activity, it penalized police for "good faith" conduct. It was clear from the tenor of the opinion that the court was urging the U.S. Supreme Court to consider making a policy change, which it did in *Leon* (1984).

Secondly, and perhaps more significantly, the justices simultaneously denied that the rule was applicable to judicial behavior (as a policy and as a deterrent) while holding that the "good faith" rule should apply to excuse judicial errors in approving warrants. Although this contradictory holding cast doubt on exactly what policy the court did apply to reach its ruling, it left no doubt that judicial integrity was not a relevant consideration in the enforcement of the exclusionary rule. A dissenting justice complained about the tone of "grudging acceptance" displayed by Justice Wilkins in writing the opinion and argued that the judge's mistakes in issuing a warrant in *Sheppard* were clearly ones of "negligence" rather than ones of "good faith."

As a former SPA Director and senior official with the Massachusetts public defenders commented, the *Sheppard* case was symptomatic of the U.S. Supreme Court's laxity and state court indifference with respect to judicial responsibility for warrants:

> A very high percentage of cases for many of the district court judges in this state get reversed. It implies a breakdown of the appointment power for one. Some are qualified, but you really have to be politically consistent with the governor in order to get approved by the Executive Council. There are a lot of lousy judges that know nothing about the law. That's also where the problem is. What's more, they don't feel in any way punished if they don't follow the law, because it doesn't make any difference to them. There is a special screening court between them and the intermediate appeals court so they get shielded from direct attack.
> *Q. Are you saying judicial integrity is irrelevent in exclusionary rule cases*? The U.S. Supreme Court says that defense attorneys can't delve into the basis of the issuance of

warrants once they are issued. Today magistrates just issue them automatically. They never really investigate whether there is "probable cause." They just assume there is.

Although having to rule against its own philosophical inclinations (in *Sheppard*), the Massachusetts state court nevertheless continues to mount its attack on the exclusionary rule. In two other recent cases (*Commonwealth v. Upton*, 1983 and *Commonwealth v. Nowells*, 1983) the state court had an opportunity to apply the two-pronged test developed by the Warren Court in *Aguilar* (1964) and *Spinelli v. U.S.* (1969), to determine whether there is sufficient "probable cause" to issue a warrant.

The two-pronged test consists of determining (1) the underlying circumstances for the informant's conclusions ("basis of knowledge" test) and (2) whether the informant's information is credible or reliable ("veracity test"). While acknowledging that it was unclear whether *Gates* merely qualified or entirely abrogated the test, the state court interpreted *Gates* to mean that each test was independent of the other, and that it was sufficient to satisfy just one to obtain a warrant. Fortunately for the court, it found *Upton* lacking in both dimensions and therefore did not have to show just how to decide how the deficiencies to satisfy one of the two tests was compensated by the strengths of the other—an interesting problem indeed since the two tests appear interdependent. A state public defender characterized the state court's approach in these cases:

Our supreme court has not used the state constitution to develop independent state policy. They tend to pick and choose U.S. Supreme Court cases in their decisions. I would say our state court is reasonably liberal—not liberal but reasonable.

The majority added in *Upton*, however, that if *Gates* really does eliminate the Aguiler test:

And the *Gates* test proves to be unacceptably shapeless and permissive, this court may have to define the protections guaranteed to the people against unreasonable searches and seizures by Article Fourteen of the Massachusetts Declaration of Rights and the consequences of the violation of those protections (1983: 724).

Implementation and Reaction

Some structural and cultural constraints account for the Supreme Judicial Court's style and the scope of its policy making as well as the philosophical issues already identified. Structural limits consist of the mandatory screening of all appeals through a special tribunal standing between the local and intermediate appellate courts. The tribunal's powers effectively limits the number and types of cases that reach the intermediate appeals court and the Supreme Judicial Court.

Cultural limits involve a tradition of local autonomy (dating back to the New England town meeting) which probably contributes to more extensive local variation in civil liberties policies than the other states examined here. In fact, the potential interaction between these two constraining factors may reinforce the state court style of consensualism and pragmatism. Where there is strong autonomy and, thus, variation in local policies, the state court may have no choice but to develop minimum guidelines instead of imposing ideologically identifiable policy.

Some limited evidence has already been presented in Chapter 2 to support the notion that a court structure which insulates lower court decisions from direct review by state appellate courts contributes to more extensive local court policy variation. But the consensual political culture, protective of diversity and local variation, combined with these structural characteristics, furnishes the state court sufficient latitude to avoid making hard policy decisions while enjoying continued widespread legitimacy.

What is striking and intriguing about the respondents involved in the Massachusetts research is their seemingly unanimous acceptance of the legitimacy of state court policy-making despite ideological differences in attitudes toward the U.S. Supreme Court. One Boston Superior Court judge provided some thoughtful insights as to what factors motivated state court decision-making in their reaction to U.S. Supreme Court policy:

> In speculating, our courts are conservative institutions. Once they assert themselves in the area of confessions, which was ahead of the Supreme Court, then they are not likely to back off on it, even if the U.S. Supreme Court does so because of their inherent conservatism. I don't see any change short of a constitutional amendment or legislative action as happened in the case of the court's ruling on capital punishment to change its policy approach. Maybe this is a hint of what would happen if the underpinnings of *Mapp* and *Miranda* got eroded by the U.S. Supreme Court. . . . The underlying theme here is stability and consistency. Yes, from time to time the court changes its rules but you get clear warnings but there aren't any signs yet.

Although other officials, including judges, were less sanguine about the willingness of the state court to use state constitutional grounds to assert their independence from the U.S. Supreme Court, few thought that if it did an initiative such as Proposition 8 in California would be launched or successfully challenge state court authority in Massachusetts.

The message that emerges from Massachusetts is that the Supreme Judicial Court thrives best when the U.S. Supreme Court provides enough flexibility so that the state court can avoid having to disrupt existing state practice. The U.S. Supreme Court's "good faith" doctrine (*Leon* 1984) simply vindicates the state court's reservations about the exclusionary rule, without undermining its pragmatic style and political support. The state court might be forced, as was Washington's, to weigh the risks and decide whether existing state practice can withstand lower federal requirements or if the floor must either change or remain the same. However, the *Sheppard* and *Upton* cases provide only mixed signals on this question. Moreover, it is not really clear that the Massachusetts state court even has a *coherent* policy that would be threatened by further Supreme Court changes.

In this instance, ambiguity can serve some important practical purposes, shielding the court from unpleasant political realities.

CRIMINAL RECORDS POLICY: THE PROBLEM OF AUTHORITY IN INDEPENDENT AGENCIES

Washington: The Dual Problem of Elite Indifference and Institutional Conflict

Washington's policy response to the federal criminal records privacy mandate is sort of a hybrid between that of California and Massachusetts. Similar to California, gubernatorial interest and support were lacking. Instead the attorney general assumed leadership of state policy development largely because of his role as chair of the Governor's Committee on Law and Justice, which gave him responsibility for the state LEAA program.

Yet, like Massachusetts, as described below, state legislative policy resulted in vesting the state planning agency (SPA) with administrative control for privacy while providing a theoretically effective set of regulatory tools to conduct an aggressive implementation and enforcement effort. Unfortunately, however, the SPA initiatives were prematurely but effectively extinguished. The absence of elite support combined with institutional conflicts between courts and police created an insoluble situation ripe for legislative exploitation. The SPA's skillful leveraging of procedural compromise among opposing interests was only temporarily successful. The SPA was neither able to overcome elite indifference capable of suppressing institutional conflicts over the separation of powers, nor able to sustain its authority unsupported by tradition.

Policy Development

In many respects it is surprising that the state of Washington ever adopted a criminal records privacy policy. By 1976 state executives had grown accustomed to the numerous LEAA conditions of aid and thus responded to the Title 28 mandate with an air of routine resignation. There were several features of the political environment which made passage of state legislation a rather dim prospect. For example, in late 1976, liberal Republican Governor Dan Evans, was nearing the end of his third term as governor, and about to be replaced by upstart conservative Democrat, Dixie Lee Ray. Evans was not enthusiastic about enlarging an already swollen state bureaucracy with additional federal guidelines. In fact there was little incentive to take an aggressive approach while a great deal of political capital could be made from a posture of mild defiance. Slade Gorton, the popular Republican Attorney General, was ambivalent about security and privacy regulations (which he criticized in testimony before the U.S. Senate a year before), but was delegated responsibility by the governor to develop a privacy plan recommending an appropriate state policy response.

In spite of the widespread indifference, a state plan was developed. A committee composed of diverse interests, chaired by the state court administrator actually strengthened the prospects for legislative action. Nonetheless, the attorney general's special advisory committee encountered one very significant problem: The inability to find an agency willing and suitable to assume administrative and regulatory authority for criminal records privacy. A memo from Attorney General Gorton to State Court Administrator Winberry made the reasons clear:

> The Governor asked whether or not the state of Washington is required to have a specific agency undertake continuing security and privacy responsibilities within the state, and/or whether it is required to have an advisory committee to such an agency.
>
> The Governor, with my concurrence, is opposed to the creation of an independent commission on the subject in any event, feeling that the state already has too many board and commissions. For my part, I do not wish such a responsibility assigned to the Office of Attorney General. Therefore, it is a preference of both the Governor and myself, choosing among your alternatives that the responsibility to the extent required be delegated to the Office of Community Development (Gorton, 1976).

Nearly every other state agency with some criminal justice responsibilities was canvassed and gave the same negative reply. The State Highway Patrol (responsible for the central state repository) claimed that such a role would undermine the rapport it had developed with local criminal justice agencies (Bachofner, 1980). Even the Governor's preferred alternative, the Office of Community Development and the SPA's administrative home, suggested that some other agency be found.

The legislative hearings went surprisingly well for the proposed state legislation. The Senate Judiciary Committee was controlled by a respected liberal Democrat who was sympathetic to ACLU concerns about records abuses. Significantly, given the absence of a designated administrative agency in the proposed legislation, the state court administrator persuaded the Judiciary Committee to list the Judicial Council (staffed by the Court Administrator) as the implementing agency. This gesture helped keep the legislation alive while a better prospect could be found.

Yet interest group divisiveness did break out, threatening to undermine the chances of successful passage. The press, the ACLU and public disclosure interests were locked in conflict over competing interpretatons of privacy invasions. Consequently, the press held criminal records legislation hostage because of concerns that the bill would not protect the press from liability for publication of criminal justice information.

The confluence of several factors, however, insured the survival of the Washington Criminal Records Privacy Act (WCRPA). First, some influential staff members of Governor Ray's newly elected administration had been placed in control of the Office of Community Development. Sympathetic to the criminal records privacy bill, they agreed to support the move of the state planning agency to acquire administrative control—a move calculated to ensure survival of the state office beyond the anticipated end of the LEAA program. Next, the State Court Administrator, the legislative shepherd of the bill, graciously deferred to replacement of the Judicial Council by a more appropriate executive agency. Also, the chair of the House Institutions Committee, who saw a strengthened state planning agency contributing to his hope of creating a state department of justice, kept the bill alive in the House and delivered a unanimous floor vote. And finally, the Senate Judiciary Chairman was made an offer he couldn't refuse, prompting him to override an attempt by the press to hold the bill hostage in the Senate in exchange for withdrawal of a threatened gubernatorial veto of the Juvenile Justice Reform Act, for which he had been the prime sponsor.

Enabling Legislation

The legislation which resulted from this rather fortuitous set of circumstances was largely identical to that recommended by the Attorney General's advisory committee. The law was comprehensive and forward looking, incorporating many of the LEAA recommendations. Like California, it included a restrictive policy towards access to and dissemination of arrest records, and required that all transactions be monitored, logged and audited by the state planning agency. Also included were procedures for a record subject to obtain access to and correction of his criminal file. Although failing to incorporate sealing or purging provisions like Colorado, the statute did prohibit the dissemination of arrest records if a final disposition had not been obtained within one year.

In addition, the law capitalized on the existing technological capabilities of the central state repository (CSR) by requiring pre-dissemination queries by local agencies to the CSR prior to release of the information. A preexisting statutory requirement that all arrests be reported to the CSR obviated the need for formal policies in this regard. Notwithstanding these provisions, a significant oversight involving the inability to specify the court's record reporting responsibilities, ultimately precipitated a legitimation crisis in 1979, undermining an already weakened and suspect SPA state regulatory role.

Implementation and Reaction

Development of implementing regulations proved to be difficult because virtually no one in the criminal justice community supported the law and none wanted to assume a leadership role. The Governor's Committee on Law and Justice (which included numerous state officials including a Supreme Court Justice and two Superior Court judges) seemed ill at ease in accepting a regulatory role and chose instead to assume a low profile. The observations of a Superior Court judge who had been a Governor's Committee member typified these concerns and problems:

> Theoretically it would have been better to have an independent agency or commission implement criminal records privacy law and regulations. The state planning agency was more appropriately a planning and monitoring body. The Governor's Committee was not

capable of providing consistent policy direction to the SPA privacy staff. The Committee was more of a political group in which different points of view emerged each time they met to consider security and privacy policy. In addition, Governor Ray didn't really put a lot of trust in the group or solicit its advice in criminal justice matters. Besides these concerns, as a member of the judiciary, I didn't really feel comfortable being involved in what was essentially an executive function.

Evidently skepticism about the SPA role was shared by a former SPA administrator:

The SPA was handicapped in two ways with respect to implementing criminal records privacy. First, it had no real power to bring about compliance. This probably contributed to tolerance of its authority since it had never been a real threat in the enforcement of other LEAA conditions of aid. Second, the SPA lacked credibility; it had no real expertise in the administraton of criminal justice. The law enforcement community was frustrated by the SPA guideline development and compliance process. They did not think the SPA staff was knowledgeable about law enforcement functions and problems. Because of this, they weren't worried about compliance; they would simply continue to do the same things they always did.

The Governor's Committee could not easily avoid the development and application of state dissemination policy. The law had left it up to the SPA to spell out a process for approval of non-criminal justice access to non-conviction information. Thus, a certification process was specified involving ultimate review and approval by the Governor's Committee. Unfortunately certification quickly deteriorated into a controversy over politically volatile decisions. The Committee was faced with problems including such diverse issues as whether federal agencies could get access to state records, or whether federal control over an eastern Washington Indian reservation entitled their police force to obtain criminal records. With almost every application considered, there was conflict, intensive lobbying of SPA officials including members of the Governor's Cabinet, frequent opinions from the Attorney General's office, and occasional concessions to agencies with political clout but mostly denials. Needless to say, it was not a happy situation for the Governor's Committee, accustomed to approving grants, to have to say *no*.

SPA development of regulations in other areas proved equally difficult. Even the creation of a forty-member Ad Hoc Advisory Committee comprised of a wide assortment of criminal justice and civil liberties groups proved to be a forum which simply exacerbated conflict. One policy which became a lightning rod for conflict was that pertaining to the rules implementing individual right to access, review and challenge of records. The conflict over this issue was symptomatic of a criminal justice policy divided by divergent ideological commitments and expectations about probable outcomes of enforcement of due process protections.

Differences in belief, attitude and policy consequence were involved in the

SPA attempt to produce rules which would implement the individual access provisions. Civil liberties interests, predisposed to believe that rules for individual access constituted the most effective way to enforce the management and dissemination of criminal records, sought the most permissive rules possible. Law enforcement interests were equally assertive that such decisions, if implemented, would constitute an intolerable administrative burden. Consequently, a great deal of time and energy were expended to reach agreement on the issue. Ultimately it took an opinion from the attorney general's office to resolve the dispute. That opinion favored the more permissive regulations supported by civil liberties groups, ruling that the public disclosure law governed the way that access should be handled. But this controversy and its resolution did nothing to address the more important but less visible issues of record quality, management, dissemination and audits.

In light of the turmoil surrounding the development of the access and inspection provisions, it would not have been surprising to find evasion. To the contrary, there has been far more acceptance than anticipated. Asked to evaluate his experience with these provisions in light of original expectations, an eastern Washington records manager observed:

> We all cried "wolf" when we got the *Miranda* decision because this was going to impact us to the point where we couldn't do a damn thing. And this was the attitude we were taking on the WCRPA. I was the first one to say that the *Miranda* decision made better cops out of us and that consequently, the WCRPA would make better cops out of us if it was done rationally. I fought for that approach and to some degree it was accepted. It was a necessary evil that we found ourselves cleaning up the loose-lipped attitude that prevailed within criminal justice which was that, by saying all this data is mine and no one can tell me what to do with it. I think we have needed some discipline in this regard.

When asked to state more specifically how civil liberties and criminal records policies compared in terms of effects on law enforcement practice, the same respondent provided this elaboration:

> It (the WCRPA) compares only to the extent that it was expected to impact us so we couldn't do our job. *Miranda* required us to warn a person of his rights before taking him in for questioning. Similarly, we could have been impacted by the WCRPA to the point that we were supposed to be handcuffed like we were supposed to be by *Miranda*. What *Miranda* made us do was clean up to make sure we had the right guy and we had to go through these procedures so we didn't lose the right guy before going any further. Privacy and security gave us the same type of obligation. We had to make sure the record was clear and make sure the record was available. Prior to the WCRPA, criminal justice record keeping was an almost ran.
>
> If the WCRPA had preceded the *Miranda* decision, we probably wouldn't have had that decision. *Miranda* came about in part because an officer acted on the basis of prior knowledge that the suspect was a known criminal in the community. Because of that knowledge, the arresting officer acted in a totally disrespectful manner, failing to ac-

knowledge his rights. If there had been an environment conducive to accuracy and completeness, abuses of this kind may have been less likely to occur.

But the successful conclusion of rule making did not end the SPA difficulties. In early 1978 a gubernatorial reorganization moved the state planning agency into the Office of Financial Management and SPA power began to dissolve. The state Sheriffs and Chiefs Association capitalized on this move to intensify its efforts to undermine SPA regulatory momentum. A blunt letter sent to the Office of Financial Management administrator expressed their attitudes:

> The Sheriffs and Chiefs Association ask that you spend a few days with representatives of the law enforcement community making an in depth study of the monster you are creating for criminal justice agencies to live with. The only way to effectively implement the Security and Privacy Act of 1977 (WCRPA) is through mutual understanding and agreements by all agencies involved; this has not been accomplished by the forty-five plus member Ad Hoc Committee (Cotton and Webb, 1978).

Needless to say this put the Office of Financial Management in a very difficult and unwanted position. But all that could be done at that point was to slow rather than eliminate SPA regulatory activities.

But these conflicts captured only the appearances of underlying political realities involving ongoing conflict between police and courts. One dimension of that conflict surfaced in Seattle with an unsuccessful effort by the police to use the criminal record statute to thwart access to its intelligence and investigative files. Several community activists had brought a lawsuit challenging the practice whereby intelligence information was collected regarding political, sexual, religious and other beliefs and private behavior of persons with no known criminal record. The King County Superior Court found that the criminal records act pertained not to rules regulating *intelligence* information but the *accuracy* and *completeness* of information maintained by law enforcement agencies. Moreover, the court found that the public disclosure law made intelligence information publicly accessible. On appeal, the State Supreme Court affirmed the lower court's decision, thus opening the way for creation of a city ordinance regulating the collection of intelligence and investigative information—the first of its kind in the country. Not surprisingly however, the greatest opposition to criminal records requirements for dissemination controls, continues to involve the exchange of intelligence information.

Another way in which a police vs. court conflict surfaced involved the court's responsibility for furnishing disposition information to local police and to the central state repository. This dimension of the conflict not only dramatized the real difficulty involved in achieving improvements in record quality, but was an important factor contributing to the takeover of SPA administrative authority by the State Patrol in 1979.

The problem started early on in the SPA rule making process when the State

Court Administrator, citing the LEAA exemption of the courts in 1976, used the power of the state Supreme Court to get the SPA to withdraw regulations which would have given the state court system statutory responsibility to furnish disposition information to state and local criminal justice agencies. The practical effect was to rob police and prosecutors of a uniform way to get up-to-date disposition information to satisfy criminal records quality guidelines. Moreover, it put the police in an awkward position of assuming liability for incomplete records for which the courts had responsibility.

The observations of an eastern Washington police sergeant best expressed police resentment of the courts:

> There are more and more of us saying now we can't give out arrest or conviction information because it isn't accurate even though we know the source of accurate records. Again, that may be challenged in the courts, especially where it involves data subjects requests. But right now, apparently, it is a good enough reason because the courts aren't arguing with us. The smallest amount of everything the courts do—criminal cases—is the information they won't give us—not without some damn good working relationships. If they were mandated by law, they would do it. That's what probably made the thing so ridiculous when they (LEAA) excluded them. In our county, it is less than 1600 dispositions a year that they would have to give us. We're only looking at three to four transactions a day that they would have to deal with.
>
> The courts won more than we ever expected. The development of regulations was going to be the one place where we could get the information we needed. But throughout the whole process, we were the bastards that . . . had the criminal liability placed on us because of infraction, but yet we had no control over court records, so how could we be wrong? So we felt utter frustration when the committee exempted the courts. What's even sadder is that the trial courts in (my) county wanted to participate—they were willing to assist in getting disposition information. What is unfortunate is that we let a state court administrator make the decision for the courts of the state of Washington.

Law enforcement ultimately confronted this and other issues along with the SPA administrative control by supporting amendment of the statute, replacing the SPA with the State Patrol and making the courts legally responsible for furnishing disposition information. In addition to these changes, the Sheriffs and Chiefs Association tried to take advantage of a friendly legislature to avoid satisfying requirements for completeness and accuracy. This was attempted by permitting dissemination of specific facts or incidents within the direct knowledge of the criminal justice agency without having to acquire complete disposition information from the central state repository. If a quickwitted staff counsel to the House Judiciary Committee had not recognized its implications, this amendment would have virtually gutted the WCRPA of its central objectives. The Chairman of the House Judiciary Committee quickly intervened and suggested that the association propose "refinements" in the language to avoid these implications.

Overall these changes had several consequences for the implementation and enforcement of the WCRPA. First, most of the regulations pertaining to individual access and challenge were sacked and other modifications made consistent with conservative law enforcement views. In fact, one eastern Washington sheriff, who had participated in the original SPA rule-making process but who was excluded from this latest effort, remarked in a 1981 interview:

> Although I looked upon the guideline revisions as a beneficial thing to clean them up, what I objected to was the fact that they were done without any formal input from the major users. I never knew the legislature had amended the WCRPA and revised its rules until they were published. As a result, I have great trouble, even today, deciding which version of the WCRPA and administrative rules prevail.

In addition, efforts at active enforcement have grown dormant. One of the more important statutory responsibilities to capitulate to these pressures was the audit requirement. One western Washington sheriff expressed the concerns this way:

> The auditor placed way too much emphasis upon what we did with our records, how we recorded it and the accuracy and completeness of our files. . . . What would have been appropriate was a survey to generally assure that each agency had adopted procedures to carry out the objectives of the law.

Finally, it is quite clear that the law is being ignored by many local police. This attitude was particularly manifested in law enforcement attitudes toward State Patrol administrative control. One local law enforcement official interviewed about how dissemination policy had been handled by the State Patrol observed:

> I'd say the role of the State Patrol, based on law enforcement attitudes, is almost non-existent. They aren't cops so they can't tell us to do anything, which includes how we use and disseminate the information in our own files.

Thus, the attempt at criminal records reform in Washington was swallowed by organizational power conflicts between courts and police over control of state policy making and regulation.

Massachusetts: The Erosion of Reform by Managerial Indifference

Although Massachusetts anticipated the federal criminal records guidelines, as did California, the circumstances of their choices were quite different. Massachusetts was not forced to adopt state policies but, instead, actively developed a far reaching policy as protection against an *expansion* of federal information systems which lacked coherent controls and safeguards. Massachusetts' experimentation with the LEAA-SEARCH guidelines made them natural but unintended allies with LEAA in the struggle for control over the development of NCIC/CCH. There are three important implications of the Massachusetts experience for understandinng factors influencing state policy outcomes of federal guidelines.

First, the probability of initial success of state policy is increased by the extent to which its implementation is joined to electoral politics. This occurs because incumbent state executives are likely to take a more active role in policy leadership (given a federal mandate) if there is the possibility of subsequent electoral payoffs. This incentive may become particularly compelling if the policy involves a ''state's rights'' issue.

Second, such leadership must be sustained and renewed over time. If not, the substantive focus is likely to be lost and slippage, evasion and non-compliance are likely to occur. The Massachusetts experience is a good example of how changing policy styles of state executives can quickly undermine a substantive, result-oriented policy approach. Although bureaucratization of innovative programs is not inevitable, a combination of political organizational and structural forces at work in criminal justice make it likely.

Finally, it is clear in contrasting Massachusetts with Washington and Colorado, for example, that conflicts over separation of powers issues involving courts and executives can be resolved in ways that support rather than undermine criminal justice policies. This is particularly likely in a consensual political culture where there is mutual respect and trust, and common ideological affinities among courts, executives and legislators.

Policy Development

Governor Francis Sargent was a liberal Republican with an overriding interest in national policies affecting the states. This was partly due to his political ambitions as well as to his personal connections with Nixon appointees such as former Governor John Volpe and Elliott Richardson.

Congressional inquiries into the incipient development of national data banks (and later, the NCIC/CCH policy conflict) in the late 1960's, provided an avenue by which Sargent could gain national visibility as the liberal, states-rights conscience of a conservative administration. In fact, by the end of his term as Governor, Sargent had introduced and passed several pieces of related legislation addressing areas which included a fair information practice law (1975), a public records law (1973) as well as the Criminal Offender Record Information Act (1972).

The criminal records issue in 1971 provided Governor Sargent the opportunity to show the Nixon administration's insensitivity to individual privacy rights. Sargent's SPA director, joined by Arthur Miller, a Harvard law professor and outspoken critic of national data banks (Miller, 1971), informed Sargent about FBI plans to develop the NCIC/CCH in the absence of a viable national policy. The director of the state LEAA agency, aware of the LEAA-SEARCH model legislation, and suspecting that a federal policy would soon be promulgated, convinced Sargent to establish a special security and privacy committee to formulate a state criminal records policy. The committee persuaded Sargent to request wholesale adoption of the SEARCH model by the legislature. Two factors facilitated its swift passage in 1972: The legislature was told that such a law would be required by LEAA eventually and that it was a necessary element of a comprehensive approach to the regulation of public and private information. Also, the legislature was almost entirely ignorant of the technical details and controversy surrounding state and federal criminal records information systems.

Enabling Legislation

The Criminal Offender Record Information Act (CORI) constituted the most far reaching approach to criminal records information systems of any in the nation. Dissemination policy was more restrictive than the initial regulations produced by LEAA in 1974 which were quickly withdrawn in subsequent versions. Neither *arrest* nor *conviction* information could be disseminated by criminal justice agencies unless for criminal justice purposes or in accordance with a statute specifically authorizing access for a particular purpose.

The interstate exchange of criminal records was also to be strictly controlled by CORI. Extensive access provisions were also specified. But what was most unique was the creation of an independent Criminal History System Board to promulgate regulations and serve in a quasi-judicial capacity—handling decisions on certification of agency access and hearings of record challenges.

In addition, a special Security and Privacy Council was established to make policy recommendations and conduct research on development of new standards. The CORI regulations (approved in 1976) are very detailed with some thirty-three pages devoted to defining board procedures, council powers, personnel security classifications, and agency responsibilities for providing access to record information.

The political implications of criminal records policy became clear after a controversy between Sargent and Richardson emerged in 1973. An alert and politically astute policy advisor to Sargent informed him about the development of the NCIC/CCH system by reading investigative press stories by Nate Hentoff in the *Village Voice*. The upshot of these stories was that then U.S. Attorney General Mitchell was going ahead with plans for the FBI to operationalize its national criminal history record system. This was being done in spite of LEAA criticisms and Congressional concerns that the proposed system lacked uniform policies for record quality and management, dissemination controls and other privacy protections.

Realizing the political opportunities that this controversy presented for Sargent, one aide persuaded him to publicly challenge Richardson's continuation of the FBI plans in late 1973. A letter sent to Richardson raising a number of privacy and states' rights issues was subsequently published in the *Boston Globe* in a front page story. Surprisingly, instead of drawing fire from law enforcement it was praised even by the American Legion. Importantly, press distortion of the conflict catapulted the controversy to national attention.

During this period the press also uncovered a Justice Department lawsuit brought against Massachusetts, challenging the legality of the CORI dissemination policy which barred access to state criminal records by the Defense Investigative Services Agency. Although the suit had been filed long before the controversy erupted between Sargent and Richardson, the press juxtaposed the lawsuit and the Sargent letter and concluded that the suit was Richardson's retaliation for Sargent's refusal to participate in the NCIC/CCH. Nothing was further from the truth: Massachusetts did not have the technical capability to join the national system if they wanted to.

Nevertheless, Sargent decided to ride the wave of national publicity resulting from this fortuitous misinterpretation. Sargent capitalized on the Richardson lawsuit as a way to mobilize other state governors against the development of the NCIC/CCH. In September 1973, Governor Sargent solicited the support of other governors in a letter underscoring the privacy issue and states' rights implications of the development of a national CCH. While nearly one third of the governors responded to Sargent's plea by expressing serious concern about these developments, only a handful of governors actively joined the petition along with three congressmen, Senator Brooke and local civil liberties groups. Subsequently, when Sargent was not re-elected, the issue failed to sustain much interest in the National Governor's Conference despite continued efforts by Governor Raye of Iowa to keep it alive.

In addition to national exposure there were some immediate political and policy payoffs for Sargent. First, it made good political sense, for it gave him an opportunity to rob then Attorney General Quinn, a political rival for governor in 1974, of dramatic and useful issue. Also, it gave Sargent the opportunity to take new policy initiatives. He established a legislative commission on privacy and personal data to create a coherent state information policy. The efforts of the commission resulted in the substantial overhaul of a 1893 public records law and passage of a Fair Information Practices Act specifying uniform due process principles and management practices to be observed by all such legislation (Brant et al., 1981: 36).

Implementation and Reaction

Sargent was unable, however, to translate the enormous publicity from the Richardson affair, into a re-election victory in 1974. Michael Dukakis, a young Democrat, defeated Sargent on more pragmatic issues of concern to the state such as economic development and management effectiveness. The main problem that the Sargent defeat presented to CORI was the maintenance of continuity and continuation of momentum. Fortunately, Francis X. Bellotti, the newly elected Attorney General, was sympathetic and willing to provide the necessary support and continuity.

Therefore, Sargent's SPA director and Arthur Miller, continuing to advocate about criminal records issues, approached Dukakis about appointing Bellotti to chair the Criminal History Systems Board. In an initial meeting Dukakis reluctantly consented to the appointment, but his disinterest in the policy was evident. A former counsel to the Criminal History Systems Board at the time characterized Dukakis's attitude this way:

> Governor Dukakis was detail oriented; he was much more interested in hard management issues than doctrinaire, ideological ones. . . . He didn't want to use state funds to support the administration of the CORI act. . . . Dukakis's crimnial justice appointments were very politically motivated without regard for competence. His weakest cabinet appointment was the Commissioner of Probation. His appointment of Secretary of Public Safety was a man who could be manipulated—who wouldn't create trouble. Overall, he was disinterested in criminal justice and distanced himself from the entire area.

The imporance of Bellotti's role in saving CORI, on the other hand, could not be overstated:

> Bellotti took up the point when Sargent left. He was a front line advocate; CORI would have died had he not taken it. Bellotti had run a close race for Attorney General, in 1974, so everyone thought his appointments would be political but he made them instead on the basis of professionalism and commitment to issues. He gave staff a free hand to do things as long as they helped people.

Indeed, in creating a special privacy division, Bellotti brought Sargent's former policy staff along with him while appointing a civil liberties proponent to head the Security and Privacy Council. He also assigned a bright young attorney from the SPA staff as legal counsel for the CHSB in order to commence the development of implementing regulations.

As with the Washington experience, conflict and opposition to CORI did not really surface until the rule-making process got going in earnest nearly three years after passage. The Security and Privacy Council made regulatory recommendations considerably to the left of the more conservative and law enforcement dominated CHSB, putting Bellotti in an awkward position with the law enforcement community. Also, once the LEAA regulations were finalized it became clear to law enforcement that Massachusetts state policy went far *beyond* minimum federal guidelines. A former CHSB Council member characterized their reaction this way:

> The law enforcement community saw CORI as a thorn in their side. They saw it as imposing unilateral controls over their records but they had to accept them in order to get LEAA money. They felt for the first time that people from the liberal community were going to impose their policies on them and restrict the way they would use their records. One of their primary law enforcement weapons was being threatened.

The recollection of one member of the Security and Privacy Council (and chair from 1977 to 1978) showed how strikingly similar law enforcement opposition was in all four states. The rules for individual access were stubbornly opposed and the consequences of compliance extremely exaggerated. The civil liberties proponents won on the procedural issues while state and local law enforcement prevailed on technological ones as well as those involving certification of agency access. At one meeting, an assortment of some 440 criminal justice and quasi-investigatory agencies were all certified with little time for discussion. The Security and Privacy Council's obvious disenchantment with these results of rule making prompted one member to observe:

> I came to realize that although the civil liberties proclivities of state leaders is important and strong, there is a tendency to capitulate to law enforcemennt pressure. State law enforcement uses a cloak of ''state security'' just as effectively as does the President in invoking ''national security.''

CORI's overly broad definition of criminal history record information combined with its restrictive dissemination policies were particularly important strategic targets of the courts and press. The first confrontation between executives and courts emerged in a 1974 opinion by the state court requested by the legislature to determine whether the CHSB could proceed with the consolidation of state criminal records into a central state repository for the purposes of fulfilling CORI statutory objectives. The state court contended that executive branch control over electronic data processing in all branches, including the judiciary, would violate the separation of powers doctrine enunciated in the Massachusetts state constitution. But in a concilliatory, cooperative gesture, the state court did not preclude voluntary judicial participation in sharing data processing facilities, as long as it did not interfere with the internal functioning of the judicial branch.

Two years later, in 1976, Attorney General Bellotti skillfully engineered a ''statement of understanding'' to which the Commissioner of Probation, and Executive Secretary of the State Court agreed, defining the basis of voluntary cooperation. That agreement simply provided that the courts would maintain control over all dissemination of records internal to the courts, while it would observe CORI regulations with respect to external disseminations. Significantly, this agreement also enabled the court and probation commissioner to exercise sole responsibility for the maintenance and quality of their disposition records.

The next confrontation involved a conflict between the press and the executive branch over the CORI dissemination policy. In what was admittedly an oversight, CORI had made it impossible for the public or press to gain access to court records. This policy was inconsistent with LEAA regulations which had exempted all court records from dissemination restrictions in its 1976 regulations, so there was precedent supporting the press' challenge. In particular, the *New Bedford Times* was not happy with this disparity and brought a suit in 1977 challenging the definition of criminal records found in CORI.

The *New Bedford Times* case advanced two arguments to challenge the constitutionality of CORI: (1) that it violated the separation of powers doctrine by interfering with the internal recordkeeping function of the court; and (2) that it interfered with the paper's First Amendment right to publish criminal record information. The use of the separation of powers argument was unusual, but reflected silent collaboration with Probation Department officials. In Massachusetts the Probation Department has responsibility for court records and was not supportive of the CHSB assumption of control over court disposition records through the central state repository. As one observer put it: "It is likely that the Probation Department coached the *New Bedford Times* in putting together their case."

Anticipating a way to get the suit dropped by rendering the issue moot, CHSB officials quickly obtained a legislative amendment declaring court records maintained in *chronological listings* available for public access. This did not placate the publisher's concern and the suit went forward anyway, claiming that access to *alphabetical files* must also be unrestricted.

While the Superior Court ruled in favor of the newspaper, the Supreme Judicial Court reversed and remanded the case in March 1979. It was obvious that the statement of understanding reached three years before between the state court and the Attorney General Bellotti had strongly influenced the state court's decision. First, the state court held that the limits to access and dissemination of alphabetical files did not violate the separation of powers doctrine because they did not involve the *internal* functioning of the judicial branch, but rather pertained to policies regarding *external* use. As such, the court stressed that a prior agreement reached between the executive branch and state court had rendered the issue moot, and that the press did not have *standing* to bring an issue that was exclusively the court's prerogative.

Secondly, the state court denied that these limitations violated the freedom of the press. The court ruled that CORI acknowledges the need to balance individual privacy and the public right to know. Therefore, the court held that its obligation was to insure that the public have an opportunity to oversee the judicial process only while cases are pending:

> But with termination of the proceedings, the utility of the glare of publicity fades after the trial is over. After that, the interest of the individual in privacy rights weighs more heavily in the balance, particularly if an individual is not convicted. In case of conviction, that interest is reinforced by the public interest in rehabilitation (*New Bedford Times v. Clerk*, 1979: 116).

This ruling is in stark contrast to the California State Court's decision in *Loder* which weighed effective law enforcement more heavily in the balance.

While the case clearly shows the state court's strong philosophical support of the principles underpinning criminal records privacy, the legislative and executive erosion of CORI has continued nonetheless. Additional amendments to dissemination policy in 1977, for example, established a new category for release of criminal record information authorizing certification of agencies when the *public interest* in dissemination outweighed *privacy interests*. What is problematic about this amendment, as one observer points out, is how to identify what constitutes "compelling public interest" (Brant et al., 1981: 68–69). Although the Board and Council have attempted to develop standards to balance the competing values, these provisions remain vague and difficult to apply. Ironically, as a result of the 1977 amendments the Defense Investigative Agency—the controversial subject of the Sargent-Richardson lawsuit—was finally granted access to Massachusetts criminal record information.

Changes in state leadership and shifting public priorities have also contributed to increased bureaucratization of CORI and diversion from original statutory purposes. Governor King's term from 1978 to 1982 was an uneventful one for privacy. His appointments to public safety and especially to the CHSB and the Security and Privacy Council revealed a general disinterest in CORI. A positive action was taken to secure a full time executive director for CORI through a 1979 legislative amendment. But this decision was matched by a questionable one to move CORI from the Executive Office of Administration and Finance to the Executive Office of Public Safety. Clearly, with this change, state and local law enforcement interests have gained leverage over CORI denied to them in the past.

Dukakis's re-election as governor in 1982 also ushered in a renewed era of managerialism in state government. One of his campaign pledges was to finally operationalize a state criminal justice information system which had long languished because of unresolved jurisdictional and managerial conflicts between the CHSB, Commissioner of Probation and Commissioner of Public Safety. Ironically, however, CORI continues to be a law with sophisticated, cadillac type regulations governing a Model T information system because Dukakis has been unable to resolve these conflicts.

Almost inevitably, changes in executive leadership and shifts in public mood are bound to be expressed in the policy priorities of incumbents and neither Attorney General Bellotti nor Governor Sargent were immune from such forces. A former SPA director reflected on the evolution and change of the leadership and policy priorities this way:

> Attorney General Bellotti was interested in privacy at first but he lost interest because the issue just wasn't hot for him. At one time, it was a politically good place to be. He believed in privacy but it became a liability. For Sargent it was the right time, the right place. There was federal money and momentum but that died down and priorities had to change.

6

Understanding the State Implementation of Judicial and Legislative Policy

This study has sought to identify interests and factors which determine the politics of state implementation of federal policy in criminal justice and what that implies for an understanding of policy implementation processes. Chapter 2 presented a number of political factors likely to constrain the implementation of national criminal justice policies. These factors provide a means to explain variations in state performance because they allow us to theorize about the relative significance of the common conditions of effective implementation described in Chapter 1.

Briefly put, theories stressing the importance of statutory clarity and change emphasize the importance of conflicts over constitutional rights and cross-cutting policies and law enforcement practice to explain variations in state implementation. For example, as Chapter 3 intimates, organization and communications theories provide persuasive but incomplete explanations when focused on these factors alone because they fail to reflect the significance of elite responses and political culture in shaping outcomes. Utility theory finds more significance in the relationship between the extent of change and possibility of enforcement. Accordingly, factors such as beliefs about law enforcement practices and costs and benefits of compliance with institutional authority take on greater importance. Yet, explanations of implementation based on these factors alone overestimate the possibility of rationally estimating the costs and benefits of compliance and the actual incidence of policy impacts. Also, they exaggerate the capacity of implementers to anticipate the institutional consequences of decisions while underestimating the importance of conflicting beliefs implementers have about the legitimacy of originating and intervening policy sources in explaining outcomes.

Instead, when variations in state implementation result from a confluence of ideological, institutional, psychological factors, and political culture, an alternative explanation is needed which gives more attention to the role of state and local elites as they are reflected in conflicts over the separation of powers, federalism and governance. These factors accentuate the importance of power structural conflict and beliefs about the legitimacy of institutional authorities inherent in the implementation of intergovernmental policies advancing structural reform.

Our comparison of court and legislative policies suggests that the outcomes of public policy are products of multiple factors involving reciprocal relationships between originating institutions, state intermediaries and local implementers. The processes by which federal policy is translated into state policy and ultimate practice cannot be understood nor explained simply in terms of a hierarchical system, involving mechanical and abstract calculations of the relative utility of acceptance and adoption, or rejection and resistance or evasion. Nor is it the case that state elites' or implementers' responses and behavior result from cognitive impulses which result in adaptation to policy changes reconciling dissonance between beliefs and behavior. Rather, inconsistency is often an acceptable concession in order to avert unacceptable losses in institutional power.

Our focus on processes by which federal mandates are converted into state policy and practice suggests that state policy implementation is an important focus for explanatory theories of intergovernmental policy. Key factors and interests which affect responses to and outcomes of policies regulating the state administration of criminal justice may operate with similar influences and results in other policy arenas. Or, it may be that the criminal justice system exhibits structural relations which make it particularly resistant to change initiated by institutions *external* to the policy system. Consequently, the connection between our findings and studies of other policy systems must take into account the uniqueness of such institutional features and relationships in the attempt to generalize about American politics. Nevertheless, as Chapter 1 suggests, each policy system entails a particular configuration of power structural and institutional relationships which both limit and support the possibility of change.

This chapter concludes with an explanatory framework constructed to show how policy and institutional factors condition the responses and actions of state intermediaries in dealing with political constraints involved in the state implementation of national policy. Subsequently, Chapter 7 will advance a theory with which to explain the dynamics of policy change in criminal justice and examine what that implies for a more general understanding of the American political system.

EXPLAINING VARIATIONS IN STATE RESPONSE AND PERFORMANCE

An explanation which focuses on power structure and the institutional roles of state and local elites draws upon four important variables which have shaped the outcomes of national policy regulating criminal justice processes. They include (1) policy form or configuration, (2) beliefs and expectations of state elites and implementers, (3) interests and priorities of state executives, legislators and court justices, and (4) institutional structure and relationships. Each of these variables is described below as it encompasses the political constraints identified earlier.

Policy Form

This study shows that there are three dimensions of policy which may contribute to our ability to identify relationships between factors shaping implementation processes and outcomes. First, federal policy may define the *substantive* mandate and goals of the implementing organization by specifying the policy or program approach, treatment philosophy or rights and the specific kinds of services to be delivered or regulations to be enforced. Second, federal policy may influence the *structure* of an organization, for example by prescribing or attempting to change its location with respect to state or local government, its governance or decision making structure, the actual functions it performs, or its position within a policy system. Finally, federal policy may attempt to dictate or alter *procedural* aspects of how an organization performs, how routine tasks are conducted and discretion exercised in applying procedures to individual situations or clients.

Most studies seeking to explain the politics involved in implementation processes treat the substance of the policy as a *given* or unalterable feature of the context. However, as this study suggests, the policy which actually gets implemented is largely the product of the actions of state and local rather than federally mandating institutons. We have also found a problematic relationship between policy objectives enunciated by policy originators and the expectations of implementers. Therefore, it is misleading to assume that implementer's responses are governed largely by the clarity of policy or their understanding of its intent. Implementers may respond instead according to expected political consequences of implementation. Adaptive behavior resulting from such anticipatory reactions to the redistribution of power is largely the product of ongoing political relationships between institutions within a policy system.

Over the last two decades, federal criminal justice policy has been increasingly concerned to specify both structural and procedural characteristics of implementing organizations as well as the substantive approach. Thus, federal policy makers have expanded their intervention through mandates and conditions of aid which prescribe the structural and procedural means by which they expect policy to be implemented as well as the ends they desire to achieve. As I shall demonstrate in Chapter 7, these types of policies are not always carefully distinguished nor acknowledged by either policy originators or implementers. Nevertheless, they have important implications for the efficacy and legitimacy of policies designed to reform the criminal justice system.

Our analysis of criminal records privacy and Supreme Court civil liberties policies illustrates the importance of the procedural and structural dimensions of policy for understanding variations in state response and outcome. First, the *Miranda* decision did not really involve or implicate state courts in direct supervision of police practice. Therefore, consideration of state court organizational interests did not enter into the equation regarding an appropriate response. In the absence of potential role conflicts between adjudication and supervision, the state courts have been able in some states to avoid interference with police conduct.

Second, *Miranda* has been generally interpreted to apply only to police procedures. Therefore, the decision imposed constraints on police discretion but did not put them in a structural bind. Police and particularly prosecutors have discovered that the *Miranda* warnings have had only negligible effects on their ability to dispose of cases. Yet when state courts have chosen to increase prosecutorial responsibility for enforcement of *Miranda* rights by holding them liable for police errors, as in California and Colorado, then the possibilities of institutional conflict and change increase.

Mapp has involved much broader implications for the criminal justice system than *Miranda*. The ambiguity of the decision, combined with its attempt to draw police and courts into a closer supervisory relationship, has made it difficult for state courts to be consistent in their efforts to limit the impact of burgeoning Supreme Court search and seizure decisions. Unable to avoid infringing upon police practices, state courts have had to consider the effects of their post-*Mapp* decisions on their credibility, policy authority and ability to effectively supervise lower court and police behavior.

Thus, the exclusionary rule has created conditions conducive to structural conflict between state courts, trial courts and police with respect to organizational interests, loyalties, enforcement responsibilities and prevailing practice. The search and seizure decisions suggest that state courts are unable to reconcile their need to maintain their constitutional policy-making role with the desire to avoid making decisions which collide with trial court and law enforcement preferences. States such as California, seeking to reduce the reach of federal enforcement, have expanded their control over lower court behavior. Others, such as Massachusetts, have tried unsuccessfully to develop policies consistent with the spirit of the U.S. Supreme Court rulings without specifying the means of enforcement. Overall, state court attempts to limit the *Mapp* decision have still increased rather than limited their regulatory supervision over police practice.

The *Mapp* decision has set in motion a dialectic which has put police increasingly in a bind, while straining the capacity of the criminal justice system to effectively absorb its impact and evade its objectives. Perhaps it is these structural effects which account for the continued controversy over *Mapp* rather than the *Miranda* decision. *Mapp* has had the effect of spreading the burdens of compliance as well as the risks of resistance and evasion. In this respect, *Mapp* has drawn the components of the criminal justice system into interorganizational relationships which involve uncertainty and contradiction—where policies designed to limit the conduct of one organization may ultimately undermine the capacity of the others to absorb or deflect its central objectives.

We see similar forces at work in the implementation of federal criminal records policy, albeit with different structural consequences. The way that state courts have chosen to get involved in the state implementation of criminal records privacy is an important factor in explaining variations in state outcomes. The political benefits which accrue to state courts who successfully avoid separation of powers conflicts with state executives and legislatures over implementation of criminal records policy seem attractive and compelling (as occurred in California). However, as the Massachusetts case underscores, state court deference to executive prerogatives is no guarantee of effective enforcement if state executives fail to sustain a commitment to aggressive enforcement.

In contrast, the Washington and Colorado cases are good examples of the paradox of attempts to anticipate separation of powers conflicts by redistributing the burdens of implementation. For example, the efforts by the Colorado Supreme Court to steer clear of separation of powers conflicts has had the unanticipated consequence of forcing them to assume quasi-administrative authority. This has cast the state court in an overlapping policy-making role with state executives which it had consciously tried to avoid. In Washington unintended organizational consequences also ensue from successful state court avoidance of responsibility for implementation. Given the exemption of the state court from furnishing disposition information, police were forced into a bind. The way out involved two mutually reinforcing strategies: the capture of state regulatory authority by law enforcement and redistribution of responsibilities for implementation. In essence, conflicts over regulatory responsibilities in Washington resulted in some changes in organizational relations. Ironically, the collision over institutional roles and conflicting priorities between courts and police have worked in conjunction to achieve some of the agendas which neither LEAA nor the Washington SPA were able to accomplish.

Beliefs and Expectations

Our comparison of the policies also suggests that beliefs and expectations of state policy intermediaries, state and local criminal justice officials, and civil liberties groups bear an important relationship to outcomes. Ideological differences, predicated on preconceptions and projected images of law-enforcement practices, influence perceptions about the distribution of the responsibilities and burdens for implementation, the balance struck between defendants' rights, privacy and public safety, and efficacy of civil liberties groups in advancing reform agendas.

Differences between federal policy-makers and states reflect their underlying conceptions of routine criminal justice processes. One conception sees the search for truth impeded by the regulations and limitations placed by courts on interrogations, searches and criminal records because of the belief that police and prosecutors are primarily dependent upon these means to secure convictions. Another conception holds that due process and fairness are impeded by involuntary confessions, warrantless searches and inaccurate criminal records and that they are neither routine or indispensible to effective law enforcement.

The ambiguity of constitutional rights is one of the political factors discussed in Chapter 2 as an important constraint to implementing intergovernmental policies in criminal justice. Such ambiguities might help to explain differences between Warren and Burger court policies and account for variations in state court civil liberties policies. Similar arguments can be employed to explain variations in state criminal records privacy policies, given divided court and congressional policies.

Mapp seems afflicted by greater problems of ambiguity than *Miranda*. This problem has seemingly only worsened with Burger Court decisions, whose attempt to limit the exclusionary rule has increased uncertainty about constitutional principles governing its application. This has not precluded state courts such as Colorado from developing their own policies which avoid such ambiguities or inconsistencies.

State court policy in California and Washington illustrates the difficulty of trying to square competing conceptions of law enforcement projected in Supreme Court decisions involving constitutional rights. The California state court manifested its uncertainty about the incompatibility between its conception and that of the Supreme Court by cautiously citing parallel provisions of the state constitution to support the application of its search and seizure policy until confrontations with the U.S. Supreme Court forced it to end its equivocation in *Brisendine*. The ''doctrinal amnesia'' of the Washington state court in dutifully adopting Burger Court decisions increasingly at odds with its original policy foundations (stated in *Gibbons* and *Michaels*) underscores the importance of conflicting conceptions of the administration of criminal justice. The Washington state court's justification of independent state grounds in *Ringer* emphasizes how the continual erosion of *Mapp* by exceptions has clearly sanctioned the expansion of law enforcement practices inimical to the Fourth Amendment. In contrast, the Massachusetts Supreme Judicial Court has made it clear in *Sheppard* that it shares rather than rejects the Burger Court's underlying conception of effective law enforcement most recently stated in *Leon* (1984). Therefore, we find fewer restraints on police investigative practices in Massachusetts than in Washington.

Conflicts over constitutional policy can reflect underlying political differences between state courts and state and local criminal justice implementers. We see these differences expressed most clearly in confession and interrogation policy in Washington. Here police and prosecutors have considered the Burger Court rulings to provide greater clarity than their own state court rulings largely because they reinforce underlying conceptions of law enforcement practices. As Chapter 3 would lead us to expect, the consistency of state court interrogation policy with Burger Court directives seems the best indicator of state and local implementers' support for state court policies. For example, where state courts have remained within Burger Court post-*Miranda* policy boundaries (as in Washington and Colorado), there are few concerns about clarity. However, where the state court has adopted policy variations of its own, as in Massachusetts and California, then complaints by police and prosecutors about the ambiguity of state policies have surfaced because they trigger underlying conflicts involving divided loyalties and legitimation problems.

The state implementation of criminal records privacy regulations has occurred despite the lack of specific constitutional guidance. Federal and state court decisions interpreting due process and privacy rights exhibit a common caution in balancing these rights against the needs of effective law enforcement. This caution, however, has not prevented some state courts from reaching different conclusions about where that line should be drawn despite the Burger Court's unwillingness to acknowledge the privacy rights of criminal records subjects. In this respect, the contrast in decisions reached by Massachusetts in *New Bedford Times*, California in *Loder* and Colorado in *Davidson* illustrate the differences in organizational considerations which divide courts on the constitutional ramifications of legislative policy for criminal justice.

One additional point should be stressed in conjunction with our analysis of state implementation of criminal records privacy policy. Pluralist theory contends that policy ambiguity is a likely by-product of the bargaining and partisan mutual adjustment characteristic of legislative processes. Consequently, rule-making and implementaton continue a process by which a policy is further disaggregated to appease contending interest groups (Bardach, 1977).

In their study of school finance reform, Elmore and McLaughlin (1982) make clear their proclivities toward a view of politics as coalition-formation, bargaining and compromise. They contend that progress toward implementing *Serrano v. Priest* (1971)—the California school funding equalization decision—was possible *only* after the legislature was faced with competing proposals to equalize school financing. Result-oriented court decrees were not sufficient to achieve concrete results; policy change had to originate from the less than rational world of political action and compromise. The sub-optimal results of state legislative solutions to *Serrano* reflect the limits of the process. Therefore, the authors contend that state legislative solutions to *Serrano* reflect the limits of court reform. This conclusion, however, downplays the importance of separation of powers conflicts and the instrumental and significant rolcs of state court justices and state executives in establishing, through indifference and equivocation, a climate ripe for the interest group politics of piecemeal and inadequate solutions.

Similarly, the case studies presented here show that criminal records policies exhibiting the greatest clarity and specificity happen to be in those states (i.e., Massachusetts and Washington) using an independent agency or commission, which conducted rule-making processes accessible to and strongly influenced by contending interests. These cases illustrate that real interests are less likely to be suppressed under these conditions, smoking out specious arguments and imagined obstacles, and increasing the possibility of change. Importantly, however, in the absence of elite support, the integrity of rule-making processes is likely to be undermined or overwhelmed by law enforcement interests, as was the case in California and in Massachusetts and Washington after 1979.

The strength of civil liberties interests, facilitated by access to state legislative and rule-making processes, is by no means a sufficient condition to achieve policy success or institutional change. We have found evidence in Colorado of the relative disadvantage of civil liberties interest groups (i.e., ACLU) in attempting to achieve restrictions on the dissemination of criminal records. In addition, while the strength of the press as an interest group no doubt heavily influenced the policy which emerged in Colorado, the underlying political culture of accountability and open government increased the likelihood of the adoption of policies with few dissemination restrictions.

The other states' experiences seem to reinforce this idiosyncratic dimension of Colorado policy, for in those states the influence of the press was largely restricted to the legislative process with little effect on dissemination policy. Moreover, as the Massachusetts case makes clear, the press has been unable to exploit latent separation of powers conflicts between courts and executives to challenge dissemination restrictions precisely because that strategy underestimates the potential for the state courts and state executives to reach a compromise about the institutional distribution of power. Underlying state court support of privacy policy and willingness to defer to legislative supremacy in this policy area was an important factor in preventing the gutting of the privacy law. Further, as the Colorado state court is drawn more into the administration of criminal records privacy, it is unable to avoid accepting responsibility for the interpretation of and adjudication of conflicts over privacy policy. Therefore, the initial success of the press in limiting dissemination restrictions in Colorado may be a hollow victory given the prospect of having to defend its preferred policy on a case by case basis. Thus, the continued dominance of non-criminal justice interests in dissemination policy is likely to remain uncertain.

In contrast, controls placed on the dissemination and exchange of criminal records *between* law enforcement agencies appears most susceptible to evasion. Here interest group pressure seems least effective and oversight by state elites most necessary. State regulation of police information exchanges and record management processes appears most ineffective where there is executive indifference and state law enforcement control over administration and regulation. The California and Massachusetts case provide the most striking contrast in this regard.

The need to maintain effective public safety while avoiding undue discrimination is another consitutional rights issue which appears to have limited state implementation of national criminal justice policy. Competing conceptions of criminal justice distribute the burdens of implementation differently, striking a different balance between citizen rights and public safety. The "truth" conception minimizes regulatory controls while maximizing police and prosecutor discretion. The "due process" conception enlarges the responsibility for judicial supervision and controls the discretion of police and prosecutors in solving crimes. The "truth" conception shifts the burden of protecting or justifying observance of civil liberties and privacy rights to the accused. The due process conception puts the burden on the state to justify overriding citizens' expectations of constitutional rights in the interest of public safety.

As discussed in Chapter 2, Burger Court limitations on Warren Court civil liberties policies created the space within which conflicting images of routine law enforcement practice could be projected onto state policy making. The relative weight given to the protection of due process and privacy interests was formulated on the basis of crucial distinctions between routine and non-routine practices. State and local law enforcement interests presented an image of law enforcement work which maximized the adverse impact of the exclusionary rule, especially as it pertains to the enforcement of the warrant requirement. However, the images which are projected by law enforcement interests exaggerate the importance of unfettered searches which would actually magnify the social costs (i.e., discrimination) of rules which govern police contact with citizens. This was especially true when the state court espoused policies which were more expansive than federal policy.

The Washington case illustrates this phenomenon well given recent state court decisions at odds with local law enforcement preferences. In an expression of obvious disdain for the implications of *Ringer*, one prosecutor predicted that citizens involved in vehicle stops could expect to be detained for longer periods until a warrant could be obtained to validate a search. Assertions like this exaggerate the frequency of such stops compared to their actual incidence and have the potential of becoming self fulfilling prophesies. Such responses create uncertainty among policy-makers about precisely where the boundaries or routine law enforcement begin and end. They also cast doubt on whether the benefits of the policy are really worth the costs, thus shifting the burden of justification and policy consequences onto the state court.

When the state court fails to articulate unequivocal policies, reflecting reticence to sanction judicial misconduct in issuing warrants, it is not surprising to discover evidence of wide variations in performance and uncertainty among lower courts about how to deal with violations of the exclusionary rule. Thus, the Massachusetts state court used *Sheppard* to advance a conception of law enforcement practice contrary to the exclusionary rule as an unofficial policy guideline for police practice.

The efficacy of civil liberties interests is likely to be compromised when their strategies for reform rest on misconceptions of law enforcement based on misleading stereotypes. In particular, the attempts of these interests to insure observance of due process rights may be misplaced if designed primarily to change procedural practices rather than institutional structures which offer better prospects for reform. I will examine the sources of these misconceptions about reform in more depth in Chapter 7.

Civil liberties groups in most of the states we examined accentuated the due process dimensions of criminal records regulations because they believed that the inspection provisions constituted the strongest mechanism to secure enforcement and compliance. No doubt similar perceptions by police reinforced their views. On one hand, proponents of strengthened due process rights fully expected liberally construed procedures for record access to instigate needed reforms in record management practices. On the other hand, law enforcement steadfastly resisted these attempts, expecting such procedures to inundate law enforcement agencies with record requests and time consuming challenges and appeals.

The popular paradigm among students of criminal justice system which explains outcomes of policies regulating criminal justice in terms of the conflict between crime control and due process values (Packer, 1968) misses the extent to which justifying ideologies may deceive their proponents and mislead their opponents. Operating in tandum, these opposing perspectives justify beliefs and expectations about the possibilities and realities of change.The simplistic dichotomy of efficiency versus fairness locks participants in the comfort of appearances by establishing the boundaries of how the path toward reform is conceived and repudiated. Thereby the process of reform becomes a caricature in which the proponents and opponents of change act out their beliefs in self-fulfilling ways.

Cast in these terms, the conflict between opposing interests over state criminal record guidelines has had paradoxical results. Law enforcement interests in Washington and Massachusetts attempted to derail efforts to create burdensome guidelines imposing due process protections. But in the process they were drawn into an ever-widening spiral of interpretative regulations as a defense against having alternative interpretations of due process rights imposed upon them and as an offense to contain efforts to enlarge regulatory access to intelligence files. Also, the single-mindedness of civil liberties proponents in pursuing their goals all but obscured the path toward real reforms which lay in the improvement of the quality of records used in the entire criminal justice process. Unfortunately, record quality provisions are not self-enforcing but need elite support, permanent administrative mechanisms, enforcement and long term oversight.

Law enforcement's political agenda was revealed in other ways as well. Under pressure of potential court sanctions resulting from community activist pressure to end the collection and maintenance of information resulting from political surveillance, law enforcement interests in Washington were intent upon preserving discretion thought to be inherent in the investigative function. Therefore, they used criminal records privacy regulation as a tool to deny access to material accessible through public disclosure laws. When success in this effort was thwarted by an unfavorable state court opinion, police resorted to the one weapon that really mattered—evasion of provisions which regulated interdepartmental dissemination of investigative material.

These insights underscore the importance of the reality of appearances of law enforcement in constituting a political factor influencing the effectiveness of policy regulating criminal justice and their import for understanding the interests influential in the ultimate outcome of such reform efforts. Additional political realities, which unfold when examining issues of separation of powers, federalism and governance provide the space in which to further understand reasons for the gap between procedural compliance and institutional change.

The Interests and Priorities of Elected Officials

Another factor common to the policies compared in this study concerns the role of state elected officials. Federal policy originators attempted to increase the policy discretion and enforcement responsibilities of state policy intermediaries in all three policies. As a part of that alteration, elected officials were expected to initiate and enforce state implementation and compliance processes. However, there are significant variations in the degree to which state intermediaries assumed such responsibilities. This analysis suggests that responses of state officials are governed by their perception of the organizational interests at stake, policy priorities, and political consequences which adoption of federal policy may impose by disrupting existing state policy or practice.

State intermediaries are unlikely to treat federal regulatory policy with structural implications with a sense of urgency unless their organizational interests are directly threatened or advanced. Federal policies may alter the boundaries of institutional policy-making, creating the conditions in which organizational and jurisdictional conflicts are likely to emerge. But state official responses and actions are conditioned by the opportunities created and limits imposed by such alterations on state political culture. Federal policy may provide opportunities for expansion of the policy-making of state intermediaries while imposing new responsibilities and constraints which make that expansion politically unrealistic and unfeasible.

It is commonly argued that one of the reasons why the Supreme Court civil liberties decisions have been so controversial is that they involve the attempt by the Supreme Court to *legislate* policy. The *Miranda* decision is most often cited in this regard because of its positive prescriptions for police observance of suspects' and defendants' in-custody rights. Legislators claim that decisions such as these violate the separation of powers concept. They say that the court has overstepped its legitimate authority to adjudicate the constitutionality of law and robbed the Congress of its exclusive power to create statutes and regulations to achieve particular social and economic objectives.

Notwithstanding this theoretical distinction, it is not always easy in practice to determine when the boundaries are crossed between judicial and legislative prerogatives. *Mapp* is a case in point because, unlike *Miranda*, it largely prohibits rather than prescribes appropriate judicial and law enforcement behavior. Consequently, it is not precisely clear when the judiciary is merely setting forth rules to guide trial court procedure (a commonly acknowledged prerogative) and when its prescribing *substantive* goals to regulate and guide prosecutorial and police conduct.

Importantly, however, the way these questions about policy content are construed turns upon questions which go beyond judicial and legislative distinctons to conceptions about the desirable scope of intervention in criminal justice. What governs how issues pertaining to the separation of powers surface in the state implementation of federal policies depends upon the nature of on-going political relationships between courts, executives and legislators with respect to the acceptable boundaries of policy-making authority in the state political system.

In California, the attorney general and state court have been locked in ideological and political conflict over civil liberties policy for almost two decades. While differences over policy substance find open and continuous expression in thes disputes, they are insufficient to explain why these conflicts are *repeated.* For the political culture of the state reveals a long and colorful line of attorney generals including Pat Brown, Evelle Younger and George Deukmejian who have used the public visibility of conflicts with the state court to advance their gubernatorial ambitions.

In Massachusetts it is precisely the pressure toward consensus and absence of electoral political conflict between the state court, attorney general and governor which has stabilized the boundaries of institutional powers. Consensus and deference are accentuated while political conflicts are muted and suppressed. The fact that separation of powers conflicts in Colorado have been limited to the state court and legislature seems to be primarily a function of the greater political strength of the state District Attorneys Association compared to the office of the Attorney General. In Washington, separation of powers conflicts have been confined to state court-executive relationships with respect to state budget control and control over the LEAA program. Only more recently has the legislature been drawn into the conflict by police disaffection with recent state court decisions.

Similarly, the extent of judicial involvement in legislative-originated criminal records policies, and the efficacy of executive enforcement appears to turn less upon technical issues involving court organization and technological capacity than on the nature of on-going political relationships. This finding is consistent with Laudon's (1974) seminal study. As the Colorado case suggests, there is no absolute constitutional barrier to court involvement in a quasi-administrative and enforcement capacity if that role is dictated by political realities. But the courts can just as effectively maintain their distance from executive implementation of legislative mandates, as the Washington case demonstrates, when active involvement appears to undermine management control over state court functions. Moreover, there is no guarantee as the contrasting California and Massachusetts cases exemplify, that state court review upholding state executive authority will enhance rather than detract from state enforcement efforts.

State officials do not respond unilaterally to federal policy on the basis of self-interest or utility, nor exclusively in terms of organizational power. Their sense of priorities is influenced by the reactions of other elites, implementers, interest groups and the public, especially as expressed in electoral trends. State officials, whether state court justices, administrators or legislators, search for evidence of the ways in which federal policies are likely to reshape existing practices and might affect state political culture. Changes in response which occur over time reflect not just alterations in policy-making style and ideology of incumbents, but also are shaped by feedback and evaluation of the impact as well as efficacy of initial policy. Therefore, the policies which are sustained reflect the resolution of conflicting political forces which confront policies which attempt to alter the political and organizational status quo.

There are several examples from our cases of the importance of reciprocal political relationships between state officials as they are conditioned by interests affected by implementation. The influence of electoral politics on state court policy-making is most explicitly manifested in California. As noted before, the attorney general and state court have been continually at odds in their responses to U.S. Supreme Court civil liberties policy. This has put pressure on the state court to publicly justify policies which deviate from those favored by the attorney general. Also, it has transformed the re-election of some controversial state court incumbents (esp., Chief Justice Bird) into a plebiscite on state court activism.

Political considerations appear differently in Massachusetts, but are no less important in explaining policy outcomes. Instead of establishing its own identifiable variations from U.S. Supreme Court policy, the Supreme Judicial Court has expressed its political allegiance in dicta calculated to placate law enforcement criticism of state court decisions which officially go against them. In this regard, the *Sheppard* decision had the effect of energizing police evasion of the exclusionary rule guidelines, given the expectation that the current policy is unlikely to be enforced and that major Supreme Court policy revisions are forthcoming.

Political feedback can also reshape state court policy in more insidious ways by altering interpretive judgements of constitutional issues. One former Colorado state court judge, a pragmatist in style and ideological orientation, did not find it inconsistent to hold that the "good faith" exception was necessary to further distinguish the difference between "reasonable" and "unreasonable" searches while acknowledging that such exceptions were ultimately likely to undermine the exclusionary rule. What seems to have contributed to the apparent inconsistency was the fact that the state legisature had usurped the state court's authority to rule on issues of constitutional significance. The implication was that concerns about the exclusionary rule could be accommodated by the state court if the legislature let it exercise that responsibility. Therefore, inconsistency (and the potential cognitive dissonance which may result) is sometimes an acceptable and necessary price to pay to accommodate challenges to policy-making prerogatives.

Sometimes a state court can reap significant institutional advantages from its inherent leverage over the adjudication of issues involving challenges to the policy-making authority of other state intermediaries. The *New Bedford Times* case in Massachusetts undoubtedly was instrumental in effectuating an agreement between the Criminal History Systems Board chairman, Attorney General Bellotti and the state court with respect to the boundaries of their policy-making authority.

Political conflict was averted because each institution could retain its authority and prerogatives through cooperation rather than conflict. The state court clearly established its autonomy to control state judicial record management processes while the attorney general was able to buttress his authority to limit public access to criminal records.

Neither the civil liberties policies nor criminal records privacy has mobilized a supportive public constituency. Instead, affected publics are dominated and intensely divided by special interests which include the press. Consequently, the interests which do get served tend to be those involving issues which make only marginal change in policy and practice.

State executive involvement in national CCH policy has provided few incentives and posed many risks. Incentives for involvement could include electoral advantages from a highly visible and aggressive defense of the states' rights implications of privacy rights. However, the cost may include opposition by local law enforcement to state regulation and the rejection of corresponding responsibility for regulatory outcomes. Even if a state regulatory policy is successful, it may only further alienate local law enforcement interests, costing state executives future political support. For these reasons it has been much easier and less risky for state legislatures to adopt state policies observing federal criminal records guidelines than for executives to enforce them, because legislators are more insulated from the political costs associated with implementation and enforcement.

Variations in executive involvement in state policy development and implementation appear to be explained best by problems inherent in the attempt to legitimize policies with structural implications. While both Massachusetts and California enacted criminal records policy controls *prior* to the development of federal policy, the substance of the policies and involvement of state executives differed in fundamental respects. Governor Sargent exploited the states' rights ramifications and legitimacy of a national CCH, no doubt with ambitions for higher office in mind. However, while able to generate intense support from committed civil servants, Sargent failed to generate a significant electoral constituency supporting his anti-federal policies. What also contributed to his unsuccessful bid for a second term was the inability to effectively manage state government, which no doubt included the failure to operationalize a state CCH system and the inability to adopt and enforce regulations implementing CORI.

Governor Brown of California also exploited the issue of federalism and states rights posed by Title 28. But his motivations were very different from Sargent's. Brown sought a reduced federal presence by preventing implementation of costly conditions of aid with little apparent payoff. Besides that, the attorney general had already preempted the issue by assuming state policy and administrative control, so there were strong incentives to defer to the attorney general and thereby avoid needless political conflict with potential adverse electoral consequences.

In contrast, the Colorado and Washington cases involve instances in which legislative initiatives were taken in the face of state executive indifference. Like Governor Brown, Governor Lamm was strongly opposed to federal regulatory intrusions and thus was willing to defer to policies reached through the legislative politics of interest group compromise. It is not surprising therefore that the state law was shaped largely by criminal justice interests and the press, with no executive role in administrative enforcement. The Washington case differs in an important respect because liberal interests prevailed and the executive branch obtained administrative authority almost by default. What made this possible, in part, was a state court eager to shed unwanted administrative burdens (which Colorado courts have been unable to avoid) and legislative "fixers" eager to see the SPA evolve into a Department of Justice. In both these states the legislature could maintain policy control while avoiding the liability of responsibility for implementation and enforcement.

Institutional Structure

The extent to which policies get implemented is also dependent on the configuration of on-going institutional relationships within the policy system into which the policy is injected. These include the relationships between elites with respect to leadership, governance and enforcement roles. The differences in capacity of courts and legislatures to influence implementation processes stemming from inducement and sanction systems (as discussed in Chapter 1) underestimate the significance of a commitment to enforcement in securing change. Structural policies create a variety of opportunities for courts and legislatures to provide leadership and supervision which are not solely dependent on the creation of incentives or use of coercion.

Policies with structural dimensions are also likely to set in motion opposing forces that may result in some unintended changes as well as intended consequences. These forces are likely to be manifested in contradictory ways because of the "dual" nature of the criminal justice process. Therefore, criminal justice policy reforms are typically unable to achieve comprehensiveness because they rarely fully exhaust the projected images or anticipate the potential permutations of institutional relationships involved in the state response and implementation of national criminal justice policy.

The duality of the criminal justice system can be described in the following way. There is, on the one hand, a set of formal relations between components, constituted by differences in organizational structure, mission and function in the criminal justice process. On the other, there is an informal set of relations based on policy interdependence, competing conceptions of the system's goals (e.g., "due process" versus "truth"), and varying incentives. Consequently, informal institutional characteristics largely account for the "settled" character of criminal justice. Externally initiated reforms intended to alter the formal distribution of power, responsibility and authority of the elites to make and enforce public policy are likely to be rechanneled by the informal dimensions of the criminal justice system.

Nonetheless, it is difficult for state and local criminal justice officials to totally evade policies predicated on structural reform because they are likely to put pressure on interorganizational relations in the criminal justice system. Structural policies are likely to create such effects partly because of the functional interdependence of the components of the criminal justice system and its sensitivity to disruptions in power relations. As Dolbeare and Hammond (1971) noted in their study of state implementation of the U.S. Supreme Court school prayer decisions, "style issues" provide greater leverage to state elites and local level implementers to dictate responses largely because they do nothing to alter existing structures of power and preference.

As we have shown, structural policies have a different character: they seek to alter underlying patterns of power and preference making non-decisions (or non-responses) more transparent and some limited change nearly unavoidable. Where policies impose unequal burdens or disrupt power relations between organizations which must implement them, it is likely that the institutional elites affected will attempt to redress the imbalance and restore the political equilibrium.

In studies of sentencing policies others have noted the significance of anticipatory reactions to laws specifically designed to be broken (Bynum, 1982; Zalman, 1982). What they discovered is that laws predicated on some expected degree of resistance may be better able to achieve desired goals than those requiring universal compliance. Their studies show, for example, that determinant sentencing legislation designed to limit judicial discretion may actually increase prosecutorial discretion. Thus, leverage over case outcome is simply shifted from one set of officials to another rather than eliminating it altogether. As Zalman hypothesizes in his study of sentencing reform in Michigan, the legislature perceived this to be a desirable state of affairs because it feared that imposing a law with no options would exacerbate prison overcrowding. Thus, the legislature may have expected that the law would be enforced only when prosecutors intended it to be.

Without a doubt, the Warren and Burger courts advanced contrasting policies involving basic differences in due process protections along with fundamentally different notions about federal involvement and oversight of state policy making and supervisory functions. While there may be good reasons to have expected the Burger Court philosophy of new federalism to reduce tensions between state and federal courts and increase state discretion in substantive policy matters, such expectations have not been fulfilled. Instead, some state courts now face political challenges to their policy making authority which heretofore have gone uncontested (e.g., California and Colorado). Others face opposition to the exercise of their capacity to supervise or enforce policies, which heretofore have been underutilized (e.g., Washington). Certainly, emergent ideological differences between state courts and the Burger Court have helped precipitate these difficulties, but they do not fully explain them. For example, it is difficult to explain why there has been a substantial decline of local public support of state court authority in some states, under the Burger Court when all states have now re-acquired the autonomy they once had *before* the increased intervention by the Warren Court (Canon, 1977).

The state cases provide us with some clues. What we learn from the Washington case is that a "doctrinal amnesia" had set in *after* the state court had adopted its own forward-looking exclusionary rule in *Michaels* (1962). Evidently the Washington state court had been distracted by Burger Court expansions of exceptions to the warrant requirement, sidetracking them from fully realizing the institutional implications of their policy and thereby contributing to the atrophy of the state court's authority to enforce its prior policy. This no doubt created expectations among implementers that the state court had discarded its initial policy in favor of Burger Court policy. Now that the state court has decided to resurrect *Michaels* and the enforcement implications that go with it, its *authority* to do so is being questioned.

The politics of the Washington case can be distinguished from Massachusetts because the latter state court has never really articulated a coherent and identifiable state policy and, therefore, conflicts over its authority are only incipient. Examples from the other two states suggest similar discrepancies in authority and capacity at work in explaining governance conflicts. This suggests that there is a reciprocal relationship between state court authority and capacity to enforce. Thus the extent to which state courts are able to establish the credibility of their policy making role is directly dependent on their willingness to exercise their capacity to enforce state policy.

In addition, while state court structure alone does not predict supervisory roles or case outcomes, state court authority is enhanced to the extent that efforts to strengthen court organizational structure increase the strength and credibility of their leadership in state politics. We see this most clearly in Colorado with the greater uniformity of local trial court applications of state court policy.

Problems of governance also plague the implementation of a national CCH and uniform regulatory policy. There is no doubt that the FBI has the capacity to operate a national CCH, but it has lacked the authority to do so. But for the FBI to obtain Congressional authorization, thc Bureau must be willing to accept responsibility for enforcement of record quality and privacy protections. The FBI is reluctant to accept these responsibilities because of the inconsistency with its traditional collegial relationships with local law enforcement, likelihood of increased Congressional oversight over Bureau activities and imposition of legal liability for problems of record quality in state and local systems. Therefore, what has happened instead is the piecemeal expansion of the NCIC/CCH network in the absence of a coherent national policy.

Most state law enforcement agencies have also acquired the capacity to operate central repositories for local criminal records. In addition, most have statutory authority to regulate local record management practices and enforce dissemination policy. Yet this increased capacity remains tenuous because state law enforcement lacks the traditional basis necessary to establish its legitimacy to regulate local criminal justice processes.

The Washington and Colorado cases suggest that where state law enforcement regulatory authority did not exist *before* adoption of state criminal records policy, its authority is unlikely to be acknowledged. In states such as California and Massachusetts where regulatory power *preceded* federal policy, then that authority is likely to be considered legitimate, especially when state law enforcement has influenced legislative policy. But the fact that Massachusetts and California differ in the type of regulatory agency is not as significant as the willingness of Massachusetts to exercise its capacity of enforcement.

AN EXPLANATORY FRAMEWORK: RELATIONSHIPS AMONG VARIABLES INFLUENCING OUTCOMES

While it should be stressed that the four variables which have shaped policy outcomes are interdependent, each may be isolated diagramatically to depict their relationships. Figure 1 portrays the key relationships which are enumerated for a brief explanation.

Intergovernmental policy implementation processes begin with the creation of (1) the federal mandate, statute or court decision which involves substantive, procedural and/or structural policy change. Federal policy is not given but is subject to alteration through subsequent state policy development and implementation processes. The federal mandate is also injected into (2) an institutional structure which itself is constituted by fluid rather than fixed relationships. The criminal justice policy system is constituted by organizations which vary along structural lines and institutional roles involving a set of interdependent functional relations joined by a similar policy focus. The criminal justice system within a particular state is embedded in political culture. Informal beliefs and practices involved in criminal justice processes are not infinitely adaptable; attempts to absorb the intended consequences of policies, seeking change in formal institutional structures although displaced into informal relations, may nonetheless produce changes in beliefs and conduct both consistent with and at odds with intended policy goals.

These system features create the space for (3) conflicting and tentative perceptions among policy originators, intermediaries and recipients about the system configuration and their relative policy making authority. The expectations about the impacts of policies on institutional relationships generated by these competing conceptions are particularly uncertain, inconclusive and somewhat problematic. Policy originators must make assumptions about (or accept as "given") system features and institutional practices they seek to alter. Adaptations by policy implementers calculated to avoid the burdens of compliance may actually increase such responsibilities because such responses may be predicated on preconceptions about roles and institutional structures or on faulty expectations about the con-

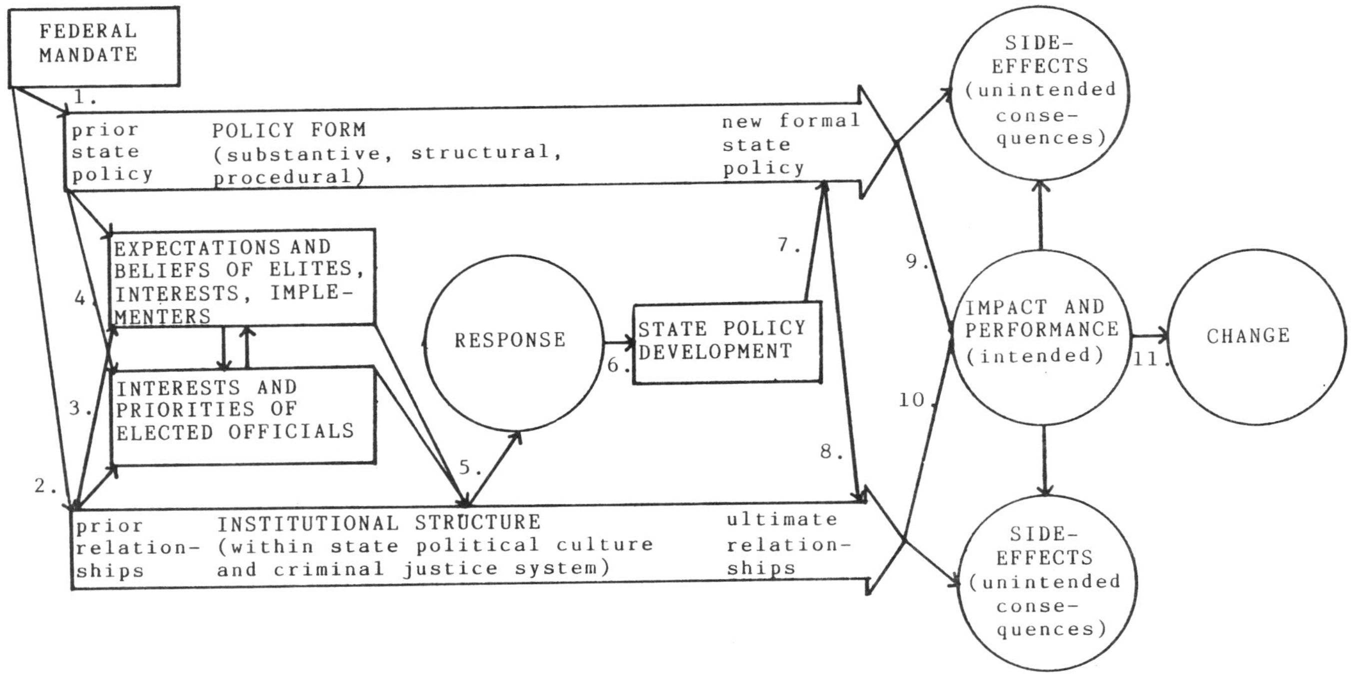

Figure 1. Explanatory Framework for Policy Implementation

sequences of the policy. Similarly, the burdens on defendants are likely to be increased if implementors are forced to accept policies which they believe to be wrong.

The conjunction therefore, of these policy and institutional factors may help crystallize the interests and priorities (4) reflected in state elected officials' responses to policy (5), and as they are later manifested in state policy (6). The interests and priorities of legislators, executives, bureaucrats and judges have a significant influence over how federal policy is translated into state policy. The power and preferences of state officials are unlikely to be imposed unilaterally but are conditioned by the constraints internal to the political culture.

The unevenness of authority and power relations between criminal justice components and the differential effects of policies regulating the administration of criminal justice set in motion an interactive process (5) in which criminal justice officials learn of each others responses, gauge the capacity, willingness and probability of support and enforcement and interact in ways which determine how the system will adjust to accommodate or absorb mandated change. This interactive process occurs through both formal and informal political channels involving consensus, conflict or both.

State policy development processes (6) both act as a catalyst, initiating a system response and reflect the refinement or evolution of a policy as refracted through behavioral, psychological and institutional factors. State policy development processes provide an arena within which to adjust the scope of the policy in terms of expected consequences. In this regard, it may take state courts as well as legislators a long time to provide policy guidance because of the incremental and indeterminate nature of litigation and bureaucratic guideline development processes. These evolving policies subsequently constitute the basis for formal policy as understood by its recipients (7).

Once the policies are adopted they must also withstand a test of public scrutiny (8). Legislative guidelines differ from state court rulings in that more extensive public review must be involved prior to adoption. In contrast, state court decisions are reviewable by the federal courts but that review must await litigation which challenges the policy only *after* it has been adopted. This institutional distinction, based as it is upon differences in susceptibility to environmental influences, may make little difference to policy substance and ultimate outcomes. For as our cases suggest, even when interests external to the criminal justice process are strategically positioned to influence policy development and oversight responsibilities, the advantage in subsequent implementation processes may shift to criminal justice organizations whose interests still prevail.

Finally, the impact and performance which result from the policy implementation processes described here will depend in part upon the characteristics of the federal policy and its state embodiment (9) and the way the institutional practices and interorganizational relations are altered or affected by the implementation of the policy (10). Ultimate change (11) is a long-term result dependent upon all of the foregoing relationships and the persistance of a policy in terms of altering behavior, beliefs, attitudes, and institutional structure, potentially recasting the contours of a state political culture. We now direct our analysis to these dimensions of change in order to show how a theory of legitimation enhances our understanding of the relationship of criminal justice policy to American politics.

7

Criminal Justice Policy and American Politics: Reform and the Dilemma of Legitimacy

It is now possible to draw together the strands of a theme begun in Chapter 1 into a general theory regarding the state implementation of regulatory policies intended to reform criminal justice and other policy systems and to address the implications for governance of the American political system.

In that chapter, I identified several difficulties in current versions of legitimation theory which must be addressed in order to strengthen its explanatory power and improve it as a guide to applied studies. Briefly, these problems include: (1) the inability to account for the apparent flexibility and responsiveness of the American political system to deal with social and economic problems through periodic critical elections which absorb disaffected constituencies; (2) the evident exaggeration of the importance of national policy-making institutions and underestimation of subnational differences in state political culture in explaining governance conflicts and the potential for institutional change; (3) the unexamined possibility that regime support can be undermined by conflicts over policies other than those involving economic problems such as symbolic morality issues or defendants' rights; and (4) the inability to account for the differential rather than unified effects that disaffection has on the level of support for national and state governmental institutions and their respective constitutional foundations. I will indicate how the findings of this study address and help resolve each of these issues.

One of the significant conclusions emerging from Chapter 6 is that federal policy originators can influence but are unable to control the state implementation of national policies regulating criminal justice processes. The *form* that federal policy takes has a profound influence on the ability of state elites to legitimate their policy choices and actions. More specifically, I will demonstrate the significance that structural policy has for legitimation theory by demonstrating how the contrasting styles and policy strategies employed by the Supreme Court and Congress contribute to an electoral cycle of reform and retrenchment.

I also identify important power-structural and institutional factors at work within the parameters of a state political culture which establish the threshold of change and determine how legitimation problems are likely to be handled. The susceptibility of states to federal policies will vary according to their political-cultural traditions and pre-existing configuration of institutional relationships. The nature and scope of legitimation problems that a state may face will depend upon the degree of elite consensus, compatibility of policy-making styles, the political resources available to justify policy-making authority and the exercise of enforcement responsibilities.

The upshot of this analysis of federal policy and state implementation contexts is that national policies with structural implications (e.g., separation of powers and federalism) tend to get displaced into state institutional conflicts over policy-making authority, capacity and substantive consequences. These conflicts tend to further disperse and fragment the authority and accountability of national and state elected officials while reinforcing the concentration of power and discretion of elites and implementers in policy subsystems.

The vulnerability of the intergovernmental policy system to problems of legitimation reveals paradoxical implications which are symptomatic of both the weaknesses of the ideology of liberal reform and limitations of accountability inherent in the American political system. These paradoxes are likely in a political system in which elite conflict over institutional leadership and policy-making authority overwhelms concern with the implementation and enforcement of controversial policies.

I will try to explain these paradoxes in the remainder of the chapter by showing first how psychological and behavioral factors interact in conflicts over criminal justice reforms to lock participants into a set of appearances which perpetuate the cycle of reform and retrenchment. Second, I will explain why the propensity of liberal reform to capitulate to the pressures of governmental withdrawal and retrenchment, with punitive crime policies, for example, is rooted in a profound ambivalence about the role of freedom in securing individual rights. Finally, I will show how the dilemma this withdrawal poses between sovereignty, rights and accountability is likely to enlarge judicial intervention in the governance of the American political system.

THE CYCLE OF REFORM AND RETRENCHMENT

One significant weakness of current versions of legitimation theory discussed in Chapter 1 is their inability to account for the apparent capacity of the American political system to respond to institutional conflicts and absorb disaffected constituencies. Key (1959), Burnham (1970) and others contend that recurring social and economic dislocations and tensions contribute to the breakup of dominent electoral conditions. They argue that critical or realigning elections are the primary instruments by which these tensions are managed and the sovereignty of its citizens preserved. Significant periods of realignment are generally considered to have followed the critical elections of 1800, 1828, 1860, 1896 and 1932. Electoral realignments typically involve changes or reversals in dominant partisan ideologies, the creation of new coalitions and a law-making majority which adopts policies consistent with its interests. Electoral realignments result in Presidential and Congressional collaboration to advance policies involving major changes in public policy. The Supreme Court reinforces the strength of the dominant majority by conferring legitimacy upon the policies enacted (Dahl, 1957).

Recent observers have challenged the premises and arguments used to support legitimation-conferring functions of the Supreme Court and critical elections in explanations of regime stability and responsiveness to public demands for policy and institutional change. Each of these challenges broadens our understanding of the underlying structural dynamics of American politics and policy processes while helping us to locate recurring features of legitimation problems in a cycle of reform and retrenchment. They demonstrate that the public has little knowledge of the judicial function of constitutional interpretation (Casey, 1974) nor of its major decisions (Dolbeare and Hammond, 1968). Most knowledge acquired by the public pertains to judicial decisions which overturn rather than support federal or state policies (Adamany, 1973) and the public shows only mixed support and confidence in the impartiality of the Supreme Court. In addition, support for the Court seems to be strongly correlated with the party affiliation of the incumbent President (Dolbeare and Hammond, 1968). These findings, plus those reached in this study, make it difficult to support the assertion that the Supreme Court primarily performs a legitimacy-conferring function in which those disfavored are reconciled to the policies of the majority coalition.

In a subsequent effort to further elaborate his thesis, Adamany (1980) suggests that we need not reconcile the conflicting appearances of court decisions seemingly delegitimating and legitimating the policies of governing majorities because the Supreme Court does both. Adamany has developed an intriguing explanation which assimilates both tendencies of Court policy-making into a cyclical theory of critical, electoral realignments.

Adamany concurs with Dahl's (1957) argument that the Supreme Court ultimately assumes partnership with the Presidential wing of the policy-making majority during long eras of stable rule, such as the post-New Deal era, thus legitimizing its policies. Nonetheless, he argues that the foundations of majority coalitions are increasingly de-stabilized by cross cutting issues, intra-party strife, and defections from party block voting on salient issues of partisan significance before Congress. This provides the Supreme Court with a leadership opportunity to address controversial issues that would otherwise prove to be divisive for other political elites. How the Court chooses to resolve such issues carries important implications for continued viability of the governing majority. If the Court's decisions and those of successive Presidents misread the drift of public opinion, the majority coalition will probably collapse, giving rise to an electoral realignment.

If, on the other hand, the Supreme Court decisions retain enough support for the governing majority by legitimating their policy approach, then a "converting election" will result (see Pomper, 1967). Such elections reshuffle long-standing party loyalties while maintaining control by the dominant majority over governmental policy. According to Adamany, examples of "converting elections" occurred in 1964 and 1968 which were characterized by massive sectional changes in traditional sources of support for the Democratic Party. Supreme Court decisions involving controversial issues such as school prayer, criminal procedure, abortion and integration (followed by substantial governmental policy intervention) which preceded the 1968 election contributed to abandonment of the Democratic Party in the South and increased electoral appeal of third party conservative candidates such as Alabama Governor George Wallace in other parts of the country. Nonetheless, the governing coalition remained intact, despite Nixon's election, to continue to sustain major social policy interventions. Although many observers now see signs of the breakup of the New Deal coalition and public support for its policies, there is little agreement as to whether a critical election with realigning consequences has occurred or is likely soon.

Given its present membership, it is doubtful that the Burger Court will advance policies which undertake any additional structural reforms which alter the prevailing mode of federal-state relations or increase the possibility of electoral realignment. Thus, while the philosophy of decentralization is likely to continue in the short run, a substantial change in the membership of the Court during Reagan's second term, combined with new national policy initiatives for economic renewal (e.g., industrial reorganization or the restructuring of the financial community through alteration of the powers of the Federal Reserve Board), could result in a re-nationalization of Supreme Court policy comparable in scope to the Warren Court initiatives. Under such circumstances the Court would be faced with adjudicating constitutional issues of fundamental significance to the economic and political order comparable with those faced by the Supreme Court during the Progressive Reform era.

An important catalyst in Adamany's theory, determining the prospects for whether de-stabilization of the governing coalition will result in realigning or converting elections, is the resolution of structural conflicts between the branches of government over regime norms (e.g., constitutional issues such as the separation of powers). Preceding electoral realignment, conflicts between elites over institutional structures and powers appear to establish the framework with which subsequent policies can emerge. These conflicts create centrifugal tendencies pulling the political system apart, because they involve issues pertaining to the separation of powers, federalism, and governance.

For example, during the post-1800 and 1828 realignments the Supreme Court's attempt to nationalize public policy conflicted with the state decentralization policies of the Jefferson and Jackson administrations. Conversely, the Court's attempt to support states' rights claims was undermined by the nationalizing policies of the Civil War and Reconstruction presidencies of Lincoln and Grant.

Separation of power issues were manifested in conflicts between the Court and President Jackson over use of the veto power as well as in conflicts over state and federal court jurisdiction involving Lincoln's suspension of the writ of habeas corpus. Differences over governance issues were accentuated with respect to the Court's challenge of Lincoln's power to impose a Reconstruction program on the South or in its attempted rollback of Roosevelt's New Deal programs.

The legitimacy-conferring functions which the theory of critical elections and realignment entails have also been significantly revised from another direction by Burnham (1981) and Kleppner (1982). Burnham contends that since the election of 1896 a new set of political and institutional relationships sponsored by the Progressive Reform era have emerged, contributing to a gradual process of erosion and delegitimation of parties and a demobilization of significant segments of the electorate. One upshot is that electoral processes conceal underlying institutional trends at odds with democratic representation. Another is that the bonds of identification with the political system through party affiliation and the legitimating functions of elections are gradually being broken.

Burnham traces the origins of party decomposition to the system of 1896 which resulted in the adoption and implementation of progressive reforms which undermined the possibility of forming stable partisan majorities. These reforms attempted to reconcile the evident groundswell for mass democracy with the drive for modernization undertaken by corporate technocratic elites (1981: 166). Reform which included direct primaries, registration laws, non-partisan elections, the initiative and referendum, and governmental consolidation rationalized politics at the expense of reducing two-party competition and fragmenting the electoral base.

Kleppner identifies some important underlying institutional changes resulting from the process of party disintegration and voter demobilization. His historical study shows how the traditional socialization and integration functions of party affiliation based on ethno-religious subculture, quasi-confessional partisanship and high turnout, climaxing during the Populist period (1870's to 1890's) were irreversably replaced by progressive reforms based on secular, technocratic values rooted in national rather than state and local perspectives (1982: 143–145). An additional important consequence of this was the demobilization of lower socio-economic classes as measured by declining electoral turnout (1982: 149).

Ironically, Republican party tactics of the past twenty years have favored demobilization strategies (e.g., changes in voting laws) calculated to erode the bases of traditional Democratic party strength. Moreover, Republican strategists have exploited the disaffection with government intervention and policies, which numerous single-issue interest groups represent, by emphasizing valence or life style issues such as abortion, crime, school prayer and criminal defendants' rights, to increase abstention or defection among traditional bases of Democratic Party support. Overall, these strategies have been successful in undermining the New Deal coalition but have failed to result in realignment (Phillips, 1982).

These deconstructive pressures have wrought institutional change including the centralization of policy-making, insulation of electoral elites, dealignment, and implementation of policies with a distinct professional, technocratic bias. Kleppner contends that the New Deal helped strengthen the penetrative capacity of bureaucracy with its ability to mobilize particularized clienteles in support of its policies. In fact, with the exception of the grassroots civil rights movement, Kleppner argues that policy initiatives of the last twenty years have been originated either by the judiciary or executive bureaucracy themselves (1982: 157–158). Studies by numerous observers substantiate the notion that a professionalization of reform based on the mobilization of temporary majorities of single-issue interests has replaced the politics of coalition building predicated on enduring partisan loyalties (see especially King, 1978), for a synthesis of views).

If these analyses are correct, then it is unlikely that the two-party framework of electoral politics alone is capable of reorganizing partisan loyalties and reintegrating disaffected citizens to support a new set of institutional priorities to address persistent economic and social dislocations. Instead, political conflicts are likely to be directed at the constitutional foundations of the political system.

Progressive and Regressive Change

The foregoing analysis provides an historical perspective with which we can determine the implications of our findings about policies intended to reform the administration of criminal justice for American politics. I contended at the beginning of Chapter 2 that the Warren Court civil liberties policies among others be understood as an effort to implement the New Deal policy reform agenda. Thus, the Warren Court strategy complemented the nationalization of federal policy initiated by the New Deal and renewed through the anti-poverty policies of the 1960's through conversion of economic inequalities into equality of political rights and uniform protection of civil liberties. I contend that, for the most part, these policies resulted in progressive institutional change. In contrast, the Burger Court and Congressional policies of crime control of the 1970's and early 1980's carry forward the substantive viewpoint of the post-1896 Progressive Reform era. The policies share a common strategy of decentralizing policy control in the attempt to strengthen management and enforcement capacities of state and local agencies. The common substantive theme is that of minimizing federal regulation and maximizing the discretion of state and local elected and administrative officials. On balance, these strategies and policies are having regressive institutional consequences.

Let me clarify what I mean by the terms progressive and regressive change so that we can better grasp their relationship to the notions of reform and retrenchment. The terms progressive and regressive are used to help characterize and appraise the values and interests embodied in policies and their institutional consequences. As such, they contribute to our understanding of the direction of change as the connotations of reform and retrenchment imply.

By *progressive* change I mean the maintenance or enhancement of technical or administrative capacity of implementing organizations along with the alteration of institutional relationships in a policy subsystem or national regime which results in greater representation or protection of the rights or interests of recipients most likely to be burdened or benefited by the policy and increased accountability of policy originators and implementers. In addition, this may entail changes in the beliefs and attitudes of the public, elites and/or organizational unit members. *Regressive* change is defined as the expansion of technical or administrative capacity of implementing organizations *without* compensating alterations either in officials' or the public's beliefs or attitudes or in institutional relationships in a policy subsystem or political order. Therefore, regressive change means that there is no improvement in representation or accountability.

Some other terms housed within these definitions require additional elaboration. *Policy system* here refers to a set of organizations involved in executing the same or related policies. A policy system is characterized by internal tensions among organizations distinguished by dissimilar structures and roles somewhat functionally interdependent, divided by an unequal distribution of authority, power, discretion and esteem of unit members. The policy system is joined by a common history and exhibits an evolving pattern of formal and informal institutional relationships. By *organizational structure* I mean the formal governance and management characteristics, staff composition, decision-making procedures, roles, tasks and routines involved in the execution of an organization's mission as well as informal beliefs, attitudes, goals and expectations. Therefore, changes in technical or administrative capacity require alteration in one or more of an organization's formal characteristics whereas changes in conduct require alteration of informal ones. (For a more detailed analysis of the politics of policy systems, see Dalton and Fitzpatrick, 1983; 1985).

Accountability refers to mechanisms of enforcement, oversight and independent evaluation which can result in periodic turnover of implementers as well as policy-makers. These mechanisms can consist of a variety of strategies which may include supervision, inducements and sanctions, appellate review, countervailing policy styles, and alterations in the burden of proof.

In contrast, *representativeness* pertains to the distribution of interests or rights advanced or burdened by a policy in terms of outputs as well as outcomes. Changes in the substantive focus of a policy can bring about alterations in the designation of organizations responsible for implementation or in the socioeconomic composition of target groups.

The Dynamics of Legitimation

There are four related levels of legitimation problems which elites and implementers may encounter in their attempt to adopt and implement national policies which entail substantial controversy and institutional change.

First, *conflicts* may arise among national elites or between national and state elites and local implementers (and/or consumers or secondary populations) because of differences over the desireability and consequences of the substantive, procedural or structural focus of public policies. Structural and substantive policies are more apt to produce conflicts with regime threatening implications than procedural policy. This is so because substantive policy typically redefines the rights and/or relationships among dominant and subordinate societal or economic interests. Structural policy attempts to alter institutional roles and positions which entail power redistributing consequences within policy subsystems or the political system.

In contrast, procedural policy is largely confined to the form of policy-making processes or the discretion of implementers. A combination of procedural and substantive policies together establishes the *potential* distribution of the burdens, benefits, responsibilities and opportunities of public policies among implementers and recipients. Structural policy helps determine the *actual* patterns of distribution which result from the implementation of policy. As we shall see, what is significant about conflicts over criminal justice policy is that they convert problems of social and economic inequality into political issues of rights, thus potentially rechanneling the expression of disaffection toward the constitutional foundations of the political system.

Second, a *deficit* in regime support is likely to arise if one or more of the elements of political stability are weakened by conflict. As discussed in Chapter 1, these elements include justification of authority and generation of support; personal identification with the political system; a distribution of interests served; a process for policy adoption, evaluation and change; and the capacity to implement and enforce policy. Persistent conflicts over substantive policy issues contribute to the weakening of mechanisms of identification (e.g., party affiliation) and gravitate around the interests benefited or disadvantaged by the policies. Disputes over procedural policy issues are typically focused on the processes by which regime values and public policies are adopted, changed and evaluated. In contrast, conflicts over structural policy affect the mechanisms by which authority is justified, support generated and the capacity of governmental institutions used to implement public policies. The weakening of these latter mechanisms of support contributes to the depletion or withdrawal of the resources necessary for elites to justify and enforce their policies.

Third, deficits in regime legitimacy do not necessarily result in crises which threaten the stability of the political system. The weakening of some of the elements of stability may be *compensated* by the strengthening of others. This is particularly so with respect to substantive or procedural conflicts. For example, the weakening of participation in the political system which the decline of party affiliation poses may be offset temporarily by the organization of single-issue interest groups which attempt to gain a more favorable distribution of burdens and benefits of public policies. In contrast, the effects of structural conflicts on political stability are potentially more problematic because they threaten to undermine regime values and the basis of support for authority. It is my contention that legitimation crises are usually averted because conflicts between national, institutional elites over structural issues, (e.g., separation of powers and federalism) tend to get *displaced* into conflicts between state elites over their policy-making authority, capacity and the distributive consequences of their policies. This has the negative effect of reinforcing the dispersal and fragmentation of the authority of national and state elected officials while further concentrating the power, discretion and control that administrative elites exercise over policy subsystems.

Finally, a legitimation *crisis* is likely to occur when the contradiction between regime values and norms, institutional processes, and policy consequences becomes transparent to and opposed by significant segments of elites and the public. A crisis can be averted through additional compensating displacements; lead to fundamental alterations in regime values (e.g., constitutional framework); involve basic changes in institutional power and individual rights; or result in revolutionary change.

The historical analysis of the implementation of judicial and Congressional privacy policies presented in this book effectively illustrates these dynamics of legitimation. The Warren Court generally sought to advance the values, interests and aspirations represented by the policy coalition of the post-New Deal era (i.e., unions, poor, blacks, liberal intellectuals, and small businessmen). But it lacked a sufficient or self-evident Constitutional or institutional justification of authority to do so. On the one hand, the Warren Court was laboring against a well-entrenched judicial conservatism which held that the Court must defer to Congress with respect to issues and policy pertaining to economic rights (see Shapiro, 1978b). On the other, the Warren Court inherited a judicial policy originating with the Progressive Reform era which interpreted the Fourteenth Amendment due process clause narrowly to limit federal regulation of state business and governmental activities (Paul, 1960: 235–236).

The Warren Court's strategy to overcome the first constraint involved the conversion of economic rights into civil rights through the development of the "preferred position" doctrine first articulated by Justice Stone in 1938 (Shapiro, 1978b: 190–194). This doctrine consisted of review of underlying civil liberties issues concerning equal protection and due process in such areas as employment, school prayer, integration and the rights of indigent criminal defendants. This had the effect, for example, of triggering strict construction of statutes on cases falling under "suspect" racial classifications (e.g., *Brown*, 1954) and conferred automatic standing on criminal defendants to challenge the admissibility of evidence obtained through police searches (see *Jones v. U.S.*, 1958, in Chapter 2). The ultimate objective of this doctrine was unmistakably clear: the removal of institutional constraints inhibiting the aspirations of some citizens for equal opportunities, the right to free expression and expectation of due process protections. Accordingly, the states had to demonstrate that a "compelling necessity" justified intervention which overrides these interests and claims.

The route by which the Warren Court overcame the constraining application of the due process clause of the Fourteenth Amendment was to employ the ''selective incorporation'' doctrine (Funston, 1977: 137–141). This doctrine held that the states must meet the same standards under a given provision of the Bill of Rights as were required of the federal government. The first significant test of this doctrine with respect to criminal defendants' rights came with the *Wolf* (1949) and especially *Mapp* (1961) decisions, subsequently followed by others including *Gideon* (1963) and *Miranda* (1966). What ''selective incorporation'' achieved was a gradual federalization of the Bill of Rights. Many state courts resisted this federalization process because of its refusal to judge separately the ''fundamental fairness'' of each state's standards (Funston, 1977: 139–140).

What contributed to the controversy surrounding these substantive and procedural doctrines was the Warren Court's policy of federalism adopted to implement and enforce the policies advanced under these doctrines. Expansion of federal injunctive relief with civil rights (*Brown*, 1954) and reapportionment (*Reynolds*, 1964), and the enlargement of federal court jurisdiction over state court criminal procedures through expansion of habeas corpus relief, established in the *Brown* (1953), *Fay* (1963) and *Townsend* (1963) decisions, greatly expanded the Court's capacity to enforce its decisions. Therefore, while public controversy centered largely on substantive issues (e.g., racial equality and defendants' rights), national and state elites (especially state court judges) were locked in conflict over structural issues pertaining to the separation of powers, federalism and, especially, governance.

The significance of the governance implications (i.e., authority and capacity) of these changes became clear only after the Warren Court decided *Mapp*. In contrast, the *Miranda* decision marks a later stage in Warren Court policy making whereby a preoccupation with proceduralism displaced its earlier structural emphasis. For, as Chapter 3 demonstrates, *Mapp* put many state courts in one of two awkward positions. State courts with pre-existing but under-enforced policies would now face potential reversal by federal courts if they continued to observe the procedural form rather than the substance of federal policy. State courts facing adoption for the first time were now confronted with the possibility of having to justify their authority to intervene and supervise the criminal justice process in unprecedented ways. Consequently, many state courts have, in fact, seized their new authority openly through invocation of state constitutional grounds to gain their independence from federal and Supreme Court appellate review. Some courts have also instituted new forms of enforcement and supervision of police and prosecutorial conduct. Significantly, there is little evidence that *Miranda* has had similar consequences.

These policies have also set into motion further changes in judicial roles as well as organizational capacity which the Burger Court is finding difficult to reverse. Though evidence of this kind is not sufficient to pronounce *Mapp* or other changes in federal court jurisdiction a success, it does suggest that Warren Court policies made it difficult for state courts to avoid implementing structural changes which increased their accountability while enhancing representation of the interests in civil liberties protections.

The criminal procedure and other decisions made by the Burger Court have been guided and shaped by the political philosophy of the "New Federalism" ushered in by the Nixon Administration and have moved toward a laissez-faire economic philosophy. In theory the principles of state decentralization and deregulation are not inconsistent with progressive change as I have defined it. However, there is an unmistakable tendency for managerial and disciplinary strategies to either overwhelm or be substituted for efforts to increase accountability of elected officials or to enlarge citizens' rights.

With the election of Nixon on a law and order platform, the Burger Court perceived the emergence of a new consituency of middle Americans fearful of crime, resentful of the growing dependence of some groups on government assistance, and critical of liberalization of criminal defendants' rights. Consequently, the Burger Court has refused to sustain the Warren Court notion (and New Deal philosophy) that economic welfare is a fundamental right or that poverty or race are necessarily "suspect" categories (see especially Bennett, 1983; Shapiro, 1978a). Moreover, the Burger Court's decisions pertaining to the rights of organized labor have shown signs of a willingness to erode the power of unions and the rights of their membership (St. Antoine, 1983).

The Court has capitalized on the fear of crime by positing the connection between the rise in crime and the loss of police discretion. For the Burger Court contends, as demonstrated in Chapter 2, that the exclusionary rule has undermined public safety at the same time as it has failed to deter police misconduct. Therefore, the Burger Court has been anxious to restore a balance between the costs of increased crime and the risks of violating individual rights. The "truth" conception of justice which underlies this policy strategy lends itself to utilitarian reasoning and justification. It does so by intimating that the tradeoff which confronts us is between enabling the factually guilty to go free and allowing the police to decide when the observance of civil liberties constitutes a threat to public safety. This preserves the discretion, judgement and preferences of criminal justice officials by overriding the legitimacy of presumption of innocence and claim to due process.

To be sure, the Burger Court's arrival at this position has been gradual and marked by policy inconsistencies. In addition, it has had to overcome some structural constraints imposed by the Warren Court in order to implement a philosophy of state decentralization. Although the Warren Court changes in federal court jurisdiction have been reversed with relative ease, state court policy making has become increasingly independent from the influence of the Supreme Court as well as more vulnerable to legitimation conflicts.

Initially, the Burger Court attempted to redress the perceived imbalance between effective law enforcement and individual rights resulting from the exclusionary rule through its principle of "reasonableness" of the expectation of privacy. As Chapter 2 and the case studies demonstrate, the application of doctrine through the sliding scale of cost and benefit has proven to be too ambiguous and poorly equipped to achieve consistent judicial decisions. Consequently, it has prompted many state courts to give up the attempt to reconcile operational inconsistencies in favor of an unequivocal policy toward the use of search warrants, as has been the case in Colorado and Washington. More recently, however, the Burger Court's disenchantment with the "reasonableness" standard in effectuating its policy goals was manifested in the adoption of the "good faith" and "public safety" exceptions in *Leon* (1984) and *Quarles* (1984). These decisions have importance not only for the warrant requirement and custodial interrogation but involve the potential redistribution of policy making authority within the criminal justice system.

These new policies have been no less controversial than the "reasonableness" standard, as our cases suggest, for they have become a focal point of conflict between the Washington and Colorado state courts and the Supreme Court, although for different political reasons. What is crucially significant about this latest phase of Burger Court civil liberties policy is its near refusal to establish rules guiding the conduct of law enforcement activity. But this strategy conceals an important form of power. For, as Shapiro perceptively contends,

> Indeed, in a sense the refusal to make rules is the refusal to delegate since the subordinate unguided by rules can hardly make authoritative decisions. The disadvantage of the refusal to make rules is obviously that the work load of the top echelons is increased. Unlegitimized by rules, subordinate decisions can be challenged and appealed to the top more frequently. The advantage is that, unbound even by its own previous rules and in receipt of a large number of appeals, the top decision maker increases the area in which he can exercize his own discretion. Is a court any less activist that maximizes its discretion than one that maximizes its rule-making? (1978b: 206).

In fact, this may be one of the more realistic ways, short of additional changes in state court jurisdiction over federal, constitutional issues, by which the Burger Court can retain national policy leadership in the face of further state decentralization of policy-making authority.

Surely the shrewdest and more politically successful element of the Burger Court retrenchment has been the contraction of federal court jurisdiction to review state court decisions. No state court, no matter how liberal, was content with the prospect of federal court oversight of its decision making prerogatives. As early as 1972 in *Picard v. Connor* the Burger Court interpreted a 1966 Congressional statute sponsored by the Judicial Conference which modified the habeas corpus rule to mean that state findings would be presumed to be correct unless defects in the proceedings were demonstrated. Thus, when *Stone v. Powell* was decided in 1976, state courts had already enjoyed a diminished federal court presence, allowing them to reclaim their sovereignty to formulate civil liberties and other policies.

Nevertheless, state courts have not perceived this new freedom in the same terms nor necessarily subscribed to the new substantive conservative style practiced by the Burger Court. Instead, many state courts have perceived a decline in Supreme Court legitimacy resulting from its unwillingness to provide progressive leadership regarding issues of constitutional significance. Therefore, some state courts have advanced more progressive policies, many have maintained Warren Court policies, and some have followed the policy directives of the Burger Court. Thus, state decentralization has had the effect of causing the Burger Court to forfeit direct leverage over state court policy.

The observations of a former Colorado state court justice underscore the importance of understanding increased state court independence in the context of legitimation. When asked why many state courts have refused the Burger Court's invitation to weaken criminal defendants' rights, he attributed this trend to a historical decline in respect and authority:

> The philosophy used to be in judicial decision making that if the U.S. Supreme Court interpreted a provision of a statute in some federal areas in a certain way, that was because it was the Supreme Court. Great weight was given it by the lower courts. The Supreme Court doesn't have that kind of authority—that kind of respect they had before. . . . The Supreme Court's interpretation of various laws and the Constitution has no greater effect on interpretation of state statutes by the state courts. We are all in the same ball park now. That aura that emanated from the U.S. Supreme Court is no longer there.

However, despite these appearances of freedom under the new federalism, many state courts face new dilemmas of legitimacy because Burger Court substantive conservatism poses new and more insidious threats which promise to rob progressive state courts of their authority and capacity to continue to advance policies inconsistent with those of the Supreme Court. The onus of the Burger Court policies lies not so much in its obvious preference to deregulate police discretion as in its profound alteration of the terms within which constitutional rights are being disputed. The "truth" perspective puts the burden on the proponents of civil liberties protections to justify departures from the public safety standard. In essense, this requires civil liberties advocates to distinguish between routine and non-routine law enforcement practices. This new framework poses some potential dangers as well as opportunities for progressive reform.

First, the utilitarian mode of reasoning that the "truth" perspective incorporates robs liberals of the ability to find a place for rights which is not in continuous danger of being overridden by the necessity of law enforcement exigencies. Thus, some other principle must be employed which is capable of putting rights on a stronger footing without capitulating to an absolutist position. Although legal scholars and philosophers such as Dworkin (1977) and Parfait (1984) have sketched frameworks for principled reasoning about the rights of persons, there is little evidence of their influence on judicial opinions and decision making. Therefore, as long as liberal reformers make the case for rights in the framework of utility we can probably expect the continued erosion of civil liberties guarantees.

Second, the new framework of decision making fashioned by the Burger Court may increase the opportunity for some state courts to reconcile discrepant positions they have taken on matters concerning effective law enforcement. For example, the California state court has formulated somewhat inconsistent positions on public safety issues in its civil liberties and privacy policies, as Chapter 4 illustrates. The state court has supported the priority of administrative necessity and public protection against the threat of recidivism over that of privacy protection for holders of criminal records. Yet in its civil liberties decisions the state court has embarked upon a detailed structuring of almost every significant dimension of police discretionary contact with suspects and defendants. In contrast, the Washington and Colorado state courts have exhibited greater sensitivity in trying to establish a coherent image of law enforcement routine underlying their constitutional rights policies. To be sure, these variations in consistency are dictated by the different political and institutional circumstances of each state. Nonetheless, where such discrepancies persist, they undermine the formulation of a coherent and effective rights doctrine.

Finally, recent Burger Court decisions such as *Leon* (1984) provide the opportunity for state courts to substantially alter the way that reform might be conceived by reformulating the responsibilities of courts and prosecutors in the administration of criminal justice. The *Leon* decision offers just such an opportunity for it will necessitate the establishment of explicit standards of judicial conduct in the issuance of warrants and require prosecutors to establish the parameters of routine law enforcement practices, especially when it is claimed that public safety hangs in the balance. Moreover, as Chapter 6 suggests, the consequences of structural policies such as *Mapp* cannot be clearly foreseen nor anticipated so it is just not as self-evident as Justices Brennan and Marshall lament ''that the court's victory over the Fourth Amendment is complete'' (*Leon*, 1984: 1).

We see similar conflicts unfolding in the development of the national CCH and evolution of congressional policy to regulate the exchange of criminal history records. In 1970 the FBI was on the verge of implementing a national CCH, lacking in privacy protections and record quality regulations. The *Menard* decision halted further progress in that regard. First, the decision prompted the fledgling LEAA program to embark on an ambitious program to stimulate and underwrite informational technological reforms in criminal justice. However, weaknesses in the enforcement of standards combined with the over-development of law enforcement information systems compared with prosecutorial and especially judicial systems has slowed the development of a national system. This has had significant adverse side effects such as police overdependence on inaccurate and incomplete criminal records. Moreover, LEAA has been unable to reconcile organizational and intergovernmental conflicts necessary for cooperative informational relationships between criminal justice components and has failed to increase elected officials' knowledge of and involvement in the oversight and supervision of local, state and national systems.

The federal court decision also precipitated Congressional debate about gaps in FBI authority and the need to develop a national regulatory policy *prior* to the development of a national CCH. The limited consensus Congress was able to achieve produced a mandate which gave LEAA substantial discretion to adopt regulations implementing a uniform national policy. However, a uniform policy did not emerge primarily because the new federalism dictated that LEAA produce only minimum guidelines, giving the states maximum discretion to develop state policies best suited to their needs and circumstances. The protracted federal and state rule-making processes reveal that LEAA was ill-equipped to deal with the forces opposing uniform standards because it was unable to control the political processes and environment within which state policies are adopted.

Although LEAA intervention successfully resolved one of the most problematic institutional conflicts involving the separation of powers by exempting courts from executive regulation and influence, court and executive conflicts have not subsided. In addition, the responsibilities and discretion which LEAA conferred on governors to launch policy development processes has had mixed results. Very few governors seized the initiative to create new regulatory agencies while most deferred to state law enforcement interests. Yet the expansion of state law enforcement's regulatory involvement has not resolved governance issues regarding the legitimacy of its authority despite its increased capacity to enforce record management and dissemination guidelines. Therefore, what we continue to find in most states is the persistence of indifference, uncertainty, and institutional deadlocks over separation of powers and governance issues.

With the termination of the LEAA program in 1982, the states have had few incentives to continue to develop and implement state policy. In the face of federal withdrawal, state and federal courts reluctantly but inevitably have had to assume some oversight and/or enforcement responsibilities. Moreover, new national political forces are at work to consummate the development of a CCH network despite the lack of a uniform regulatory policy and unresolved federal and state governance issues. Of course, Congress has the opportunity to overcome these political constraints but success seems unlikely, especially when the states have now developed policies which serve the interests of state and local law enforcement.

The Threshold of Change and State Dilemmas of Legitimacy

The foregoing analysis suggests that federal policy establishes a framework within which the state implementation of national policies occurs. Structural policies in particular appear to influence the ability of state officials to legitimate their substantive policy preferences. Yet state officials do have extensive leverage over state policy responses. Current versions of legitimation theory fail to deal with the significance of subnational influences in explaining how institutional change occurs despite political conflict and instability.

These seemingly contradictory findings raise some additional questions: What features of state political systems make them susceptible to federal influence, and what accounts for the direction in which change occurs as a result of state responses to federal policy? Why have some states' policies, for example, resulted in progressive change while others' have been regressive? Why have some states avoided legitimation crises while others have not? And how should we assess the implications for American politics? The idea of political culture provides some important clues to answering these additional questions concerning legitimation and change.

A complex feature of state policy making, undoubtedly influencing the threshold and direction of change that federal policy intervention will take in a given state, is that of political culture. Although difficult to define in precise terms, a political culture appears to integrate conflicting values and interests and stabilize the processes by which conflicts over policy and institutional power are resolved (see literature references in Introduction). In essence, a political culture establishes among other things a set of expectations about the functions of governmental institutions which constitute resources upon which political elites can draw to legitimize their policies.

First, it provides a relative coherence to a set of competing political values and traditions (i.e., authority, participation, procedural compromise, leadership, accountability, sovereignty, and so forth) by assigning or ordering their priority in an institutional context. In this regard, in states such as Massachusetts, participation, compromise and consensus processes may be given greater weight than the values of sovereignty or accountability found in Colorado. In contrast, the citizens of California may expect institutional elites such as the governor and the attorney general to provide strong leadership and authority in expressing majority sentiments, sometimes at odds with the protection of individual rights.

Second, a political culture helps establish, in part, the boundaries within which policy making authority is distributed among and exercised by institutional elites. These boundaries reflect shared beliefs and expectations about appropriate roles and capacities of governmental institutions in policy making and governance processes. For example, in Colorado, replacement of electoral selection of judges by merit appointment undoubtedly reflects the belief that judicial decisions should be shielded from political influences and that they should be confined to technical and procedural rather than substantive political views. Or consider the differences between gubernatorial roles revealed in a comparison of California and Massachusetts with Washington and Colorado. In the former states, the governor is expected to exercise strong policy leadership and management control over the state bureaucracy while the role of governor in the latter states is limited to traditional party brokerage. When institutional elites overstep these established boundaries, power conflicts are likely to ensue.

Finally, state political culture provides an important linkage to institutional legitimacy by establishing the basis for citizens to *identify* with the existing authority of institutional elites and accept policy outcomes. The bonds of identification are strong when there is a high degree of diversity and tolerance, participation in governmental affairs is extensive and partisan politics structures elite behavior and public policy. (See Elazar, 1972; Litt, 1965; and Patterson, 1968).

Problems of legitimacy are likely to arise for state institutional elites involved in implementation of federal policy because they are often placed in a political bind. Federal policies with structural implications tend to have this consequence because of the dilemmas they pose for state elites. The way state elites choose to respond to federal policies involving institutional change entails the risk of depleting the resources available for the continued legitimation of their authority. Salient features of ongoing institutional relations likely to conserve or deplete the availability of the resources of legitimacy include (although not limited to) the extent of elite support or reinforcement, the scope and extent of differences in policy making styles and enforcement mechanisms.

Let us return to the cases to see how differences in the availability of the resources of legitimacy in a state political culture help account for variations between states with regard to the direction of change and the type of legitimation problems they face. First, there are substantial differences in initial responses and eventual outcomes in the way each state implemented the civil liberties and criminal records privacy policies. For example, California and Massachusetts started at polar extremes in terms of response to the two policies. Where Massachusetts has been progressive in criminal records and conservative in civil liberties, the opposite pattern applies in California.

Second, the implementation of the civil liberties and privacy policies has clearly resulted in progressive change in some states while regressive in others, with Massachusetts' civil liberties policy showing little change one way or the other. For example, change in criminal records privacy policy in Washington clearly appears to be regressive since 1979, while that in Colorado shows signs of being progressive. In contrast, examples of states now experiencing regressive change in civil liberties would be California and to a lesser extent Colorado, while Washington shows signs of progressive change.

The tendency of California politics to closely parallel, if not anticipate, national political trends makes it peculiarly sensitive to changes in federal policy. This is particularly so because the state provides an important source of policy innovation as well as recruitment of national officials. The California state court had already anticipated *Mapp* with its decision in *Cahan* (1955) and Pat Brown had been supportive of it both as state Attorney General and later as Governor. The state court's exclusionary rule policies also enjoyed a long period of stability and continuity because of its consistent approach to enforcement, the strong supervisory role it provided for trial courts, substantive policy leadership and signifcantly, elite consensus.

But this consensus was undermined by subsequent Burger Court policies which have contributed in part to the legitimation crisis the state court now faces. Political rivals such as the attorney general and governor have converted the enormous differences in policy making styles between the Burger Court and state supreme court into basic conflicts over state constitutional foundations and the policy making prerogatives of state elites. The state court now faces a severe depletion in the resources, especially public esteem, upon which it might draw to shield itself from the increased politicization and delegitimation of its policies. Criticism of state court policies, now increasingly cast by political rivals in terms of a bleak trade off between majority sovereignty and minority rights, makes continued erosion of its progressive policies likely, especially when the constitutional basis upon which its policy independence has been fundamentally altered.

The assault upon the constitutional foundations of political power has not been limited to the state court, but now includes the powers of legislative leadership as well. Proposition 24 (1984) now mandates a restructuring of the Assembly Speaker's powers. So far, Assembly Speaker Willie Brown has been unsuccessful in obtaining early judicial review of its constitutionality, no doubt because of a weakened state court, hesitant to enter yet another heavily politicized institutional conflict.

In contrast to the civil liberties area, institutional conflicts have been averted with criminal records privacy largely because of the combined state court and gubernatorial deference to the attorney general's policy authority. Governor Jerry Brown showed little interest in intruding upon the attorney general's policy authority when LEAA provided the opportunity. Not only was the attorney general's authority already well established, but his credibility as a potential political rival was clearly evident. Moreover, Governor Brown saw greater political capital to be reaped by delegitimizing the LEAA program and the federal political ideology it represented than in advancing due process issues of dubious feasibility and low political returns. Nor has the state court found discrepancies in enforcement of the criminal records privacy policy particularly egregious given its philosophical support for a law enforcement perspective and aversion to additional conflict with the attorney general.

The Massachusetts cases provide a sharp contrast to California with respect to the politics of implementation. Neither the state court nor other state elites have been drawn into legitimation conflicts over its policies. There are a number of reasons for this. Massachusetts, unlike its counterpart in California, adopted civil liberties policies which rarely exceeded and frequently fell below Warren Court standards. What has been particularly conspicuous in the development of its policies is the narrow reading of the scope of due process protections in terms of defendants' rights, the issue of standing and reasonableness of privacy expectations. Also, there has been a preoccupation with the procedural form rather than the substance of police observance of civil liberties protections and an aversion to spelling out the judicial role in enforcement. Moreover, the court's careful avoidance of enunciating an official, unambiguous policy regarding the exclusionary rule, potentially offensive to liberals, has insulated its unofficial policy of opposition to the rule from political controversy. These modes of response have conserved its esteem and public support while disarming conflict from potential institutional rivals.

It is, therefore, not surprising that the Burger Court policies would find an environment conducive to their implementation and legitimation. The policies were neither disruptive to existing law enforcement routine nor contrary to the expectations of the attorney general or even liberal Democrats. They have grown accustomed to the variations in local police and judicial practices encouraged but not condoned by an exceedingly pragmatic and politically astute state court. The possibility for progressive reform had already been well contained within the parameters of the political culture. Thus, state court inaction and indifference, combined with a supportive attorney general and only marginal differences in policy making styles (e.g., compared with the governor) has led to adoption of state court policies with little change in civil liberties protections for defendants.

The erosion of a progressive criminal records privacy policy in Massachusetts seems best understood in terms of differences in the relative strength and assertiveness of institutional leadership, policy making styles and willingness to enforce. Governor Sargent was able to generate sufficient political resources to legitimize state privacy policy, in part, because he converted his challenge of the legitimacy of the FBI controlled NCIC into an issue of federalism and states' rights. This made an independent commission politically feasible and enforcement possible, especially with the continuity of a supportive attorney general. Conversely, factors which appear to account for a reversal of the progressive direction of privacy policy principally include change in gubernatorial policy making style (managerial vs. substantive), increased administrative control by state law enforcement, and a decline in elite support (i.e., by the attorney general).

The implementation experience documented in the Washington and Colorado cases provides some additional evidence from contrasting political cultures of the significance of power structural and institutional factors in demonstrating the relationship between legitimation and the direction of change. Significantly, the authority, policy making role and political involvement of the supreme courts of both states increased dramatically during the post-Warren Court years. In addition, since 1970 both states have had progressively oriented gubernatorial leadership, sometimes closely allied with a supportive attorney general (e.g., Washington), sustaining an environment conducive to progressive reform. Despite these similiarities, legitimation conflicts over the implementation of civil liberties policies have contributed to contradictory tendencies of reform and retrenchment.

There are several reasons why the Washington and Colorado state courts faced little initial controversy in their civil liberties policies. Washington had adopted a state policy on the exclusionary rule soon after the *Weeks* decision (although construing it restrictively) and adopted a pragmatic policy response to the Warren Court civil liberties decisions. Although the state court promulgated a very liberal position on standing (*Michaels*, 1962), it subsequently abandoned this and other more liberal policies (pre-Warren Court) in favor of those dictated by the Burger

Court. This pragmatic style invited little opposition from either law enforcement or civil liberties interests and was wholly consistent with the policy styles of other state elites.

The Colorado state court also employed a similar pragmatic style with similar political consequences, exhibiting somewhat less policy innovation and expressing somewhat more sympathy to the need of effective law enforcement. One major difference was the Colorado court's propensity to cite parallel provisions of the state constitution to justify its decisions on federal due process policies. This had the subsequent effect of depriving the court of solid substantive grounds, unlike Washington, for legitimizing its departure from the Burger Court policy line. Its heretical liberal policies prohibiting searches without warrants and holding prosecutors legally liable for use of evidence illegally obtained by police were extremely unpopular with a profoundly conservative legislature and the powerful state district attorneys' association. The legislature's dissatisfaction with state court policy came in the form of a "good faith" exception which sought, among other things, to limit state court authority to advance criminal justice reforms. Ironically, at no time has Governor Lamm sought to intervene in support of the state supreme court, most of whose members owe their appointments to him. Thus far, the Colorado State court has averted a legitimation crisis but has had to accept legislative encroachment with the political consequence of undermining its authority.

The Washington state court's deviation from Burger Court policies was more abrupt and dogmatic than that of its Colorado counterpart. So far, it has not had the same political repercussions because neither the prosecutors nor police associations have acquired sufficient credibility nor legislative support to challenge its power and substantive style. Moreover, unlike the California state court, the Washington court has shrewdly anticipated the real battlefield where conflict over judicial independence from Burger Court retrenchment is likely to be fought: the state constitution. Thus, the state court stands prepared to advance increasingly esoteric constitutional interpretations to shield its policies from attack by state and federal officials.

When comparing the implementation of criminal records policies in these two states the direction of change reverses itself. Colorado exhibits signs of progressiveness while Washington shows clear signs of retrenchment. The changes in the availability of resources of legitimacy brought about by conflicts over structural factors best explain differences in the direction of change in these two states. The criminal records policy retrenchment occurring in Washington is no doubt aggravated by a state court providing philosophical rather than operational support. Also, the disruption to the existing distribution of institutional power which SPA regulatory control represented, depleted the resources available to legitimize and actively enforce state policy.

In contrast, the progressive turn of an initially weak Colorado statute seems best explained by the unintended alteration in state court power and policy making style of proceduralism, drawing the state court into a more active policy leadership role than before. This increased state court involvement, seemingly of little concern to other state elites, may continue to enhance the resources at its disposal to advance and legitimize its policy preferences in the application and adjudication of record challenge provisions. In this regard, the virtue of a procedural style is that it enables incremental change by avoiding structural conflict.

The foregoing analysis suggests that legitimation conflicts which the American political system faces are the combined result of the dispersal and fragmentation of the authority of national and state elected officials and the concentration of power and discretion in its policy subsystems. National policies with structural implications (e.g., separation of powers, and federalism) tend to get displaced into conflicts between state elected officials over their policy making authority, institutional capacity and substantive issues. These conflicts tend to reinforce the control and leverage policy subsystem elites and implementers have over the substantive and procedural dimensions and outcomes of national policy. I have discussed ways in which the characteristics of a state political culture will dictate, in part, how these institutional authority conflicts get resolved and what effect they will have in determining the changes in policy subsystems. However, institutional and power structural factors alone provide an incomplete understanding of the processes of change. Psychological, behavioral and ideological factors, to which we turn now, help fill in remaining gaps in our understanding of why legitimation conflicts get displaced to perpetuate the cycle of reform and retrenchment.

THE APPEARANCE AND REALITY OF REFORM

An important reason why the cycle of reform and retrenchment gets perpetuated is that it is firmly entrenched in a set of appearances which commits reformers and implementers to advance self-perpetuating policies. A significant reason for this cyclical feature of change is that the identities and positions of the participants (e.g., both liberal reformers and criminal justice implementers) are sustained by common expectations generated by their beliefs as to how the path toward reform is to be conceived and repudiated. This set of appearances has the dual effect of isolating police practices while insulating elected officials (including judges) from involvement in and oversight of the administration of criminal justice.

Second, a new ideological consensus is emerging among elites about the limited capacity of national governmental institutions to effectively address problems of growth and equity in the distribution of scarce resources. There is also an apparent loss of confidence by citizens in the capacity of governmental institutions to promote opportunities which satisfy individual aspirations. Both trends have intensified pressures on elites to support regressive criminal justice policies which tend to diffuse and displace this growing disaffection. Proponents of liberal reform are particularly susceptible to such pressures which put democratic processes at risk because of a profound ambivalence regarding the role of freedom in securing individual rights. Confronted with the imperatives of retrenchment, liberal reformers are likely to adopt managerial styles of policy making which promote improvements in organizational capacity potentially inconsistent with the rights of the subject and demand for political accountability.

Third, the withdrawal of political elites from active intervention, combined with policy making processes increasingly remote, inexplicit and inaccessible to non-implementers, is likely to exacerbate problems of regime authority and accountability. This is most likely to further enlarge the role of courts in governance processes of the American political system. The enlargement of judicial intervention demanded to address issues of equity and rights may put courts under new legitimation pressures which make alterations in the constitutonal distribution of powers and individual rights a more likely prospect.

The Politics of Identity and Displacement

There are four related beliefs which help constitute and reinforce the identities of proponents and opponents of criminal justice reform and contribute to self-fulfilling behavior with paradoxical consequences for the possibility of institutional change.

First, a common perspective of civil liberties and criminal justice officials emerging from this study is that criminal justice policies must originate primarily from courts. This has had the consequence of limiting the potential for reform by severely limiting executive and legislative oversight and enforcement functions. The liberal reformers' preference for courts is largely dictated by strategic considerations problematically rooted in their identity as legal advocates. Courts, unlike legislatures, provide a forum more amenable to rational debate by confining policy issues to individual cases involving procedural violations requiring expertise about criminal justice processes. Legislative forums provide far less certainty that policy arguments will be confined to procedural matters. Instead, the inherent tendency of legislative politics is to enlarge the scope of conflict surrounding substantive issues to include the outcomes and consequences of policy for the relative power positions and interests of the contestants. This is not to say that such matters never enter judicial decision making processes, but only that they rarely do so explicitly.

Many of the civil liberties attorneys I questioned expressed their disdain for and distrust of legislative policy to advance civil liberties policies. The proclivity of civil liberties attorneys, for example, to favor a litigation strategy of finding test cases with precedent-setting potential as opposed to those involving mundane and tedious follow-up of the implementation and enforcement of existing laws is really a function of the structure of incentives of the profession. For example, Halpern's (1976) study of the six-month workload of ACLU chapter affiliates revealed a distinct bias toward choosing *atypical* complaints with state or national policy implications over more problematic ones involving issues of enforcement. Significantly, these latter cases constituted 95 percent of all complaints filed, with the most frequent ones involving alleged police misconduct, denials of right to counsel, and employment discrimination (1976: 161–162). The visibility that attorneys are apt to get with breakthrough policy is more likely to advance their individual aspirations and careers than risky and unrewarding conflicts with bureaucratic implementers. Reflecting upon his seminal work, *The Politics of Rights* (1974), Scheingold (1981) now acknowledges numerous shortcomings in the use of judicial forums (especially the lack of follow-up enforcement) as means by which activist lawyers may achieve social reform.

Law enforcement officials also have a vested interest in confining criminal justice issues to court adjudication processes. Police and prosecutors can expect to restrict issues of salience to defendants' rights to the narrow parameters of the specific facts of the situation. They can also expect such decisions to generally have a marginal effect upon routine behavior and roles, entail few sanctions from superiors and involve wide variations in judicial interpretation and enforcement (e.g., approval of warrants or ruling on the admissability of evidence). This is not to say that police or prosecutors eschew the legislative policy forum, for they will exploit it to redistribute the burdens of judicial actions or the policies or prerogatives of other criminal justice agencies (e.g., corrections, probation, parole) they oppose. Nonetheless, they run the risk of enlarging the scope of intervention (e.g., through rule-making processes), decreasing their leverage and control over internal organizational matters as illustrated by the Washington and Massachusetts criminal record privacy cases.

Second, both civil liberties advocates and law enforcement interests share a propensity to favor specific and unambiguous judicial and legislative policy. This has had the effect of reinforcing a preoccupation with procedural and substantive rather than structural policy issues. While this propensity might be explained by the fact that people have a low tolerance for ambiguity and dissonance, our analysis suggests a different explanation. Advocates for increased civil liberties and privacy protections exhibit an eagerness to exploit the rule-making powers of state courts and bureaucrats to tighten the language in order to enlarge (or contract) the substantive emphasis of federal policy. Moreover, this kind of strategic intervention is adopted mainly to further clarify and structure police discretion rather than address broader issues of power, responsibility and enforcement.

Law enforcement interests also demonstrate a similar tendency to favor more rather than less clarity, albeit for different strategic reasons. The contrasting state policy responses to *Mapp* and *Miranda* illustrated in this study best capture the strategic considerations involved. *Mapp* and *Miranda* were nearly always distinguished by implementers in terms of differences in clarity. But *Miranda* was clearly preferred not merely because of its precision and specificity, but because its impact on police investigation activities and performance could be *minimized* and assimilated. In contrast, *Mapp* offered no such clear cut possibilities and, therefore, continues to be opposed by law enforcement.

These conflicting expectations have paradoxical consequences for legislative reform. For example, vagueness of focus and uncertainty of impact of the criminal records privacy legislation presented more troublesome difficulties because of the added policy leverage which bureaucratic regulatory processes gave to non-criminal justice interests. As the Washington and Massachusetts cases demonstrate, the consequence was an overspecification of due process procedure (dictated in part by a defensive law enforcement strategy) and an inattention to and underspecification of internal changes in record practices oversight and enforcement mechanisms. Or, as a Massachusetts legal activist and one-time participant in the regulatory development process charactrized it: "Civil liberties interests won on procedural matters while law enforcement won on technological, organizational and oversight issues."

Third, there is a consensus among police and reform advocates that *discretion* is the pivot upon which effective law enforcement turns. The paradoxical effect that this shared belief has is to perpetuate policies which continue to isolate police from the broader forces of professionalization, while releasing courts and prosecution from the burden of responsibility for supervision and enforcement.

Advocates of police reform typically view law enforcement activities through stereotypical and simplistic images which limit their role to crime prevention or reduction, or maintenance of law and order. This results in an almost exclusive emphasis on policies which structure or eliminate discretion. This exaggerates (if not tacitly justifies) the influence police exercise over the outcomes of criminal justice policy while imposing a disproportionate burden of responsibility for compliance. It also appears to lend support to the common political contention that civil liberties decisions have dealt a devastating blow to law enforcement effectiveness. Yet it is clear that other criminal justice officials must share the blame for this mistaken image. Judges and prosecutors claim that crime control suffers because they consider these policies to affect only police conduct, albeit through a vastly oversimplified and stereotypical image of law enforcement. Moreover, as the privacy policy illustrates, judicial resistance to the assumption of regulatory responsibilities may produce police resentment of unevenly distributed compliance responsibilities. Thus, the manifestation of these role conflicts suggests that the displacement of legitimation conflicts is rooted in a political psychology in which projected self-images of freedom and policy authority are sustained by a common conception of law enforcement practice.

It is not surprising, therefore, that reform policies formulated almost entirely in terms of the exercise of police discretion in crime control would simply reinforce police beliefs in the importance of protecting discretion. James Q. Wilson (1968) among other observers, has demonstrated the integral relationship between views about discretion and police self-images as a "craft" rather than a profession. The boundaries of professions, unlike crafts, are determined by mastery of a discipline or field of knowledge, standards of ethical conduct and a set of common practices. Interestingly, Wilson found that police resistance to professionalization seems strongly rooted in their fear that it will expose them to increased outside regulation. Although we see these fears and anxieties expressed in numerous and contradictory ways, such responses are certainly not unique to law enforcement. For state courts are just as sensitive to interference with their freedom by their federal judicial superiors or encroachment by other branches of government. What this suggests is that the politics of policy making and institutional reform are bound up in the identities of their contestants. Therefore, what makes institutional change problematic in the criminal justice system is that it entails (as Connolly and Harre contend) an alteration in roles and identities through the redistribution of power, freedom and responsibilities, and respect and contempt among its organizational participants.

Fourth, both police and reform groups share the common expectation that the politicization of crime through electoral politics will mobilize public support in favor of their preferred policy agendas. Police influence on electoral outcomes through exploitation of the fear of crime is expected to result in the commitment of an increased level of resources. Criminal justice reformers expect the politicization of crime to dramatize the need for policies to deal with the sources of crime through social and economic reforms by drawing attention to ineffectiveness of crime reduction strategies and the abuse of minority rights. Significantly, the expectations of both sides are fulfilled. Elections which make law and order the central issue tend to result in larger allocations for crime control with little payoff in increased effectiveness (as the Massachusetts privacy policy case suggests) and a more conspicuous rise in punitive law enforcement, particularly for the poor and minorities, as suggested by the California and Colorado cases. (See also: Heinz, Jacob and Lineberry, 1983 for similar findings).

In evaluating these policy initiatives, Scheingold concludes that federal and local crime programs have probably done more harm than good for the cause of progressive policy. For he contends that "the net effect of the policies of law and order has increased rank and file discretion leading to heightened tensions particularly in high crime areas" (1984: 142). This also contributes to subsequent erosion of public confidence in crime control policy and increased public support for addressing issues concerning the protection of minority rights.

The Politics of Exclusion

The effects of the historic reversal of national governmental policy leadership and programmatic intervention which recent national elections embody are now being expressed in ways which are having differential effects on policy making institutions and the constitutional foundations of the political system. The most important political consequence this reversal has had is the breakup of New Deal coalition held together by the common aspirations and support for governmentally stimulated economic growth, increased opportunities for the poor, enlarged civil rights and racial justice for minorities and strengthened civil liberties protections. Thus far, that breakup has not been translated into an electoral realignment (Mollenkopf, 1983; Burnham, 1982).

The policy implications are also beginning to appear. There is a general reduction of the scope of government intervention through across the board deregulation and narrowing of its programmatic responsibilities to those considered within its capacity to manage such as national defense and public safety.

We also see an increased emphasis upon productivity improvement and other managerial approaches designed to strengthen the disciplinary capacity and enforcement mechanisms of bureaucratic routine organizations such as employment, welfare, public health and others which must handle dependent populations (Dalton and Fitzpatrick, 1985). This emergent managerial style is most clearly manifested in the gubernatorial politics of California and Massachusetts where issues of organizational capacity have displaced those of rights.

Finally, there appears to be a growing sense of individual insecurity and loss of confidence in the capacity of government to deal effectively and fairly with problems of allocation and distribution stemming from the withdrawal of government intervention and preoccupation with control of the public debt. This insecurity and doubt was expressed in contradictory ways in the 1984 Presidential election. National public opinion polls conducted a few weeks before the election indicated that while the majority of respondents agreed with Mondale's criticisms of the unfairness of Reagan's social policies and ineptness in reducing the federal deficit, Reagan still commanded overwhelming public support for his re-election.

But this doubt has also manifested itself in more profound ways which threaten to alter the constitutional foundations of the American political regime. One way this is demonstrated is by the growing political movement to pass a Constitutional amendment to require a balanced budget. Other proposed amendments include voluntary school prayer, and the prohibition of abortion and of the use of minority quotas. As the California case illustrates, the impulse toward constitutional change is not limited to substantive issues, but includes institutional ones as well.

What is most striking about these expressions of doubt and insecurity is the contradictory impulse toward freedom *and* support of new regime norms which enlarge disciplinary and punitive approaches toward marginal populations and criminal offenders. Scheingold suggests that these contradictory impulses and their expression in a punitive crime policy stem from deeper anxieties about personal identity in a changing social order. For the politicization of crime has increased since the mid 1960's even though crime rates have fallen. Scheingold explains this phenomenon in the following way:

> It might seem at first that the explanation is obvious, since politicization began to develop as the crime rate took off in the mid 1960's. But law-and-order rhetoric at that time extended beyond crime to the social turmoil stemming from the Vietnam War and urban traumas. It is also true that politicization has continued well beyond the plateauing of crime in the mid 1970's. Accordingly, the politicization of crime, and especially the public's punitive predispositions, are best understood in broad cultural terms that are only tangentially linked to the actual incidence of crime. . . . Crime is, moreover, a convenient symbol for focusing more general concerns about unwelcome changes in the social order. Given a broad social malaise, crime draws our attention because of the consoling lesson provided by the culture which teaches us that punishment is a necessary and sufficient response to a fundamental problem. *Punitive responses are liberating*

because they are so simple. We yearn to believe that seemingly intractable problems are actually responsive to direct and forceful action. The attractions of punishment are more expressive than instrumental (1984: 226, emphasis added).

There is a seeming inconsistency between the self-images of freedom citizens project and their support of a punitive approach to crime. Yet this inconsistency conceals a set of appearances in which a sense of freedom (enjoyed by the release from frustration resulting from the inability to achieve aspirations) and a secure identity (which the emerging order blocks) is purchased by the exclusion of marginal populations whose disaffection persists. Significantly, individuals demonstrating the least psychological flexibility and greatest intolerance of civil liberties protections (especially for those exhibiting weaknesses, social peculiarities and deviance) are most likely to be people who experience feelings of unworthiness, status frustration and a lack of self-esteem (McClosky and Brill, 1983: 368).

These contradictory public impulses are particularly problematic for liberals who substitute managerial solutions for progressive reform. I contend that this is because of a deeper ambivalence in the philosophical foundations of liberalism toward the idea of freedom and its role in securing the rights of citizens in a democratic state. More specifically, the inability to reconcile positive and negative notions of freedom has put mechanisms of democratic accountability at risk through policies which enlarge organizational capacity and control at the expense of individual rights.

Isaiah Berlin (1958) first brought attention to the competing conceptions entailed by the idea of freedom. One conception views freedom *negatively* as the absence of restraints on what people want to do. In contrast, a *positive* conception of freedom assumes that persons have the capacity to autonomously conceive and pursue their individual aspirations. Berlin contends that these notions have developed in divergent directions, ultimately coming into conflict. He suggests that positive freedom was discredited when it was translated into the political ideologies of Rousseau and Marx who advocated the use of the state to realize the "general will" or to liberate some groups or classes at the expense of others.

Connolly (1983) advances an argument which incisively rejects Berlin's contention. The nerve of this disagreement centers upon the misleading image that the dichotomous conception of freedom conveys about the role and level at which potential constraints to individual freedom operate. His alternative formulation of freedom sees constraints operating at two levels which liberals tend to obscure:

> There are constraints operating on the character of the agent himself, impeding his ability to conceive and to choose reflectively among alternatives. There are also those operating upon his actual and potential actions, limiting his ability to act upon his choices. While these two levels are not always easy to distinguish in practice, liberals have often emphasized the second and ignored the first (1983: 157–158).

Freedom construed in these terms must include the constraints imposed on thought and action by political ideologies and policies which construct and justify the necessity of a merely contingent institutional configuration of power and prevailing interests. Therefore, what becomes essentially contested between cognitive dissonance, utility and expressivist theories, for example, is to what extent government policy creates or removes obstacles in the way of individal autonomy.

Cognitive dissonance theorists tell us that the cause of increased disaffection in times of social and economic stress lies in unrealistic desires and expectations about individual freedom (Elster, 1983) grounded in an overzealous faith in "idealistic" constitutional norms and founding values and in an almost irrational distrust of authority (Huntington, 1981). Thus, the threats to public authority and individual satisfaction are removable to the extent that the regime is successful in cultivating a new set of beliefs consistent with a less ambitious public agenda and more realistic individual aspirations. Utilitarian principles dictate that a public agenda for social and economic renewal entailing varying degrees of sacrifice can be accomplished if some constitutional constraints preventing institutional collaboration (i.e., the separation of powers) are lifted or relaxed. In addition, the middle class must be provided sufficient economic incentives to support necessary institutional changes. And, finally, the underclass must be faced with sanctions credible enough to discourage their expression of disaffection through criminality or other forms of economic or social disruption which might threaten the viability of such initiatives.

One political implication issuing from this study is that the liberal policy agenda advanced in a period of retreat and withdrawal of national governmental intervention is apt to reflect an ambivalence regarding the duality of freedom. That ambivalence is most clearly reflected in a punitive crime policy which enables citizens to retain the appearance of freedom of choice while supressing doubts about the legitimacy of the political order. Thus, such a strategy can have the double effect of saving the appearances of freedom and personal security by restricting the life chances of others. It does so by redistributing the resources of respect and contempt by redefining the legal, economic and civil rights of some of its citizens.

Judicial and Congressional Policy-Making: The Dilemma of Sovereignty, Rights, and Accountability

Political systems face many potential dangers and troublesome paradoxes when confronted with the inability to legitimate their policies. This study suggests that national and state policy making processes and institutions are increasingly vulnerable to certain dangers which issue from structural constraints generated by intractable conflicts over the distribution of power and continued erosion of citizen identification through electoral dealignment.

There is likely to be a three-fold effect of power structural conflicts, demobilization and dealignment on the ability of governmental institutions to authoritatively allocate societal values. First, institutions increasingly deadlocked in conflict over policy making prerogatives are likely to increase the hesitancy and reluctance of national and state political elites to advance progressive national policy reforms because of the fear of retaliation by entrenched interests and challenges to their power and subsequent policy decisions. Second, institutional elites are likely to avoid implementation and enforcement of policies imposing regulatory burdens on politically dominant interest groups (including policy implementers) because of the political liabilities involved.

Third, the insecurity of liberals combined with the disaffection of intensely committed single-issue minorities is ripe for exploitation by unscrupulous demagogues promising institutional change through authoritarian solutions. Although the politics of civil liberties in California has not reached this extreme situation, such possibilities are intimated if the state court takes a future opportunity to challenge citizen initiatives such as Proposition 8 and 24 designed to restructure the constitutional powers of state judicial and legislative institutions.

Therefore, the real danger to the American political system is not the fluidity of the boundaries between the branches of government and capacity of each institution to influence the implementation of public policy, but rather institutional deadlocks over achieving policy objectives which result in perpetuating the power and preferences of administrative and professional elites in policy subsystems. Therefore, power structural conflicts over the authority, capacity and boundaries between policy making institutions only exacerbate legitimation problems which tend to enlarge rather than diminish the role of the courts. This is so for two reasons.

First, if legislators and executives are unable or unwilling to accept responsibility for the enforcement of public policies they originate because of the unacceptable risk of political conflict with policy subsystem elites, then disputes over those outcomes will be converted into litigation in the courts. The abundant evidence today of courts overwhelmed by litigation is symptomatic, in part, of the breakdowon of authority resulting from the depletion of the resources of legitimacy and lack of confidence citizens have in governmental institutions effectively and fairly translating collective policy objectives into individualized consequences.

Second, intervention by the courts is increasingly required (and demanded by some disaffected minorities) to fashion detailed policy solutions with extensive enforcement provisions to insure equal protection of their rights because of legislative and executive default. This has the consequence of expanding the presumptive "rights" of selected interests such as those involved in contacts with the criminal justice system. Other interests are likely to oppose this expansion because it legislates rights. But it is often forgotten that issues of constitutional rights apply not just to the criminal defendant, the welfare dependent, or minority, but to all citizens in common.

Some observers have expressed concern that the erosion of legislative policymaking which the expansion of judicial intervention represents is altering basic governance processes (Gambitta, May and Foster, 1981). There are strong differences of opinion as to whether judicial policy making actually poses such implications for governance processes in a democratic state. The contrasting arguments advanced by Dworkin (1978) and Walzer (1981) nicely frame the contours of the dilemma of rights, accountability and sovereignty which underpin arguments about distinctions between judicial and congressional reform.

Dworkin argues that the purpose of a liberal democracy is to insure equal concern and respect for each of its citizens. Therefore, some rights must be removed from majoritarian legislative processes because of the risk of resulting in inegalitarian outcomes. Such rights serve as "trump cards" held by individuals to resist the consequences of legislative policies contrary to equal protection under the law (Dworkin, 1978: 134).

Walzer proposes a different interpretation of democracy which stresses the priority of sovereignty over that of equality and rights. According to Walzer, the people's right to adopt laws through legislative processes cannot be circumscribed or limited in advance in terms of preconceived philosophical or judicial notions of the reasonableness or rationality of substantive outcomes. To do so would be to rob the citizens of their sovereignty and the "right to be wrong" (Walzer, 1981: 386). According to Walzer, therefore, judicially enforced rights must not intrude upon legislative prerogatives.

The difficulty we face in trying to adjudicate between these conflicting but persuasive arguments is that they are predicated on two different conceptions of democracy. Dworkin's conception is based on the premise that democracy is guided by the ideal of procedural equality and respect for persons. Walzer denies that such ideals can be coherently formulated in concrete terms, insisting instead that democracy is best approximated when citizens have the opportunity to exercise their sovereignty (e.g., control over governance processes) through majoritarian decision making for the common good.

It is possible that the values Dworkin endorses are best protected in judicial processes, therefore resolving the apparent conflict between competing conceptions. But the difficulties are not disposed of this easily, for it is equally clear that notions of equality and respect as substantive goals have a place in collective decisions promoting the common good. Clearly, rights must be capable of individualized application to make sense of the concept, but it also encompasses the collective capabilities of citizens to exercise their sovereignty. If some citizens are deprived of the capacity to exercise their rights as a result of majoritarian decision making processes then that puts their sovereignty in doubt. By Walzer's reckoning then we must sometimes accept the risk of minority oppression in order to preserve the sovereignty of the majority. The problem with Walzer's conception is that if the boundaries of court intervention are predetermined in advance, then there is no guarantee that intended or unintended losses of rights can be challenged and remedied. Moreover, it is likely to merely exacerbate the problems of legitimation courts now face in their attempt to address controversies which legislators and executives are likely to avoid.

References

Adamany, David (1973). "Legitimacy, Realigning Elections and the Supreme Court." *Wisconsin Law Review* 1973: 790–846.

——— (1980). "The Supreme Court's Role in Critical Elections." In *Realignment in American Politics: Toward a Theory*, ed. by Bruce Campbell, and Richard Trilling. Austin, TX: University of Texas Press.

Allison, Graham T. (1971). *Essence of Decision*. Boston: Little Brown.

Altman, Drew, and Harvey M. Sapolsky (1976). "Writing the Regulations for Health." *Policy Sciences* 7: 417–437.

Atkins, Burton M., and Henry R. Glick (1976). "Environmental and Structural Variables as Determinants of Issues in State Courts of Last Resort." *American Journal of Political Science* 29: 97–115.

Baar, Carl (1980). "The Scope and Limits of Court Reform." *The Justice System Journal* 5: 274–290.

——— (1982). "Judicial Activism in State Courts: The Inherent-Powers Doctrine." In *State Supreme Courts: Policymakers in the Federal System*, ed. by M.C. Porter, and G.A. Tarr. Westport, CT: Greenwood Press.

Baar, Ellen, and Carl Baar (1981). "Judges as Middlemen?" *The Justice System Journal* 6: 210–225.

Bachofner, William, former Chief of Washington State Patrol (1980). Letter to P. Winberry, Washington State Court Administrator, January 22.

Bailey, Stephen, and Edith K. Mosher (1968). *ESEA: The Office of Education Administers a Law*. Syracuse: Syracuse University Press.

Ball, Howard (1980). *Courts and Politics: The Federal Judicial System*. Englewood Cliffs, NJ: Prentice-Hall.

———, et al. (1982). *Compromised Compliance*. Westport, CT: Greenwood Press.

Bardach, Eugene (1977). *The Implementation Game: What Happens After a Bill Becomes a Law*. Cambridge, MA: MIT Press.

Baum, Lawrence (1976a). "Decisions to Grant and Deny Hearings in the California Supreme Court: Patterns in Court and Individual Behavior." *Santa Clara Law Review* 16: 713–744.

——— (1976b). "Implementation of Judicial Decisions: An Organizational Analysis." *American Politics Quarterly* 4: 86–114.

——— (1976c). "Lower Court Responses to Supreme Court Decisions: Reconsidering a Negative Picture." *The Justice System Journal* 3: 208–219.

——— (1977). "Judicial Impacts as a Form of Policy Implementation." In *Public Law and Public Policy*, ed. by J.A. Gardiner. New York: Praeger.

——— (1979). "The Impact of Court Decisions on Police Practices." In *Determinants of Law-Enforcement Policies*, ed. by F.A. Meyer, Jr., and R. Baker. Lexington, MA: D.C. Heath.

——— (1981). "Comparing the Implementation of Legislative and Judicial Policies." In *Effective Policy Implementation*, ed. by D.A. Mazmanian, and P.A. Sabatier. Lexington, MA: D.C. Heath.

Baumer, Donald, and Carl Van Horn (1984). *The Politics of Unemployment*. Washington, DC: Congressional Quarterly Press.

Bennett, Robert W. (1983). "The Burger Court and the Poor." In *The Burger Court*, ed. by Victor Blasi. New Haven: Yale University Press.

Berkson, Larry, Steven Hays, and Susan Carbon (eds.) (1977). *Managing the State Courts*. St. Paul, MN: West.

Berlin, Isaiah (1958). *Two Concepts of Liberty*. Oxford: Clarendon Press.

Berman, Paul (1980). "Thinking About Programmed and Adaptive Implementation: Matching Strategies to Situations." In *Why Policies Succeed or Fail*, ed. by H.M. Ingram, and D.E. Mann. Beverly Hills, CA: Sage.

Bice, Scott H. (1972). "Anderson and the Adequate State Grounds." *Southern California Law Review* 45: 750–766.

Blasi, Vincent (ed.) (1983). *The Burger Court: The Counter Revolution that Wasn't*. New Haven: Yale University Press.

Bloom, Robert M. (1982). "Warrent Requirement—The Burger Approach." *University of Colorado Law Review* 53: 691–744.

Brant, Jonathan, et al. (1981). "Public Records, FIPA and CORI: How Massachusetts Balances Privacy and the Right to Know." *Suffolk University Law Review* 15: 23–77.

Brennan, William J. (1977). "State Constitutions and the Protection of Individual Rights." *Harvard Law Review* 90: 489–504.

Brown, Don W., and Robert V. Stover (1977). "Court Directives and Compliance." *American Politics Quarterly* 5: 465–480.

Burnham, Walter Dean (1970). *Critical Elections and the Mainsprings of American Politics*. New York: W.W. Norton.

——— (1981). "The System of 1896: An Analysis." In *The Evolution of American Electoral Systems*, ed. by Paul Kleppner. Westport, CT: Greenwood Press.

——— (1982). *The Current Crisis of American Politics*. New York: Oxford University Press.

Burnham, Walter D., and Martha W. Weinberg (eds.) (1977). *American Politics and Public Policy*. Cambridge, MA: MIT Press.

Bynum, Timothy S. (1982). "Prosecutorial Discretion and the Implementation of a

Legislative Mandate.'' In *Implementing Criminal Justice Policies*, ed. by Merry Morash. Beverly Hills, CA: Sage.

California, Department of Justice (1983). ''Agencies Authorized to Receive Criminal History Information.'' Memorandum, September.

California (1982). Voters' Guide.

Canon, Bradley C. (1973). ''Reactions of State Supreme Courts to a U.S. Supreme Court Civil Liberties Decision.'' *Law and Society Review* 8: 109–134.

——— (1974a). ''Is the Exclusionary Rule in Failing Health? Some New Data and a Plea against a Precipitous Conclusion.'' *Kentucky Law Journal* 62: 681–730.

——— (1974b). ''Organizational Contumacy in the Transmission of Judicial Politics: The *Mapp, Escobedo, Miranda* and *Gault* cases.'' *Villanova Law Review* 20: 4–79.

——— (1977). ''Testing the Effectiveness of Civil Liberties Policies at State and Federal Levels: The Case of the Exclusionary Rule.'' *American Politics Quarterly* 5: 57–82.

——— (1979). ''The Exclusionary Rule: Have Critics Proven that it Doesn't Deter Police?'' *Judicature* 62: 398–403.

Carter, Lief H. (1974). *The Limits of Order*. Lexington, MA: D.C. Heath.

Casey, Greg (1974). ''The Supreme Court and Myth: An Empirical Investigation.'' *Law and Society Review* 8: 385–419.

Cavell, Stanley (1979). *The Claim of Reason*. New York: Oxford University Press.

Cimino, Richard D. (1973). ''Confessions—Right to Counsel—The Impact of *Miranda* in Missouri.'' *Saint Louis University Law Journal* 17: 572–583.

Colton, Kent W. (ed.) (1978). *Police Computer Technology*. Lexington, MA: D.C. Heath.

Connolly, William E. (1981). *Appearance and Reality in Politics*. London: Cambridge University Press.

——— (1983). *The Terms of Political Discourse*. Lexington, MA: D.C. Heath, 2nd ed.

———, and Glen Gordon (1974). *Social Structure and Political Theory*. Lexington, MA: D.C. Heath.

Cotter, Cornelius P. (ed.) (1974). *Political Science Annual: An International Review*. Vol. 5, Indianapolis, IN: Bobbs-Merrill.

Cotton, Eugene, Chair, and William A. Webb, Executive Director, Washington Association of Sheriffs and Police Chiefs (1978). Letter to T.C. Dalton, Washington Law and Justice Planning Office Privacy Administrator. May 18.

Cover, Robert M., and T. Alexander Aleinikoff (1977). ''Dialectical Federalism: Habeas Corpus and the Court.'' *Yale Law Journal* 86: 1035–1102.

Dahl, Robert (1957). ''Decision-Making in a Democracy: The Supreme Court as a National Policy-Maker.'' *Journal of Public Law* 6: 279–295.

Dalton, Thomas C., and Linda C. Fitzpatrick (1983). ''The Effects of Federal Policy on State and Local Organizations and Representation Processes.'' Paper presented at Western Political Science Association conference, Seattle, March.

———, and ——— (1985). ''The Politics of Measuring Public Sector Performance: Productivity and the Public Organization.'' *In Productivity in the Public Sector: Problems, Strategies, and Prospects*, ed. by Rita Mae Kelly. Port Washington, NY: Kennikat Press.

Davis, Kenneth C. (1969). *Discretionary Justice*. Baton Rouge: Louisiana State University Press.

Derthick, Martha (1975). *Uncontrollable Spending for Social Services Grants*. Washington, DC: Brookings Institution.

Deukmajian, George, and Clifford K. Thompson, Jr. (1979). "All Sail and No Anchor—Judicial Review under the California Constitution." *Hastings Constitutional Law Quarterly* 6: 975–1010.

Deutsch, Karl (1966). *The Nerves of Government*. New York: Free Press.

——— (1970). *Politics and Government*. Boston: Houghton Mifflin.

Dolbeare, Kenneth M. (1974). "The Impacts of Public Policy." In *Political Science Annual: An International Review*, Vol. 5, ed. by C.P. Cotter. Indianapolis, IN: Bobbs-Merrill.

———, and Phillip Hammond (1968). "The Political Party Basis of Attitudes Toward the Supreme Court." *Public Opinion Quarterly* 32: 16–30.

———, and ——— (1971). *The School Prayer Decisions: From Court Policy to Local Practice*. Chicago: University of Chicago Press.

Downs, Anthony (1967). *Inside Bureaucracy*. Boston: Little Brown.

Dubois, Philip L. (1980). *From Ballot to Bench: Judicial Elections and the Quest for Accountability*. Austin: University of Texas Press.

Dworkin, Ronald (1977). *Taking Rights Seriously*. Cambridge, MA: Harvard University Press.

——— (1978). "Liberalism." In *Public and Private Morality*, ed. by S. Hampshire. Cambridge, MA: Cambridge University Press.

Dyke, Charles F. (1981). *Philosophy of Economics*. Englewood Cliffs, NJ: Prentice Hall.

Easton, David (1965a). *A Framework for Political Analysis*. Englewood Cliffs, NJ: Prentice Hall.

——— (1965b). *A Systems Analysis of Political Life*. New York: John Wiley and Sons.

Edwards, George C., III (1980). *Implementing Public Policy*. Washington, DC: Congressional Quarterly Press.

Elazar, Daniel (1972). *American Federalism: A View From the States*. New York: Crowell, 2nd ed.

Elmore, Richard F. (1978). "Organizational Models of Social Program Implementation." *Public Policy* 26: 185–228.

——— (1979). "Backward Mapping: Implementation Research and Policy Decisions." *Political Science Quarterly* 94: 1–18.

———, and Milbrey Wallin McLaughlin (1982). *Reform and Retrenchment: The Politics of California School Finance Reform*. Cambridge, MA: Ballinger.

Elster, Jon (1983). *Sour Grapes: Studies in the Subversion of Rationality*. New York: Cambridge University Press.

Everson, D.H. (ed.) (1972). *The Supreme Court as Policy-Maker: Three Studies on the Impact of Judicial Decisions*. Carbondale, IL: Southern Illinois University, Public Affairs Research Bureau. 2nd ed.

Feeley, Malcolm M., and Austin D. Sarat (1980). *The Policy Dilemma: Federal Crime Policy and the Law Enforcement Assistance Administration*. Minneapolis, MN: University of Minnesota Press.

Festinger, Leon (1957). *A Theory of Cognitive Dissonance*. Evanston, IL: Row, Peterson and Company.

Folan, Rita, and Michael A. Lettre (1981). *Status of Offender Based Transaction Statistics (OBTS): System Development in the States*. Washington, DC: Criminal Justice Statistics Association, August.

Foucault, Michel (1972). *The Archeology of Knowledge*. New York: Pantheon.
——— (1977). *Discipline and Punish*. New York: Vintage.
Funston, Richard (1977). *Constitutional Counter Revolution*. New York: John Wiley.
Gambitta, Richard A.L., Marlynn L. May, and James C. Foster (eds.) (1981). *Governing through Courts*. Beverly Hills, CA: Sage.
Gardiner, John A. (ed.) (1977). *Public Law and Public Policy*. New York: Praeger.
Gazell, James A. (1978). *The Future of State Court Management*. Port Washington, NY: Kennikat Press.
Glick, Henry R. (1982). "Supreme Courts in State Judicial Administration." In *State Supreme Courts: Policymakers in the Federal System*, ed. by M.C. Porter and G.A. Tarr. Westport, CT: Greenwood Press.
——— (1983). *Courts, Politics and Justice*. New York: McGraw-Hill.
Goffman, Irving (1968). *Asylums*. London: Penguin Press.
——— (1969). *The Presentation of Self in Everyday Life*. London: Penguin Press.
Goodin, Robert E. (1982). *Political Theory and Public Policy*. Chicago: University of Chicago Press.
Gorton, Slade, Washington Attorney General (1976). Letter to P. Winberry, Washington State Court Administrator. January 29.
Gray, Virginia, and Bruce Williams (1980). *The Organizational Politics of Criminal Justice*. Lexington, MA: D.C. Heath.
Gruhl, John and Cassia Spohn (1981). "The Supreme Court's Post-*Miranda* Rulings." *Law and Policy Quarterly* 3: 29–54.
Habermas, Jurgen (1973). *Legitimation Crisis*. Boston: Beacon Press.
——— (1982). "A Reply to My Critics." In *Habermas: Critical Debates*, ed. by John B. Thompson and David Held. Cambridge, MA: MIT Press.
Halpern, Stephen C. (1976). "Assessing the Litigative Role of the ACLU Chapters." In *Civil Liberties Policy and Policy Making*, ed. by Stephen L. Wasby. Carbondale, IL: Southern Illinois University Press.
Hampshire, Stuart (ed.) (1978). *Public and Private Morality*. Cambridge, MA: Cambridge University Press.
——— (1983). *Morality and Conflict*. London: Basil Blackwell.
Hargrove, Erwin C. (1975). *The Missing Link: The Study of the Implementation of Social Policy*. Washington, DC: Urban Institute.
———, and Michael Nelson (1984). *Presidents, Politics, and Policy*. New York: Alfred A. Knopf.
Harmon, M. Judd (ed.) (1978). *Essays on the Constitution of the United States*. Port Washington, NY: Kennikat Press.
Harre, Rom (1980). *Social Being: A Theory for Social Psychology*. Totowa, NJ: Littlefield, Adams.
Hays, Steven W. (1978). *Court Reform: Ideal or Illusion?* Lexington, MA: D.C. Heath.
Hebert, Scott (1978). "Impact and Implications for Future Criminal Justice Reform Efforts." In *Police Computer Technology*, ed. by K.W. Colton. Lexington, MA: D.C. Heath.
Heinz, Anne, Herbert Jacob, and Robert L. Lineberry (eds.) (1983). *Crime in City Politics*. New York: Longman.
Held, David (1982). "Crisis Tendencies, Legitimation and the State." In *Habermas: Critical Debates*, ed. by John B. Thompson, and David Held. Cambridge, MA: MIT Press.

Hollis, Martin (1983). "Rational Preferences." *The Philosophical Forum* 14: 246–262.

Horowitz, Donald (1977). *The Courts and Social Policy*. Washington, DC: Brookings Institution.

Huntington, Samuel P. (1981). *American Politics: The Promise of Disharmony*. Cambridge, MA: Harvard University Press.

Ingram, Helen, and D.E. Mann (eds.) (1980). *Why Policies Succeed or Fail*. Beverly Hills, CA: Sage.

Jacoby, Joan E. (1980). *The American Prosecutor: A Search for Identity*. Lexington, MA: D.C. Heath.

Johnson, Charles A. (1979). "Judicial Decisions and Organizational Change." *Law and Society Review* 14: 27–56.

———, and Bradley C. Canon (1984). *Judicial Policies: Implementation and Impact*. Washington, DC: Congressional Quarterly Press.

Johnson, Richard (1967). *The Dynamics of Compliance*. Evanston, IL: Northwestern University Press.

Kagan, Robert A., Bliss Cartwright, Lawrence M. Friedman, and Stanton Wheeler (1978). "The Evolution of State Supreme Courts." *Michigan Law Review* 76: 961–1001.

Kamisar, Yale (1983). "The Warren Court (Was It Really So Defense-Minded?), and Burger Court (Is It Really So Prosecution-Oriented?) and Policy Investigatory Practices." In *The Burger Court: The Counter Revolution That Wasn't*, ed. by V. Blasi. New Haven: Yale University Press.

Katz, Michael (1966). "The Supreme Court and the States: An Inquiry into *Mapp v. Ohio* in North Carolina: The Model, the Study and the Implications." *North Carolina Law Review* 45: 119–151.

Kaufman, Herbert (1960). *The Forest Ranger*. Baltimore: Johns Hopkins University Press.

Kelly, Rita Mae (ed.) (1985). *Productivity in the Public Sector: Problems, Strategies, and Prospects*. Port Washington, NY: Kennikat Press.

Key, V.O., Jr. (1959). "Secular Realignment and the Party System." *Journal of Politics* 21: 198–210.

King, Anthony (1978). "The American Polity in the Late 1970's: Building Coalitions of Sand." In *The New American Political System*, ed. by Anthony King. Washington, DC: American Enterprize Institute.

Kleppner, Paul (1982). *Who Voted? The Dynamics of Electoral Turnout 1870–1980*. New York: Praeger.

Kramer, Daniel C., and Robert Riga (1982). "The New York Court of Appeals and the U.S. Supreme Court, 1960–1976." In *State Supreme Courts: Policymakers in the Federal System*, ed. by M.C. Porter, and G.A. Tarr. Westport, CT: Greenwood Press.

Krislov, Samuel (1971). "The Perimeters of Power: The Concept of Compliance as an Approach to the Study of the Legal and Political Processes." In *Compliance and the Law: A Multidisciplinary Approach*, ed. b S. Krislov, et al. Beverly Hills, CA: Sage.

———, K.O. Boyum, et al. (eds.) (1971). *Compliance and the Law: A Multidisciplinary Approach*. Beverly Hills, CA: Sage.

LaFave, Wayne R. (1965). "Improving Policy Performance through the Exclusionary Rule—Part I: Current Police and Local Court Practices." *Missouri Law Review* 30: 391–458.

Laudon, Kenneth C. (1974). *Computers and Bureaucratic Reform*. New York: John Wiley and Sons.

——— (1980a). "Privacy and Federal Data Banks." *Society* 17: 50–56.

——— (1980b). "Survey of Management Policies and Practices: 50 State Surveys of Criminal History Repositories." New York: New York University, Graduate School of Business Administration.

Lindblom, Charles (1968). *The Policy Making Process*. Englewood Cliffs, NJ: Prentice Hall.

Lipsky, Michael (1980). *Street Level Bureaucracy: Dilemmas of the Individual in Public Services*. New York: Russell Sage Foundation.

Litt, Edgar (1965). *The Political Culture of Massachusetts*. Cambridge, MA: MIT Press.

Lloyd, Christopher (ed.) (1983). *Social Theory and Political Practice*. Oxford: Clarendon Press.

Lowi, Theodore J. (1969). *The End of Liberalism*. New York: W.W. Norton.

——— (1979). *The End of Liberalism*. New York: W.W. Norton, 2nd ed.

MacIntyre, Alasdair (1983). "The Indispensibility of Political Theory." In *The Nature of Political Theory*, ed. by David Miller, and Larry Siedentrop. London: Clarendon Press.

Manwaring, David R. (1964). "California and the Fourth Amendment." *Stanford Law Review* 16: 318–354.

——— (1972). "The Impact of *Mapp v. Ohio*." In *The Supreme Court as Policy-Maker: Three Studies on the Impact of Judicial Decisions*, ed. by David H. Everson. Carbondale, IL: Southern Illinois University, Public Affairs Research Bureau.

Marchand Donald A. (1980). *The Politics of Privacy, Computers and Criminal Justice Records*. Arlington, VA: Information Resources Press.

Mays, G. Larry (1983). "*Stone v. Powell*: The Impact on State Appellate Court Judges' Perceptions." *Journal of Criminal Justice* 11: 27–34.

Mazmanian, Daniel A, and Paul A. Sabatier (eds.) (1981). *Effective Policy Implementation*. Lexington, MA: D.C. Heath.

———, and ——— (1983). *Implementation and Public Policy*. Glenview, IL: Scott, Foresman.

McClosky, Herbert, and Alida Brill (1983). *Dimensions of Tolerance*. New York: Russell Sage.

McFeeley, Neil D. (1980). "A Change of Direction: Habeas Corpus from Warren to Burger." *Western Political Quarterly* 31: 174–188.

Medalie, Richard J., L. Zeitz, and P. Alexander (1968). "Custodial Police Interrogation in Our Nation's Capitol: The Attempt to Implement *Miranda*." *Michigan Law Review* 66: 1347–1422.

Medsger, Betty (1983). *Framed: The New Right Attack on Chief Justice Rose Bird and the Courts*. New York: Pilgrim Press.

Meyer, Fred A., Jr., and Ralph Baker (eds.) (1979). *Determinants of Law Enforcement Policies*. Lexington, MA: D.C. Heath.

Miller, Arthur (1971). *The Assault on Privacy*. Ann Arbor: University of Michigan Press.

Milner, Neal A. (1971a). *The Court and Local Law Enforcement*. Beverly Hills, CA: Sage.

——— (1971b). "Supreme Court Effectiveness and the Police Organization." *Law and Contemporary Problems* 36: 467–487.

MITRE Corporation (1977a). *Implementing the Federal Privacy and Security Regulations:*

Vol. I: Findings and Recommendations of an Eighteen State Assessment. McLean, VA.

——— (1977b). *Implementing the Federal Privacy and Security Regulations: Vol. II: Problem Analysis and Practical Responses*. McLean, VA.

Mollenkopf, John H. (1983). *The Contested City*. Princeton, NJ: Princeton University Press.

Morash, Merry (ed.) (1982). *Implementing Criminal Justice Policies*. Beverly Hills, CA: Sage.

Mosk, Stanley (1978). "Contemporary Federalism." *Pacific Law Journal* 9: 711–721.

Muir, William (1967). *Prayer in Public Schools*. Chicago: University of Chicago Press.

Murphy, John T. (1975). *Arrest by Police Computer: The Controversy over Bail and Extradition*. Lexington, MA: D.C. Heath.

Murphy, Michael J. (1966). "Judicial Review of Police Methods in Law Enforcement: The Problem of Compliance by Police Departments." *Texas Law Review* 44: 939–953.

Nakamura, Robert T., and Frank Smallwood (1980). *The Politics of Policy Implementation*. New York: St. Martin's Press.

National Center for State Courts (1974). "Memorandum Re: National Center for State Courts position on proposed LEAA Information systems Regulations; Justice Department Order No. 561–74." Denver, CO.

Navasky, Victor (1976). *Law Enforcement: The Federal Role*. New York: McGraw Hill.

Neiman, Max, and Catherine Lovell (1981). "Mandating as a Policy Issue: The Definitional Problem." *Policy Studies Journal* 9: 667–681.

Neustadt, Richard (1960). *Presidential Power*. New York: John Wiley and Sons.

"Note: Courting Reversal: The Supervisory Role of State Supreme Courts." *Yale Law Journal* 87: 1191–1218.

Oaks, Dallin H. (1970). "Studying the Exlcusionary Rule in Search and Seizure." *University of Chicago Law Review* 37: 665–757.

O'Brien, David M. (1980). "Crosscutting Policies, Uncertain Compliance, and Why Policies Often Cannot Succeed or Fail." In *Why Policies Succeed or Fail*, ed. by H. Ingram, and David E. Mann. Beverly Hills, CA: Sage.

Office of Technology Assessment (OTA) (1982a). *An Assessment of Alternatives for a National Computerized Criminal History System*. Washington, DC.

——— (1982b). *An Assessment of Alternatives for a National Computerized Criminal History System: Summary*. Washington, DC.

O'Toole, George (1978). *The Private Sector*. New York: W.W. Norton.

Packer, Herbert (1968). *The Limits of the Criminal Sanction*. Stanford, CA: Stanford University Press.

Parfait, Derek (1984). *Reasons and Persons*. London: Oxford University Press.

Patterson, Samuel C. (1968). "The Political Cultures of the American States." *Journal of Politics* 30: 187–209.

Paul, Arnold (1960). *Conservative Crisis and the Rule of Law*. Ithaca, NY: Cornell University Press.

Phillips, Kevin (1982). *Post Conservative America: People, Ideology and Politics in a Time of Crisis*. New York: Vintage.

Pomper, Gerald (1967). "Classification of Presidential Elections." *Journal of Politics* 29: 535–566.

Porter, Mary Cornelia (1982). "State Supreme Courts and the Legacy of the Warren

Court: Some Old Inquiries for a New Situation.'' In *State Supreme Courts: Policymakers in the Federal System*, ed. by M.C. Porter, and G.A. Tarr. Westport, CT: Greenwood Press.

——— and G. Alan Tarr (eds.) (1982). *State Supreme Courts: Policymakers in the Federal System*. Westport, CT: Greenwood Press.

Posner, Richard A. (1982). ''Excessive Sanctions for Governmental Misconduct in Criminal Cases.'' *Washington Law Review* 57: 635–667.

Powell, Lee (ed.) (1980). *Court Reform in Seven States*. Washington, DC: American Bar Association and National Center for State Courts.

Pressman, Jeffrey L., and Aaron B. Wildavsky (1973). *Implementation: How Great Expectations in Washington Are Dashed in Oakland*. Berkeley, CA: University of California Press.

''Project: The Effect of Court Structure on State Supreme Court Opinions: A Re-Examination,'' (1981) *Stanford Law Review* 33: 951–965.

Rabinovitz, Francine, Jeffrey Pressman, and Martin Rein (1976). ''Guidelines: A Plethora of Forms, Authors, and Functions.'' *Policy Sciences* 7: 400–416.

Rapoport, Roger (1982). *California Dreaming: The Political Odyssey of Pat and Jerry Brown*. Berkeley, CA: Nolo Press.

Rawls, John (1971). *A Theory of Justice*. Cambridge, MA: Harvard University Press.

Rein, Martin, and Francine Rabinovitz (1977). ''Implementation: A Theoretical Perspective.'' In *American Politics and Public Policy*, ed. W.D. Burnham, and M. Weinberg. Cambridge, MA: MIT Press.

Ripley, Randall B., and Grace Franklin (1982). *Bureaucracy and Policy Implementation*. Homewood, IL: Dorsey Press.

Rodgers, Harrell, and Charles Bullock (1972). *Law and Social Change: Civil Rights Laws and Their Consequences*. New York: McGraw Hill.

——— (1976). *Coercion to Compliance*. Lexington, MA: D.C. Heath.

Romans, Neil T. (1974). ''The Role of the State Supreme Courts in Judicial Policy Making: *Escobedo, Miranda*, and the Use of Judicial Impact Analysis.'' *Western Political Quarterly* 27: 38–59.

Rosenthal, Alan, and Maureen Moakley (1984). *The Political Life of the American States*. New York: Praeger.

Rourke, Francis (1976). *Bureaucracy, Politics and Public Policy*. Boston: Little Brown, 2nd ed.

Scheingold, Stuart (1974). *The Politics of Rights: Lawyers, Public Policy and Political Change*. New Haven, CT: Yale University Press.

——— (1981). ''The Politics of Rights Revisited.'' In *Governing through Courts*, ed. by R.A.L. Gambitta, M.L. May, and J.C. Foster. Beverly Hills, CA: Sage.

——— (1984). *The Politics of Law and Order*. New York: Longman.

SEARCH Group, Incorporated (1975). *State Judicial Information Systems: State of the Art*. Technical Memorandum No. 11. Sacramento, CA.

——— (1976). *The American Criminal History Record: Present Status and Future Requirements*. Technical Report No. 14. Sacramento, CA.

——— (1978). *Standard for Security and Privacy of Criminal Justice Information*. Technical Memorandum No. 12. Sacramento, CA. 2nd ed.

Seeburger, Richard H., and R. Stanton Wettick, Jr. (1967). ''*Miranda* in Pittsburgh—A Statistical Study.'' *University of Pittsburgh Law Review* 29: 1–26.

Sen, Amartya, and Bernard Williams (1982). *Utilitarianism and Beyond*. New York: Cambridge University Press.

Sennett, Richard, and Jonathan Cobb (1972). *The Hidden Injuries of Class*. New York: Vintage.

Shapiro, Martin (1968). *The Supreme Court and Administrative Agencies*. New York: The Free Press.

——— (1978a). "The Constitution and Economic Rights." In *Essays on the Constitution of the United States*, ed. by M. Judd Harmon. Port Washington, NY: Kenikat Press.

——— (1978b). "The Supreme Court: From Warren to Burger." In *The New American Political System*, ed. by Anthony King. Washington, DC: American Enterprize Institute.

——— (1983). "Fathers and Sons: The Court and Commentators, and the Search for Values." In *The Burger Court*, ed. by Vincent Blasi. New Haven, CT: Yale University Press.

———, and D.S. Hobbs (1974). *The Politics of Constitutional Law*. Cambridge, MA: Winthrop.

Silberman, Charles E. (1978). *Criminal Violence, Criminal Justice*. New York: Random House.

Simmons, Thomas (1984). "Colorado." In *The Political Life of the American States*." ed. by Alan Rosenthal, and Maureen Moakley. New York: Praeger.

Skoler, Daniel L. (1977). *Organizing the Non-System*. Lexington, MA: D.C. Heath.

Skolnick, Jerome (1974). *Justice Without Trial*. New York: John Wiley and Sons. 2nd ed.

St. Antoine, Theodore J. (1983). "Individual Rights in the Workplace: The Burger Court and Labor Law." In *The Burger Court*, ed. by Victor Blasi. New Haven: Yale University Press.

Starr, Paul (1982). *The Social Transformation of American Medicine*. New York: Basic Books.

Stolz, Preble (1981). *Judging Judges: The Investigation of Rose Bird and the California Supreme Court*. New York: The Free Press.

Storing, Herbert J. (1981). *What the Anti-Federalists Were for*. Chicago: University of Chicago Press.

Stromsdorfer, Ernest (1981). *Minnesota Work-Equity Project: Second Interim Report, a Summary of Findings*. Cambridge, Ma: Apt Associates.

Stross, Pamela A. (1982). "The Colorado Statutory Good-Faith Exception to the Exclusionary Rule: A Step Too Far?" *University of Colorado Law Review* 53: 809–821.

Talarico, Susan M., and Christopher R. Swanson (1979). "Styles of Policing: An Exploration of Compatibility and Conflict." In *Determinants of Law-Enforcement Policies*, ed. by F.A. Meyer, Jr., and R. Baker. Lexington, MA: D.C. Heath.

Tarr, G. Alan (1977). *Judicial Impact and State Supreme Courts*. Lexington, MA: D.C. Heath.

——— (1982). "State Supreme Courts and the U.S. Supreme Court: The Problem of Compliance." In *State Supreme Courts: Policymakers in the Federal System*, ed. by M.C. Porter, and G.A. Tarr. Westport, CT: Greenwood Press.

Taylor, Charles (1983). "Political Theory and Practice." In *Social Theory and Political Practice*, ed. by C. Lloyd. Oxford: Clarendon Press.

Thompson, John B., and David Held (1982). *Habermas: Critical Debates*. Cambridge, MA: MIT Press.

U.S. Department of Justice, Law Enforcement Assistance Administration (LEAA) (1974a). "Comments on Proposed Rules for Criminal Justice Information Systems." Washington, DC.

——— (1974b). "Title 28--Judicial Administration, Chapter I—Department of Justice, Part 20--Criminal Justice Information Systems." *Federal Register* 39: 5636–5639. February 14.

——— (1975). "Title 28--Judicial Administration, Chapter I—Department of Justice, Part 20--Criminal Justice Information Systems." *Federal Register* 40: 22114–22119. May 20.

——— (1976a). "Comments on the Criminal Justice Information Systems Regulations Relating to the Dissemination Provisions." Washington, DC.

——— (1976b). *Privacy and Security of Criminal History Information: Summary of State Plans*. Washington, DC.

——— (1976C). *Privacy and Security Planning Instructions: Criminal Justice Information Systems*. Washington, DC. April.

——— (1976d). "Title 28--Judicial Administration, Chapter I—Department of Justice, Part 20--Criminal Justice Information Systems." *Federal Register* 41: 11714–11718, March 19.

——— (1977). "Title 28--Judicial Administration, Chapter I—Department of Justice, Part 20--Criminal Justice Information Systems." *Federal Register* 41: Reprint pp. 1–6, March 19, 1976 with amendments of December 6, 1977.

——— (1978a). *Privacy and Security of Criminal History Information: An Analysis of Privacy Issues*. Washington, DC.

——— (1978b). *Privacy and Security of Criminal History Information: Compendium of State Legislation*. Washington, DC.

——— (1979). *Privacy and Security of Criminal History Information, Compendium of State Legislation, 1979 Supplement*. Washington, DC.

U.S. Senate, Committee on the Judiciary, Sub-Committee on Patents, Copyrights and Trademarks (1983). *Hearings on the National System for Interstate Exchange of Criminal History Records*. Washington, DC: U.S. Government Printing Office.

Utter, Justice Robert F. (1984). "Freedom and Diversity in a Federal System: Perspectives on State Constitutions and the Washington Declaration of Rights." *University of Puget Sound Law Review* 7: 441

Van Horn, Carl E. (1979). *Policy Implementation in the Federal System*. Lexington, MA: D.C. Heath.

Van Meter, Donald S., and Carl E. Van Horn (1975). "The Policy Implementation Process: A Conceptual Framework." *Administration and Society* 6: 445–488.

Verba, Sidney (1965). "Comparative Political Culture." In *Political Culture and Political Development*, ed. by Lucien Pye and Sidney Verba. Princeton, NJ: Princeton University Press.

Wald, Michael S., R. Ayers, D.W. Hess, M. Schantz, and C.W. Whitebread, II (1967). "Interrogations in New Haven: The Impact of *Miranda*." *Yale Law Journal* 76: 1519–1648.

Walzer, Michael (1981). "Philosophy and Democracy." *Political Theory* 9: 379–399.

Wasby, Stephen L. (1970). *The Impact of the United States Supreme Court: Some Perspectives*. Homewood, IL: Dorsey Press.

——— (1973). "The Communication of the Supreme Court's Criminal Procedure Decisions: A Preliminary Mapping." *Villanova Law Review* 18: 1086–1118.

——— (1974–1975). "Getting the Message Across—Communicating Court Decisions to the Police." *The Justice System Journal* 1: 29–38.

——— (1976). *Small Town Police and the Supreme Court*. Lexington, MA: D.C. Heath.

Washington House Judiciary Committee (1979). *Majority Report on House Bill 571*. February 22.

Weimer, David L. (1980). *Improving Prosecution: The Inducement and Implementation of Innovations for Prosecutor Management*. Westport, CT: Greenwood Press.

Weinberg, Martha Wagner (1977). *Managing the State*. Cambridge, MA: MIT Press.

Weiner, Norbert (1950). *Human Use of Human Beings*. Boston: Houghton Mifflin.

Wildavsky, Aaron (1979). *The Politics of the Budgetary Process*. Boston: Little, Brown and Co., 3d ed.

Wilkes, Donald E., Jr. (1974). "The New Federalism in Criminal Procedure: State Court Evasion of the Burger Court." *Kentucky Law Journal* 62: 681–730.

——— (1976). "The New Federalism in Criminal Procedure Revisited." *Kentucky Law Journal* 64: 729–752.

Wilkins, Herbert P. (1980). "Judicial Treatment of the Massachusetts Declaration of Human Rights in Relation to Cognate Provisions of the U.S. Constitution." *Suffolk University Law Review* 14: 887–930.

Wilson, James Q. (1968). *Varieties of Police Behavior*. Cambridge, MA: Harvard University Press.

——— (1977). *Thinking About Crime*. New York: Vintage, Revised edition.

Winberry, Phillip B. (1980). "Washington State Court Reform." In *Court Reform in Seven States*, ed. by L. Powell. Washington, DC: American Bar Association and National Center for State Courts.

Winch, Peter (1958). *The Idea of a Social Science and Its Relation to Philosophy*. London: Routledge and Kegan Paul.

Wittgenstein, Ludwig (1953). *Philosophical Investigations*. New York: Macmillian.

Wollheim, Richard (1984). *The Thread of Life*. Cambridge, MA: Harvard University Press.

Yin, Robert K., Karen A. Heald, and Mary E. Vogel (1977). *Tinkering with the System: Technological Innovations in State and Local Services*. Lexington, MA: D.C. Heath.

——— (1981). "The Case Study as a Serious Research Strategy." *Knowledge: Creation, Diffusion, Utilization* 3: 97–114.

Zalman, Marvin (1982). "Mandatory Sentencing Legislation: Myth and Reality." In *Implementing Criminal Justice Policies*, ed. by Merry Morash. Beverly Hills, CA: Sage.

Zenk, Gerald K. (1979). *Project SEARCH: The Struggle for Control of Criminal Information in America*. Westport, CT: Greenwood Press.

Case Index

FEDERAL CASES (U.S. SUPREME COURT AND FEDERAL DISTRICT COURTS)

Aguilar v. Texas, 378 U.S. 108 (1964), 43–44, 138
Bivens v. Six Unknown Agents of Federal Bureau of Narcotics, 403 U.S. 338 (1971), 45, 66
Brown v. Allen, 344 U.S. 433 (1953), 52, 186
Brown v. Board of Education, 347 U.S. 483 (1954), xviii, 51, 185–186
Carroll v. U.S., 267 U.S. 132 (1925), 42, 45, 115
Chambers v. Maroney, 399 U.S. 42 (1970), 45–47, 66, 68, 115
Chimel v. California, 395 U.S. 752 (1969), 44–46, 106
Colorado v. Bannister, 101 S.Ct. 42 (1980), 115
Coolidge v. New Hampshire, 403 U.S. 443 (1971), 45, 115, 133
Cooper v. California, 386 U.S. 58 (1967), 113
Dombrowski v. Pfister, 380 U.S. 479 (1965), 51
Doyle v. Ohio, 426 U.S. 610 (1976), 115
Edwards v. Arizona, 101 S.Ct. 1880 (1981), 49–50, 107, 114
Escobedo v. Illinois, 378 U.S. 478 (1964), 48, 76, 82, 107, 135
Fay v. Noia, 372 U.S. 391 (1963), 52, 186
Fletcher v. Weir, 102 S.Ct. 1309 (1982), 53, 115
Gideon v. Wainwright, 372 U.S. 335 (1963), 48, 186
Harris v. New York, 401 U.S. 222 (1971), 49
Illinois v. Gates, 103 S.Ct. 2317 (1983), 44, 138
Johnson v. U.S., 333 U.S. 10 (1948), 42
Johnson v. Zerbst, 304 U.S. 458 (1938), 48–49, 107, 135
Jones v. U.S., 357 U.S. 493 (1958), 43, 133, 185
Katz v. U.S., 389 U.S. 347 (1967), 44

Malloy v. Hogan, 378 U.S. 1 (1964), 48
Mapp v. Ohio, 367 U.S. 643 (1961). *See* General Index
Massachusetts v. Sheppard, Slip Opinion, No. 82–913 (July 5, 1984), 137
Menard v. Mitchell, 328 F.Supp. 718 (1971), 61–62, 66, 70, 119, 190
Michigan v. Mosely, 423 U.S. 96 (1975), 49–50, 66, 114
Michigan v. Tucker, 417 U.S. 433 (1974), 49, 69–70
Miranda v. Arizona, 384 U.S. 436 (1966). *See* General Index
New York v. Belton, 453 U.S. 454 (1981), 46, 66, 68, 114, 133
New York v. Quarles, Slip Opinion, No. 82–1213 (June 12, 1984), 50, 188
Olmstead v. U.S., 277 U.S. 438 (1928), 44
Oregon v. Hass, 420 U.S. 714 (1975), 49
Paul v. Davis, 424 U.S. 693 (1976), 62, 66, 69
Pennsylvania v. Mimms, 434 U.S. 106 (1977), 133
Picard v. Connor, 404 U.S. 270 (1972), 52–53, 188
Rakas v. Illinois, 439 U.S. 128 (1978), 43
Reynolds v. Sims, 377 U.S. 533 (1964), 51, 186
Rhode Island v. Innis, 446 U.S. 291 (1980), 50
Robbins v. California, 101 S.Ct. 2841 (1981), 46–47, 68
Schenkloth v. Bustamonte, 412 U.S. 218 (1973), 53
Spinelli v. U.S., 393 U.S. 410 (1969), 138
Stone v. Powell, 428 U.S. 465 (1976), 45, 53, 188
Tarlton v. Saxbe, 507 F. 2d 1116 (1974), 61, 119
Terry v. Ohio, 392 U.S. 1 (1968), 44
Townsend v. Sain, 372 U.S. 293 (1963), 52–53, 84, 186
U.S. v. Calandra, 414 U.S. 338 (1974), 45, 49, 66, 69
U.S. v. Chadwick, 433 U.S. 1 (1977), 46
U.S. v. Hendricks, 348 U.S. 851 (1954), 52
U.S. v. Janis, 428 U.S. 433 (1976), 45, 66, 69
U.S. v. Leon, Slip Opinion, No. 82–1771 (July 5, 1984), 47, 66, 137, 139, 160, 188, 190
U.S. v. Rabinowitz, 339 U.S. 56 (1950), 42, 44, 133
U.S. v. Robinson, 414 U.S. 218 (1973), 45–47, 68, 106
U.S. v. Ross, 456 U.S. 798 (1982), 46, 68
U.S. v. Salvucci, 100 S.Ct. 2547 (1980), 43, 133
Washington v. Chrisman, 102 S.Ct. 812 (1982), 133
Weeks v. U.S., 232 U.S. 383 (1914), xv, 42–43, 76, 106, 130, 133, 195
Wolf v. Colorado, 338 U.S. 25 (1949), 42–43, 186
Younger v.Harris, 401 U.S. 37 (1971), 52

STATE COURT CASES

Board of Selectmen of Framingham v. Municipal Court of City of Boston, 369 N.E. 2d 1145 (Massachusetts, 1977), 136
Brosnahan v. Brown, 651 P.2d 274 (California, 1982), 111

Commonwealth v. Bettencourt, 281 N.E.2d 220 (Massachusetts, 1972), 136
Commonwealth v. Bowlen, 223 N.E.2d 391 (Massachusetts, 1967), 136
Commonwealth v. Campbell, 226 N.E.2d 211 (Massachusetts, 1967), 136
Commonwealth v. Cantalupo, 420 N.E.2d 1040 (Massachusetts, 1980), 136
Commonwealth v. Daniels, 321 N.E.2d 822 (Massachusetts, 1975), 136
Commonwealth v. Femino, 226 N.E.2d 248 (Massachusetts, 1967), 135
Commonwealth v. Garreffi, 245 N.E.2d 442 (Massachusetts, 1969), 136
Commonwealth v. Harmond, 382 N.E.2d 203 (Massachusetts, 1978), 136
Commonwealth v. Meehan, 387 N.E.2d 527 (Massachusetts, 1979), 136
Commonwealth v. Morrissey, 222 N.E.2d 755 (Massachusetts, 1967), 135
Commonwealth v. Nowells, 458 N.E.2d 1186 (Massachusetts, 1983), 138
Commonwealth v. Ortiz, 380 N.E.2d 669 (Massachusetts, 1978), 136
Commonwealth v. Reynolds, 370 N.E.2d 1375 (Massachusetts, 1977), 136
Commonwealth v. Sheppard, 441 N.E.2d 725 (Massachusetts, 1982), 137–39, 160, 163, 167
Commonwealth v. Sylvia, 402 N.E.2d 489 (Massachusetts, 1980), 136
Commonwealth v. Thomas, 267 N.E.2d 489 (Massachusetts, 1971), 136
Commonwealth v. Upton, 458 N.E.2d 717 (Massachusetts, 1983), 138–39
Commonwealth v. Walker, 350 N.E.2d 678 (Massachusetts, 1976), 136
Commonwealth v. Zukoski, 345 N.E.2d 690 (Massachusetts, 1976), 136
Davidson v. Dill,, 503 P.2d 157 (Colorado, 1972), 123–24, 161
Dutil v. the State, 606 P.2d 269 (Washington, 1980), 131
Guidi v. Superior Court, 513 P.2d 980 (California, 1973), 106
Loder v. San Diego, 132 Cal. Rptr. 464 (California, 1976), 119, 153, 161
McCall v. Oroville Mercury Co., 142 Cal. App. 3d 805 (California, 1983), 120
McCall v. People, 623 P.2d 397 (Colorado, 1981), 114
New Bedford Times v. Clerk of the Third District Court, 387 N.E.2d 110 (Massachusetts, 1979), 152–53, 161, 167
People v. Bannister, 607 P.2d 987 (Colorado, 1980), 115
People v. Braeseke, 602 P.2d 384 (California, 1980), 107
People v. Brisendine, 531 P.2d 1099 (California, 1975), 105–6, 132, 160
People v. Burns, 615 P.2d 686 (Colorado, 1980), 114
People v. Cahan, 282 P.2d 905 (California, 1955), 43, 105–6, 193
People v. Casias, 563 P.2d 926 (Colorado, 1977), 114
People v. Chimel, 439 P.2d 33 (California, 1968), 106
People v. Counterman, 556 P.2d 481 (Colorado, 1976), 114
People v. Disbrow, 16 Cal.3d 101 (California, 1976), 107
People v. Edwards, 458 P.2d 713 (California, 1969), 106
People v. Haggart, 533 P.2d 488 (Colorado, 1975), 113
People v. Jimenez, 580 P.2d 672 (California, 1978), 107
People v. Krivda, 486 P.2d 1262 (California, 1971), 106
People v. Lujan, 475 P.2d 700 (Colorado, 1970), 113
People v. McGrew, 462 P.2d 1 (California, 1969), 106
People v. Medina, 496 P.2d 433 (California, 1972), 106

People v. *Parham*, 384 P.2d 1001 (California, 1963), 106
People v. *Pettingill*, 578 P.2d 108 (California, 1978), 105, 107
People v. *Quintana*, 601 P.2d 350 (Colorado, 1979), 114–15
People v. *Thompson*, 523 P.2d 128 (Colorado, 1974), 113
Serrano v. *Priest*, 487 P.2d 1241 (California, 1971), 161
State v. *Adams*, 458 P.2d 558 (Washington, 1969), 130
State v. *Canaday*, 488 P.2d 1064 (Washington, 1971), 130
State v. *Chrisman*, 619 P.2d 971 (Washington, 1980), 133–34
State v. *Gibbons*, 203 P.2d 390 (Washington, 1922), 130, 160
State v. *Gluck*, 518 P.2d 703 (Washington, 1974), 131
State v. *Michaels*, 374 P.2d 989 (Washington, 1962), 130, 133, 160, 171, 195
State v. *Patterson*, 515 P.2d 496 (Washington, 1973), 130
State v. *Ringer*, 674 P.2d 1240 (Washington, 1983), 129–30, 133–34, 160
State v. *Simpson*, 622 P.2d 1199 (Washington, 1980), 132–34
State v. *Thompson*, 601 P.2d 1284 (Washington, 1979), 131
State v. *Wilson*, 424 P.2d 650 (Washington, 1967), 131
Stewart v. *People*, 426 P.2d 545 (Colorado, 1967), 112–23

General Index

Abortion, 34, 180–81, 202

Accountability, xii, xxi, 36, 178, 192, 198, 203; Colorado, 101–2, 121–22, 162; defined, 183; law enforcement, 97; and organization theory, 22–23; state and local government policy, xiv, 17, 39–40

ACLU (American Civil Liberties Union), xvii, 68, 198; Colorado, 103–4, 122–23, 163; Washington, 141. *See also* Civil liberties interests

American Newspaper Association, 89. *See also* Press

Archibald, Samuel, 122

Bellotti, Francis X., 128, 150–54, 167

Bird, Rose, 109, 111, 167

Brennan, William, 47, 107, 113, 190

Brooke, Edward, 150

Brown, Edmund G. (Pat), 102, 166, 193

Brown, Edmund G., Jr. (Jerry), 102, 109, 118–19, 127–28, 168, 194

Brown, Willy, 101, 194

Bureau of Criminal Justice Statistics. *See* LEAA

Burger Court (1969–): civil liberties decisions, 40–41; criminal records privacy, 62, 66–67, 160–61; electoral realignment, 180; exclusionary rule, 45, 47; and federal courts, 52–53, 56–57, 84, 171, 188–89; interrogation and confession, 49–50, 69–70, 80, 160, 188; law enforcement conceptions, 66, 68, 188; policy objectives, xiv; search and seizure, 45–48, 53, 69, 160, 187–90; and Warren Court, 187. *See also* Federal courts; U.S. Supreme Court; Warren Court

California: attorney general's office, 102, 126, 166–67; Computerized Criminal History File (CCH), 116, 120, 168; criminal records privacy, xv, 87, 116–21, 140, 142, 147, 153, 193; Department of Justice, 94, 102, 116–17, 120; electoral politics, 166–67; executive-legislative-judicial relations, 102, 109, 117, 166–67; governor's office, 57, 101–2, 166, 192; independent state grounds, 57, 105–7, 109, 119, 132; interrogation and confession, xvi, 107; and Law Enforcement Assistance Administration (LEAA), 118–19, 194; legitimation crisis, 193–94; Office of Criminal Justice Planning (OCJP), 118; police, 106, 158, 162, 190; policy making style, 102, 105, 117, 202; political culture, 101–2, 104, 135, 166, 192; Proposition 8 (Victims' Bill of Rights), 109–11, 139, 205; Proposition

13, 102; Proposition 24, 194, 205; prosecutors, 106, 108, 110, 158; public opinion, 109; search and seizure, xv–xvi, 34–44, 57, 105–7, 110, 160, 193; state constitution, 57, 101, 202; state court civil liberties decisions, 84–86, 105–11, 167, 193; state court response to Burger Court, 106–7, 161, 193; state court response to criminal records privacy, 119–20, 159, 161, 166, 190, 194; state court response to Warren Court, 102, 105; state legislature, 101, 111, 194; state Supreme Court, 102, 109, 111, 193; trial courts, 106, 108–10, 158, 193; U.S. Constitution, Fourth Amendment, 101. *See also* Criminal records privacy; Interrogation and confession; Liberalism; Search and seizure; States, sample of four

Carter, Jimmy, 127

CSR (Central State Repository): California, 88, 92, 117; Colorado, 104, 121; development of, 60, 63–64, 73, 88, 171; Massachusetts, 128; quality of records, 92–95; Washington, 141–42, 145–46. *See also* LEAA; NCIC

Change (as a measure of implementation): behavioral, 9, 78, 97–98, 170; beliefs and attitudes, 8–9, 174–75; expectations, xvii–xviii, 178; institutional, xvii, 3, 11, 28–29, 36, 179, 182–83, 198; measurement, 8–9; procedural, 6, 8–9, 87, 94, 97–98; progressive, xxi, 182–83, 189–90, 193–96, 198, 200; regressive, 182–83, 193, 197. *See also* Compliance; Impact; Performance; Reform; Response

Change, extent of, as an explanation of implementation, 10–11, 25, 75–77, 97, 155

Chapman, Bruce, 126

Civil liberties decisions: Burger Court, 40–41; and criminal records privacy, xv, 9, 97–98, 144–45, 157–72, 193; search and seizure and interrogation and confession compared, xvi, 75–84, 99, 155, 165; U.S. Supreme Court, xiii, xv, xvii, 8–9, 39–40; Warren and Burger Courts compared, 65–67, 160, 163, 170; Warren Court, 8–9, 40, 186. *See also* California; Colorado; Constitutional rights; Defendants' rights; Interrogation and confession; Massachusetts; Police; Prosecutors; Search and seizure; State courts; Trial courts; U.S. Constitution; Washington

Civil liberties interests, xvii, 23, 159, 162–64, 199–200; attorneys, 198–99; criminal records privacy, 72, 96, 152; Massachusetts, 150; Washington, 127, 143–44, 196. *See also* ACLU

Clark, William C., 109

Cognitive dissonance theory, 8, 11, 25–28; adaptation, 27, 33, 157, 172; and cognitive expressivist theory, 30–31, 33, 204; and communication theory, 20; and explanations of implementation, 25, 27, 107, 156–57, 167; freedom, 26–27; and Freudian theory, 26; ideology, 27; and legitimation theory, 26–27, 34, 36–37, 107; and utility theory, 19, 204

Cognitive expressivist theory, 28–34; and cognitive dissonance theory, 30–31, 33, 204; freedom, 28, 33; and Freudian theory, 31–33, 163; ideology, 29–33; and legitimation theory, 29–32, 35, 38; politics, 28; practical and expressive orders, 29

Colorado: accountability, 101–2, 121–22, 162; attorney general's office, 103–4, 166; Bureau of Identification, 94; criminal records privacy, xvi, 87, 121–24, 142, 148, 193, 196; District Attorneys Association, 103–4, 114–15, 166, 196; executive-legislative-judicial relations, 103, 113, 115–16, 167; governor's office, 103–4, 192; independent state grounds, 113–14, 134; interrogation and confession, 114–15, 160–61; and Law Enforcement Assistance Administration (LEAA), 104, 122–23; police, 104, 122, 158; policy making style, 111–13, 115, 167, 196; political culture, 101–4, 121, 162, 192; press,

102, 122–23, 162; prosecutors, 114–15, 124, 158, 166; search and seizure, 70, 112–15, 160; state court civil liberties decisions, 84–86, 111–16, 193, 195; state court reform, xvi, 103, 112; state court response to Burger Court, 111–12, 114–16, 160–61, 188, 196; state court response to criminal records privacy, 123–24, 159, 161, 166, 169; state court response to Warren Court, 111–12; state legislature, 103, 115–16, 196; state Supreme Court, xvi, 103, 113; trial courts, 171; U.S. Constitution, Fourth Amendment, 112. *See also* Criminal records privacy; Interrogation and confession; Liberalism; Search and seizure; States, sample of four

Common good, 25, 31, 37, 206

Communication theory, 20–21; civil liberties, 99, 155; and cognitive dissonance theory, 20; communication processes, 13, 79, 99, 131; and explanations of implementation, 20, 79, 155; and Freudian theory, 20; and legitimation theory, 37

Compliance (as a measure of implementation), xix, 5–6, 17, 19, 23. *See also* Change; Impact; Performance; Response

CETA (Comprehensive Employment and Training Act of 1973), 19–20

CCH. *See* NCIC

Confession. *See* Interrogation and confession

Constitutional rights, xiv, 26, 39–40, 53, 65–67, 155, 160, 189; criminal records privacy, 61–62; U.S. Constitution, Fourth Amendment, 65–66; U.S. Constitution, Fifth Amendment, 65; U.S. Constitution, Fourteenth Amendment, 66. *See also* Defendants' rights; Privacy

Crime: clearance rates, 67, 76, 108; control, 35, 40, 79, 182, 200–1; politicization, 49, 181, 187, 200–203; punitive approach, 201–4; recidivism, 119, 190; reduction, xii–xiv, 39, 41, 200

Criminal history records: court proceedings, 90, 92, 123, 146, 152–53; defined, 87, 89–90, 149, 152; intelligence and investigative information, 68–69, 87, 96, 117, 122, 145, 164; public disclosure, xvi, 121–24, 141, 144, 150, 164; subject access, 119, 142–43, 147; uses, 57–58, 68–70, 87, 89, 96, 119–121. *See also* LEAA

Criminal justice administration, xii, 197; case disposition, 78–79, 170; federal role, 39–41, 71; intergovernmental relations, 39–40

Criminal justice information systems, 39; information technology, xvii, 41, 58–59, 61, 68, 120–121, 148; National Law Enforcement Telecommunications System (NLETS), 63–65; politics of, 96–97, 147; PROMIS, 104; technical capacity, 63, 72–73, 96. *See also* LEAA; NCIC

Criminal justice system. *See* Policy system; Reform

Criminal records privacy, xv, 39, 57–65; administration and records management, xvi, 94, 117, 123, 159, 162–63, 172, 191; audit, 72, 94, 147; dissemination, 61, 87–91, 153; dissemination, California, 118–20, 142; dissemination, Colorado, 122, 142, 162; dissemination, "compelling public necessity," 61, 66, 70; dissemination, "contemporaneousness," 89; dissemination, Massachusetts, 149–50, 152–54, 162; dissemination, "non-conviction data," 89–90; dissemination, Washington, 142, 146; employers, 89; federal court review, 61, 66, 70; governor's committee, 118–119, 122–23, 126, 132, 140, 142–43; independent commission, 92, 94, 140, 142, 161; information technology, 58–59; law enforcement conceptions, 68; pre-LEAA policy, 147, 168, 172; quality of records, 58–59, 61–63, 66, 68, 72, 90, 92, 94; quality of records, California, 119; quality of records, Colorado, 123–24; quality of records, Washington, 146–47; results, xv, 94, 96; separation of powers, 71; state planning agency (SPA), California, 118; SPA, Colorado, 122, 169; SPA, Massachusetts, 148, 150–51, 154, 159; SPA, Washington, 140–47, 196; U.S. Constitution, First Amendment, 122, 153; U.S. Constitution, Fourth Amendment, 66; U.S. Constitution, Fourteenth Amendment, 66. *See also* California; Civil liberties decisions; Colorado; LEAA; Massachusetts; NCIC; Omnibus Crime Control and Safe Streets Act of 1968; Police; Press; Prosecutors; Public opinion; State courts; Washington

Decentralization. *See* Federalism
Defendants' rights, xii–xiv, 34–35, 50–51, 65, 75, 81. 185–87; California, 105; Colorado, 112; criminal procedure, 6, 186–87; criminal records privacy, 39–41, 58, 66, 200; due process, xiv, 8, 45, 66, 163–64, 185, 194; as electoral issue, 181; Massachusetts, 129; state court reform, 54; Washington, 143. *See also* Civil liberties decisions; Constitutional rights; U.S. Constitution
Democratic Party, 35, 180–81, 195; California, 101, 117; Colorado, 102, 104; Massachusetts, 125, 128, 150; Washington, 126, 140
Duekmejian, Georgc, 102, 109, 111, 133, 166
Douglas, William O., 66
Due process. *See* Constitutional rights; Defendants' rights; U.S. Constitution: Fourteenth Amendment
Dukakis, Michael, 126–28, 150–51, 154

Edwards, Don, 116
Eisenhower, Dwight, 101
Elections, 37–38; coalitions, 35, 179–80, 182, 201; "critical" and realigning, 35, 177–81, 204
Electoral issues: crime, 181, 187, 200–203; economic, 34; symbolic/moral, 34, 180–81, 202; "style," 8, 170
Enforceability (as an explanation of implementation), xvi–xvii, 15–17, 98, 155, 178; and legitimation theory, 36
Enforcement: criminal records privacy, 87, 92, 94, 166, 169; by federal courts, 52; applies to *Mapp* and *Miranda*, 81–84, 158
Equality, xiii, 24, 40, 186, 197, 205–6
Evans, Daniel, 126, 140
Exclusionary rule. *See* Search and seizure

Fairness, 8–9. *See also* Defendants' rights
FBI (Federal Bureau of Investigation): Computerized Criminal History File (CCH), 62–64, 72–73, 116, 120–21, 148–49, 171, 190–91, 195; criminal records privacy, 58, 62, 68; dissemination, 61; National Crime Information Center (NCIC), 60, 62
Federal courts: appellate relief, 51–52; civil liberties and criminal records privacy compared, 60; "compelling necessity," 185; "full and fair opportunity," 53; "fundamental fairness," 186; habeas corpus, 51–53, 57, 188; injunctive relief, 51; jurisdiction, 51–52, 57, 71, 181, 186; "preferred position," 185; "remedial counterpart," 51; "selective incorporation," 71, 186; state court civil liberties decisions, xiv, 51–53, 83, 185–86; state court oversight, 51, 84, 174, 180, 188; U.S. Constitution, Article Three, 51; U.S. Constitution, Fifth Amendment, 71; U.S. Constitution, Sixth Amendment, 71; U.S. Constitution, Fourteenth Amendment, 71; Warren and Burger Courts compared, 71, 84. *See also* Burger Court; State courts; U.S. Supreme Court; Warren Court
Federalism, 34, 71–72, 155–56, 165, 169, 186, 197; Burger Court, 115; California, 109; Colorado, 102–3; criminal procedure, 57; decentralization, 71–72, 97, 116, 180–82, 187–89;

intergovernmental relations, 7, 11, 16, 84–85, 158; Warren Court, 52
Frankfurter, Felix, 42, 133
Freedom, 24, 27–29, 31, 33–34, 200, 202–4; individual rights, xxi, 178, 197, 203, 205; state courts, 188–89
Freedom of Information Act, 122
Freudian theory: and cognitive dissonance theory, 26; and cognitive expressivist theory, 31–33, 163; and communication theory, 20; identification, 24, 28, 32–33; introjection, 32; introspection, 31; and legitimation theory, 36, 181, 184, 192; projection, 26, 31–33, 163, 203

Gann, Paul, 109
Gezell, Gerhard, 61
Gorton, Slade, 126, 140–41
Governance, 72–73, 156, 165, 169, 181, 186, 191; authority and capacity, xiv, 18, 25, 36, 73, 81, 84, 178, 197; California, 170; Colorado, 170; and legitimation theory, 36; Washington, 170
Guideline development, xviii, 16, 20, 70, 83, 199; criminal records privacy, 72, 86, 89–90, 143, 145–47, 152, 161–62; interrogation and confession, 9; state court rule-making, 55–56, 132; by states, 97, 174. *See also* LEAA; State courts

Ideology, xvi, 45, 197, 204; California, 101, 105; and cognitive dissonance theory, 27; and cognitive expressivist theory, 29–33; Colorado, 167; ideological factors, 82–85, 155, 159, 170; legitimating ideologies, 24, 34–37; Massachusetts, 135, 137, 139, 148, 151; partisan ideologies, 24–25; state courts, 55, 79, 81–85; and systems theory, 24; Washington, 143
Impact (as a measure of implementation), 7–8, 98; unintended consequences, 7, 58, 81, 111. *See also* Change; Compliance; Performance; Response
Implementation: common conditions of effectiveness, 4, 9–17; explanatory frameworks, xx, 3–5, 156, 172–75; measurement, xix, 5–9; patterns, 4–5, 7, 11, 177; theoretical perspectives, xiii, xv, 4–5, 17–38, 155–56. *See also* Change; Change, extent of; Compliance; Enforceability; Impact; Institutional structure; Performance; Policy clarity; Policy form; Political culture; Response; State and local elites
Implementers: and cognitive dissonance theory, 107; discretion, 12–13, 21–23, 37, 98, 170, 182, 188, 200; expectations, 4–7, 11, 75–76, 155–57, 159–65; influenced by state and local elites, 13–14; responses, 6, 156–57, 172. *See also* Police; Prosecutors; Trial courts
Institutional roles, xix, 24, 29, 31, 33, 99, 184, 200–201
Institutional structure (as an explanation of implementation), 31–34, 156, 169–72, 175, 178, 180–81, 193, 197
Intergovernmental relations. *See* Federalism
Interrogation and confession: "consent to search," 49, 78; custodial interrogation, 48–50, 77, 107, 114, 136, 188; exigent circumstances, 50; "interpretive rule," 70; *Miranda* warnings, 48–49, 107; "prophylactic standard," 49; "public safety exception," 50; results, 76; "right to counsel," xiv, 48–50, 107; "right to remain silent," xiv, 48, 79; "selective incorporation," 48, 186; and separation of powers, 70; "totality of circumstances," 48–49, 130; U.S. Constitution, Fifth Amendment, 48; U.S. Constitution, Sixth Amendment;, 48; U.S. Constitution, Fourteenth Amendment, 48; voluntariness, xiv, 48–49, 107, 114, 130, 135–36. *See also* Burger Court; California; Civil liberties decisions; Colorado; Massachusetts; *Miranda v. Arizona*; Police; Prosecutors; Public opinion; State courts; Trial courts; Warren Court; Washington

Judicial and legislative processes: civil liberties decisions and criminal records privacy compared, 39–41, 97–100, 177; compared, xiv, xvii, 4–5, 73, 156, 205; criminal justice reform, 198–99; implementation, xiv–xv, 3, 5, 9–13, 15–17, 23

Judicial role: accountability, 56; activism, 21, 55, 186, 188; authority, 73, 158, 170; enlargement, xxi, 178, 198, 205–6; integrity, 43, 47, 137–38, 190; judicial impact, 3, 9, 21; "juridical democracy," 21; legislative policy making vs. judicial rule making, 165–66; legitimacy, 6, 73. *See also* Federal courts; State courts; U.S. Supreme Court

King Edward, 128, 154

Labor-management relations, 29

Lamm, Richard, 102–4, 112–13, 122–23, 169, 196

LEAA (Law Enforcement Assistance Administration), xvi, 39, 58, 159; administration and records management for criminal records privacy, 86, 92, 94, 97, 191; block grants, 98, 118, 126–28, 140, 166; California, 118–19, 168, 194; Colorado, 104, 122–23; Computerized Criminal History File (CCH), 60, 62–64, 73, 116, 147–49; court proceedings, 90, 92, 152, 191; criminal records privacy amendment, 62, 85, 117; dissemination, 69–70, 87–90, 118, 121; information technology, 58–59, 190; Massachusetts, 151; quality of records, 86, 92–95; state court reform, 53, 59; Title l28 regulations, xiv, 62, 86–87, 89–90, 94, 140, 151, 168, 191; Washington, 140–43. *See also* Criminal history records; Criminal justice administration; Criminal justice information systems; Criminal records privacy; CSR; NCIC; Omnibus Crime Control and Safe Street Act of 1968; SEARCH Group Incorporated

Law enforcement conceptions, 67–68, 161–64, 169–70, 200; California, 160, 190, 194; Colorado, 190; conception of due process, 159–60, 162–64; conception of truth, 26, 50, 66–67, 80, 159, 161–64, 187, 189; Massachusetts, 160; Washington, 160, 190

Law enforcement practice, 61, 67–69, 133, 155, 163, 190, 200. *See also* Police

Legislative and judicial processes compared. *See* Judicial and legislative processes: compared

Legitimacy: of elected officials, 98; of federal control over states, 73; institutional, 4, 21, 107, 192–93; of judicial authority, 73, 206; of national vs. state and local policy, 34–35; of policy, 21, 157, 168; of policy originator, 107, 110, 156–57; of political regime, xix, xx, 18–19, 21, 24–25, 30–31, 34, 36–38, 204; resources of, xviii, 25, 193, 196, 206; of state courts, 85, 134, 171; of state courts, California, 109–11, 161; of state courts, Massachusetts, 139, 161, 171, 193; of state courts, Washington, 130, 134, 142, 171; of U.S. Supreme Court, 179–80, 189

Legitimation theory, 5, 35–38; and cognitive dissonance theory, 26–27, 34, 36–37, 107; and cognitive expressivist theory, 29, 32, 35, 38; and communication theory, 37; compensation, 184; conflict, 183–84, 187, 197, 200; crisis, 29–30, 185; deficit, 30, 184; delegitimation, 25, 179, 181, 194; displacement, 30, 178, 185, 197, 200; electoral realignment, 178–79, 181; governance capacity, 36, 184; identification, 36, 181, 184, 192; ideology, 24, 34–37; interests served, 36, 184; judicial activism, 21; and organization theory, 37; political change process, 36, 184; political stability and policy form, 36, 177, 184; problems, xxi, 30, 34, 178, 183–91, 193, 197

Liberalism, xxi, 21, 112, 189, 203–6; California, 102, 105, 107, 118; Colorado, 103–4, 115; Massachusetts, 125, 127–29, 135, 148, 151; and reform,

197–98, 204; Washington, 126–27, 169

Magnuson, Warren, 126
Mapp v. Ohio: ambiguity, 98, 158, 160; Burger Court response, 45, 53; California response, xv, 108, 193; Colorado response, 114; and criminal records privacy, xv, 39, 97–98; Massachusetts response, 139; and *Miranda*, xii–xiv, 48, 66, 75, 78–80, 82, 99–100, 132, 158, 160–61, 165, 199; police, 76, 82, 158, 199; public opinion, 80, 100; results, 9, 45, 75–78, 160, 190; state courts, 71, 76, 80–83, 158, 186; trial courts, 70, 165; Warren Court search and seizure decision, 41, 43–44; Washington response, xv, 13–31, 133. *See also* Search and seizure
Marshall, Thurgood, 46–47, 190
Marxist theory, 29
Massachusetts: Anti-Crime Council, 126; attorney general's office, 128, 166–68; Computerized Criminal History File (CCH), 96, 149, 168; civil liberties interests, 150; Criminal History System Board, 128–29, 149, 151–54, 167; Criminal Offender Record Information Act (CORI), 129, 148–54, 168; criminal records privacy, xv–xvi, 87–88, 92, 140, 147–54, 159, 161, 168, 193–94, 200; executive-legislative-judicial relations, 128, 148, 152–53, 162, 167–68; Fair Information Practices Act, 150; governor's office, 127, 166, 192; independent state grounds, 138–39; interrogation and confession, xv, 135–36; and Law Enforcement Assistance Administration (LEAA), 128, 151; Office of Probation, 129, 151–54; Office of Public Safety, 128–29, 151, 154; police, 128–29, 136–37, 151–52, 160, 162, 164, 167; policy making style, 127–28, 135, 148, 202; political culture, 125–29, 135, 138–39, 148, 166, 192; press, 152; search and seizure, 135–40, 163, 194; Security and Privacy Council, 128, 149, 151–52, 154; state court civil liberties decisions, xvi, 84–86, 129, 135–40, 167, 193–94; state court reform, xvi; state court response to Burger Court, 135–37, 161; state court response to criminal records privacy, 152–53, 161, 166; state court response to Warren Court, 135, 194; state Supreme Judicial Court, 129, 138; trial courts, 136, 139. *See also* Criminal records privacy; Interrogation and confession; Liberalism; Search and seizure; States, sample of four
Media. *See* Press
Miller, Arthur, 148, 150
Miranda v. Arizona: Burger Court response, 45, 50, 53, 69, 80, 160; clarity, 49–50, 78–79, 199; California response, 107–8; Colorado response, 114–15; Massachusetts response, xv, 135–36, 139; police, 21, 76, 79, 157–58, 165, 199; prosecutors, 80; public opinion, 79–80, 100; results, 8–9, 75–79; state courts, 71, 79–80, 82–83, 85, 186; U.S. Congress response, 70; Warren Court interrogation and confession decision, 41, 48–49, 67; Washington response, 130–31, 144. *See also* Interrogation and confession; *Mapp v. Ohio*; and *Miranda*
Mitchell, John, 63, 149
Mondale, Walter, 202
Mosk, Stanley, 107, 111

National Association of Attorney Generals, 52
National Center for State Courts, 90, 92. *See also* State courts
NCIC (National Crime Information Center), 60; Computerized Criminal History File (CCH), 60, 68–69, 71–73, 94; CCH, California, 116, 120, 168; CCH, governance, 62–65, 148, 171, 190–91, 195; CCH, Massachusetts, 96, 149, 168; CCH, technical configuration, 64, 96, 120; criminal records privacy amendment, 62; Identification File (IDENT), 60, 64; intelligence and investigative information, 68–69; na-

tional index, 63–64, 120; press, 149–50; state governors' response, 150, 168; state participation in, 60, 120
National Governors' Conference, 103, 150
National Judicial Conference, 52, 126, 188
NLETS (National Law Enforcement Telecommunications System), 63–65. *See also* Criminal justice information systems; NCIC
New Deal, 28, 40, 135, 180–82, 185, 187, 201
New federalism, 41, 92, 105, 170, 187, 189, 191; California, 107; Colorado, 112; Law Enforcement Assistance Administration (LEAA), 191. *See also* Federalism
Nixon, Richard, 127, 148, 180, 187

OTA (Office of Technology Assessment), xvi; and CCH, 63–65, 96
Omnibus Crime Control and Safe Streets Act of 1968, xiv, 39, 49, 98; criminal records privacy amendment of 1973, 62, 85, 90, 92, 117, 121; interrogation and confession amendment, 70
Organizational structure, 7–9, 157, 171; bureaucracy, 56, 98–99, 128, 148, 182; bureaucratic type, 22–23, 202; collegial type, 23; defined, 183; and information technology, 58–59; professional expertise type, 23
Organization theory, 3, 22–23; complexity and coordination, 11; and Constitutional rights, 155; criminal records privacy, 96, 98–99; discretion and delegation, 12, 22–23, 98, 188; and explanations of implementation, 22, 155; law enforcement practice, 155; and legitimation theory, 37; and systems theory, 24

Performance (as a measure of implementation), 8, 98. *See also* Change; Compliance; Impact; Response
Police: civil liberties decisions, 21, 190; and cognitive dissonance theory, 26; conduct, 21, 43, 48, 79, 81, 89, 106, 136–37, 158, 200; criminal records privacy, 62, 87–89; criminal records privacy, California, 162; criminal records privacy, Colorado, 122; criminal records privacy, Massachusetts, 151–52, 162, 164; criminal records privacy, Washington, 144–47, 162, 164; department styles, 22, 58, 67, 200; discretion, 58, 60, 66, 76, 158, 163, 199–200; and information technology, 58–59; interrogation and confession, 21, 75–76, 78–80, 157–58; search and seizure, 75–78, 82, 158, 163, 165, 190; search and seizure, California, 106; search and seizure, Massachusetts, 160, 167; search and seizure, Washington, 131, 133–34, 144, 160, 162; search and seizure and interrogation and confession compared, 80–81, 199; and state courts, 81, 158. *See also* California; Colorado; Law enforcement practice; Massachusetts; Sheriffs and Chiefs Association; Washington
Policy clarity (as an explanation of implementation), xvii, 12–13, 85, 97, 155, 199; applied to criminal records privacy, 87, 161; applied to *Mapp*, 98, 158, 160; applied to *Miranda*, 49–50, 78–79, 199; *Mapp* and *Miranda* compared, xiv, 77–79, 82, 132, 160–61
Policy, federal, xiii, 167; conversion to state and local practice, xv, xvii, xxi, 39–40, 97; state anticipation of federal policy, xv, 6, 76, 82, 147, 168, 172; state implementation, xv, 156–57; state responses, xiii–xviii, 6–7, 193; state responses, legitimacy of, xxi, 191, 195
Policy form (as an explanation of implementation), xxi, 156–59, 177; and legitimation problems, 184; procedural, 6, 70, 157, 184, 186, 194, 199; structural, 156–57, 169–70, 177, 180, 184, 186, 190–91, 193, 197, 199; substantive, 70, 157, 184, 186, 194, 199
Policy making style, xviii, 178, 188, 195; defined, xvi; managerial, 102,

117, 127–28, 187, 202–3; pragmatic, 105, 111–13, 126, 128–29, 135, 167, 195–96; procedural, 112, 115, 135, 196; substantive, 105, 148
Policy system, 4–5, 7, 19; criminal justice system, 54, 66, 70–72, 98, 100, 156, 158, 169–70, 172, 174, 188; defined, 183; and professional interest groups, 56; stability of, 11; subsystems, 25, 35, 197
Political culture (as an explanation of implementation): California, 101–2, 104, 135, 166, 192; and cognitive expressivist theory, 30–31, 35; Colorado, 101–4, 121, 162, 192; defined, xviii, 192; differences, 5, 54–55, 83, 85; Massachusetts, 125–29, 135, 138–39, 148, 192; significance of, 155, 165, 167, 172, 175, 177–78; Washington, 125–27, 134, 140, 192
Political environment, 7, 10, 99–100, 174; national, 13, 34–35, 39, 177
Political parties, 38, 179, 181–82, 192
Political system, xix, xxi, 21, 178; defined, 20, 23–24; disaffection, 35, 177, 197, 203–5; foundations (values), 182, 185, 202; implications for, xv, 3, 37, 177, 192; and legitimation theory, 36, 197; stability, 20, 24, 27–28, 30, 33, 37, 179–80. *See also* Legitimacy: of political regime
Politics: appearances and reality, xix, 31, 33, 145, 164–65, 197; consensus, xvi, 125–26, 129, 139, 148, 166; contested concepts, 28, 31, 50, 66; defined, xix, 23; interest group, 100–101, 104, 121, 141, 161; interests served, xix, xxi, 15, 18–19, 21, 29, 36–37, 155, 158–59, 163, 184; and legitimation theory, xix, 36; national vs. state and local interests, 35, 94, 177, 191; pluralist theory, 161; real interests, xv, 18, 28, 161. *See also* Institutional structure
Populism, 101–2, 121, 181
Powell, William, 53
Power, 28; conflict over, 156, 178, 180, 197, 205; structure, xiii, xix, xxi, 5, 8, 25, 28
Press, xix, 102, 126, 152; Computerized Criminal History File (CCH), 149–50; criminal records privacy, 69–70, 89, 122–23, 141, 162, 168. *See also* Criminal history records, public disclosure
Privacy, 22, 39, 65–66; California, 119; criminal records privacy, 58, 60–62, 66, 69; Massachusetts, 153–54; public right to know, 69–70, 155, 159; U.S. Constitution, First Amendment, 62. *See also* Constitutional rights; Defendants' rights; U.S. Constitution
Progressive Reform, 40, 180–82, 185
Prosecutors, 22; civil liberties decisions, 108, 110, 114–15, 131–34, 163; criminal records privacy, 124; discretion, 59, 163, 170; information technology, 59; interrogation and confession, 76, 80, 158; search and seizure, 106, 158, 165, 190; search and seizure and interrogation and confession compared, 77–78, 80–81; state courts, 81, 158
Public opinion, 5, 99–100, 128, 168, 171; civil liberties decisions, 79–80, 109; criminal records privacy, 98; "specific" and "diffuse" support, 24–25

Quinn, Robert, 150

Racial discrimination, 68, 186–87, 194, 202. *See also* Schools; Voting rights
Rationality, 18, 26, 30–31, 34
Ray, Dixie Lee, 126, 140–41, 143
Reagan, Ronald, 102, 116–17, 127, 180, 202
Reform, xix, 164–65, 198–201; criminal justice system, 9, 39–40, 169–70, 177, 182, 198–99, 201; criminal justice system, California, 101; criminal justice system, Massachusetts, 127; criminal justice system, Washington, 126; progressive reform, 23, 31, 125–26; reform and retrenchment, xxi, 177–82, 197. *See also* Change
Regulations. *See* Guideline development
Rehnquist, William, 49
Representativeness, 183

Republican Party, 35, 181; California, 116, 118; Colorado, 102; Massachusetts, 128, 148; Washington, 126, 140

Response (as a measure of implementation), 6–7; direction and intensity, 6; evasion or resistance, 7, 78, 80–82, 162; perfunctory, 6, 27, 29, 76–78, 136. *See also* Change; Compliance; Impact; Performance

Richardson, Elliott, 148–50, 154

Rights, individual, 19, 22, 34, 183, 189, 205–6; economic, 29, 34, 182, 185; political, xiii, 182, 185. *See also* Constitutional rights; Defendants' rights

Roberti, David, 101, 117

Rule-making. *See* Guideline development

Sargent, Francis, 116, 127–28, 148–50, 154, 168, 195

Schools: desegregation, 18–19, 27, 34–35, 51, 180, 185–86; funding, 161; prayer, 8, 21, 34, 170, 180–81, 185, 202

Search and seizure: "balancing test," 44; "basis of knowledge test," 43, 138; "bright line rule," 45–46, 132; exclusionary rule, 47; "exigent circumstances," 42, 45, 68; "exigent circumstances," Massachusetts, 78, 136; "exigent circumstances," Washington, 131, 133–34; "good faith exception," 44, 47; "good faith exception," California, 106, 167, 188; "good faith exception," Colorado, 70, 77, 115–16, 188, 196; "good faith exception," Massachusetts, 136–37, 139; "good faith exception," Washington, 77, 131, 188; "plain view doctrine," 106, 115, 129, 133–34, 136; pre-*Mapp* decisions, 41–43; "probable cause," 41–42, 44, 46, 68, 82; "probable cause," California, 105, 110; "probable cause," Colorado, 113–16; "probable cause," Massachusetts, 136–38; "probable cause," Washington, 130–31; "reasonable expectation of privacy standard," 41–44, 46–47, 69, 187–88; "reasonable expectation of privacy standard," Colorado, 113–14, 167; "reasonable expectation of privacy standard," Massachusetts, 136; "reasonable expectation of privacy standard," Washington, 130–31, 133; results, 75–76; searches incident to arrest, 44–46, 68, 106, 114, 130–31, 133; and separation of powers, 70; "sliding scale," 131, 187; standing, 35, 43, 130, 133, 185; "totality of circumstances," 44; U.S. Constitution, Fourth Amendment, 41–42, 44, 47–48, 101, 112, 160, 190; U.S. Constitution, Fourteenth Amendment, 42; vehicle searches, 42, 45–47, 106, 112–13, 115, 131, 136; "veracity test," 44, 138; "warrant requirement," 41–43, 68–69, 113, 116, 163, 188, 190. *See also* Burger Court; California; Civil liberties decisions; Colorado; *Mapp*; Massachusetts; Police; Prosecutors; Public opinion; State courts; Trial courts; Warren Court; Washington

SEARCH Group Incorporated, xvi; and Computerized Criminal History File (CCH), 63–65, 116–17, 147–49; model regulations, 92, 97. *See also* LEAA; NCIC

Separation of powers, 34, 70–71, 155, 161, 165–66, 180, 197, 204; California, 111, 161; Colorado, 123, 166; court proceedings, 90, 191; criminal records privacy, 92, 159, 162; executive-legislative-judicial relations, 70–71, 90, 92; Massachusetts, 148, 152–53, 162, 166; state courts, 55–56, 59; U.S. Supreme Court, 21, 181, 186

Sheriffs and Chiefs Association, 103, 133, 145–46. *See also* Police

Sovereignty, 178, 192, 194, 206; California, 111; Colorado, 121; of state courts, 188

State and local elites (as an explanation of implementation): beliefs and expectations, 156, 159–65, 172, 174, 192, 205; and criminal records privacy, 140, 162, 169; interests and priorities, 156, 165–69, 174, 192, 205; as intermedi-

aries, xv–xvi, xviii, 79, 97, 156; support of policy, xvii, 13–15, 23, 155–56, 178, 193, 198
State courts: civil liberties decisions, 80–82, 84–85, 160; and communication theory, 21; criminal records privacy, 159, 161; executive-legislative-judicial relations, 70, 85; independent state grounds, 56–57, 73, 85, 186–90; intermediate appellate courts (IAC), xvi, 54–55, 82; interrogation and confession, xv, 79–80, 82; jurisdiction, 52, 57, 71, 181, 188; legitimacy of, 189; police, 81, 158; politicization, 53, 55–57; prosecutors, 81, 158; reform, 53–57, 59, 103, 112, 127; response to U.S. Supreme Court and Congress, 6, 21; rule-making, 55–56; search and seizure, xv, 43, 75–76, 82–83, 186; trial courts, 53–56, 80–82; unification, xvi, 55–56, 127. *See also* California; Colorado; Federal courts; Massachusetts; States, sample of four; Trial courts; U.S. Supreme Court; Washington
State executives, 168–69; Computerized Criminal History File (CCH), 64; executive-legislative-judicial relations, 70, 148, 161; and state courts, 55–56, 102–3, 109, 128, 148, 152–53, 162; and state legislatures, 103, 117, 126
State legislatures, 169; Computerized Criminal History File (CCH), 64; executive-legislative-judicial relations, 70; response to U.S. Supreme Court and Congress, 6, 194, 196; and state courts, 55–56, 103, 109, 113, 115–16, 161, 167
States, sample of four: civil liberties decision, 84–86, 132, 134, 189; civil liberties decisions and criminal records privacy compared, xv–xvii, 157–72, 193–97, 200; conflict vs. consensus, xvi; criminal records privacy, 87, 90–95, 140, 142, 147–48, 151–53; executive-legislative-judicial relations, xvi; law enforcement conceptions, 160, 190, 194; legitimation problems, 194–97; policy making style, xvi, 196; political culture, 101–5, 125–29, 135, 192; selection of, xv–xvi. *See also* California; Colorado; Massachusetts; Washington
Systems theory, 23–25; common good, 25; and communication theory, 20; ideology, 24; and legitimation theory, 24, 35, 37; and organization theory, 24

Tobriner, Matthew, 109
Trial courts: civil liberties decisions, 80–81, 108–10, 136, 139, 171; interrogation and confession, 76; police, 80; search and seizure, 106, 158, 165; and state courts, 53–56, 80–82. *See also* State courts
Tunney, John, 116

U.S. Congress, 5–6, 65, 177, 179; Computerized Criminal History File (CCH), 63–64, 96, 120, 171; crime policy, xiii–xiv, 39, 49, 182; criminal records privacy, xiii–xv, 40, 94, 148–49, 185, 190–91; federal courts, response to, 51, 61, 70
U.S. Constitution: amendments proposed, 36, 202; Article Three, 51; Bill of Rights, 34, 186; First Amendment, 62, 122, 153; Fourth Amendment, 41–42, 44, 47–48, 53, 65–66, 71, 190; Fourth Amendment, California, 101; Fourth Amendment, Colorado, 112; Fourth Amendment, Washington, 132, 160; Fifth Amendment, 48, 65, 71; Sixth Amendment, 48, 71; Fourteenth Amendment, 42, 48, 66, 71, 185. *See also* Constitutional rights; Defendants' rights; privacy
U.S. Department of Justice, 40, 150
U.S. Government Accounting Office, 47, 72
U.S. Presidents, 64, 179
U.S. Supreme Court, 5–6, 65, 99, 177, 181; activism, 35, 185; civil liberties decisions, xiii, xv, xvii, 8–9, 39–40; federal courts, response to, 51; federal

oversight, xiii, 5, 19–20, 51–53, 57, 80, 186; judicial impact, 3, 9, 21; and legitimation theory, 179–80, 189. *See also* Burger Court; Civil liberties decisions; Federal courts; Judicial role; Warren Court
Unruh, Jesse, 101
Utility theory, 18–20; and cognitive dissonance theory, 19, 204; and cognitive expressivist theory, 204; Constitutional rights, 189; and explanations of implementation, 19, 155; inducements and sanctions, 15–17, 19–20, 22, 26, 98, 169, 183, 204; law enforcement conceptions, 155, 187, 189
Utter, Robert F., 134

Volpe, John, 127–28, 148
Voting rights, 27, 35, 51

Wallace, George, 180
War on Poverty, 21, 28, 40, 182
Warren, Earl, 101–2
Warren Court (1953–1969): civil liberties decisions, 8–9, 40, 186; Constitutional rights, 66; equality and political rights, xiii, 40, 51, 66, 182, 185; and federal courts, xiv, 51–53, 56, 71, 84, 171, 185–86; interrogation and confession, 48–49, 71, 186; law enforcement conceptions, 67; legitimation, 185; and New Deal, 40, 182, 185; policy objectives, xiii, 40, 180; search and seizure, 43–44, 71, 186; U.S. Constitution, Fourteenth Amendment, 185; and War on Poverty, 40. *See also* Burger Court; Federal courts; *Mapp v. Ohio*; *Miranda v. Arizona*; U.S. Supreme Court
Washington: Ad Hoc Advisory Committee, 143, 145; attorney general's office, 126, 140–42; civil liberties interests, 127, 141, 143–44, 196; criminal records privacy, 87, 140–48, 151, 161, 166, 169, 193, 196, 200; executive-legislative-judicial relations, 126, 166; governor's office, 192; House Institutions Committee, 142; House Judiciary Committee, 146; independent state grounds, 129–30, 132–34, 160, 171, 196; interrogation and confession, 130–31, 160–61; Judicial Council, 141–42; Juvenile Justice Reform Act, 142; Law Enforcement Assistance Administration (LEAA), 126–27, 140–43, 166; Office of Community Development (OCD), 141; Office of Financial Management (OFM), 145; police, 131, 133–34, 144–47, 160, 162, 164; policy making style, 126, 129, 196; political culture, 125–27, 134, 140, 192; press, 126, 141; prosecutors, 131–34, 163; search and seizure, xv, 129–33, 160; Senate Judiciary Committee, 141–42; state constitution, 133–34; state court administrator, xvi, 127, 141, 146; state court civil liberties decisions, 84–86, 129–34, 193, 195; state court reform, 56, 127; state court response to Burger Court, 129–34, 160–61, 171, 188, 195–96; state court response to criminal records privacy, 159; state court response to Warren Court, 129, 195; State Patrol, 141, 145, 147; state Supreme Court, 127, 132, 166; U.S. Constitution, Fourth Amendment, 132, 160; Washington Criminal Records Privacy Act (WCRPA), 141–42, 144–47. *See also* Criminal records privacy; Interrogation and confession; Liberalism; Search and seizure; States, sample of four
Welfare state, 21, 31. *See also* Liberalism
White, Kevin, 127
Wilkins, Herbert P., 137
Winberry, Phil, 140

Younger, Evelle, 102, 116–17, 166